Globalization and the Rural Poor in Latin America

Directions in Applied Anthropology:
Adaptations and Innovations

Timothy J. Finan, Series Editor
BUREAU OF APPLIED RESEARCH IN ANTHROPOLOGY,
UNIVERSITY OF ARIZONA

GLOBALIZATION
and the Rural Poor
in Latin America

EDITED BY

William M. Loker

LYNNE
RIENNER
PUBLISHERS

BOULDER
LONDON

Published in the United States of America in 1999 by
Lynne Rienner Publishers, Inc.
1800 30th Street, Boulder, Colorado 80301

and in the United Kingdom by
Lynne Rienner Publishers, Inc.
3 Henrietta Street, Covent Garden, London WC2E 8LU

Library of Congress Cataloging-in-Publication Data
Globalization and the rural poor in Latin America / edited by William
   M. Loker.
      p. cm. — (Directions in applied anthropology)
      Includes bibliographical references and index.
      ISBN 1-55587-809-1 (alk. paper)
      1. Rural poor—Latin America. 2. Latin America—Rural conditions.
I. Loker, William M., 1953– . II. Series.
HC130.P6G58 1999
305.569'098—dc21   98-7511
                                                                 CIP

British Cataloguing in Publication Data
A Cataloguing in Publication record for this book
is available from the British Library.

Printed and bound in the United States of America

        The paper used in this publication meets the requirements
  ∞   of the American National Standard for Permanence of
        Paper for Printed Library Materials Z39.48-1984.

     5 4 3 2 1

Contents

Acknowledgments

The chapters in this volume represent an overview of the kinds of research occurring in the anthropological study of globalization. Most of the chapters started out as symposium presentations at professional meetings. I am grateful to the authors for their perseverance and hard work in bringing them to publishable form in a timely manner. I can truly state that working with the authors was both a pleasure and an education in the varied perspectives that characterize ethnographic research on globalization today. I trust that the reader will benefit as much as I have.

The ideas expressed in my own contribution to this volume have benefited from my interaction with the authors of individual chapters, as well as with students in my courses who were forced to endure my thoughts on these issues and who responded skeptically to my perspectives. Numerous friends and colleagues have also contributed to my ideas, including Stephen Vosti, Helen Regis, Susan Stonich, Carlos Seré, Andrés Archila, Barbara Rose Johnston, and others too numerous to mention. Needless to say, I am solely responsible for the ideas presented in my own contribution, just as the other authors bear individual responsibility for their work.

I would also like to acknowledge the constant support and inspiration of my wife, Sally, and our children in bringing this project to fruition.

This book is dedicated to my first editor, June W. Loker.

William M. Loker

Introduction

Peggy F. Barlett

The study of globalization in Latin America today presents us with paradoxes. At one moment, the powerful changes portrayed in this volume seem new, chaotic, and transformative; at another moment, the continuities with the past are compelling. Latin America as a region reflects a past form of globalization—through Iberian colonial conquest. Though rich local cultural diversity has survived, we also see the unifying pressure of Hispanic influence in economic, political, religious, and other domains. Experts on diaspora today tell us that the twentieth century marks a high point in human history with regard to people on the move—migrants seeking work, refugees displaced by war and natural disaster, and families filled with hope, searching for new beginnings. This massive dislocation fractures the unique connections of people and the land and destroys cultural traditions adapted over centuries to a particular locale. But are these traditions broken or merely stretched? Latin America's rural cultures have been formed in the crucible of past upheavals from forced labor, debt peonage, protracted civil war, and the ravages of disease. Is our sense of today's fluid lifeways built from an inattention to the fluidity of the past?

The rapidity of change is one way in which contemporary globalization strains our human capacities. When a queen's or king's policies took months or even years to arrive at a foreign shore, when pirates could sail off beyond the horizon and escape detection, and when local villages could hope to be undisturbed by predatory armies for years at a time, the pace of challenge and response was much slower. Daily life might find a rhythm that allowed for common patterns of child rearing, courtship, and shared meanings of adult life. Today, all aspects of daily life can potentially be

1

affected by new images, new beliefs, and new comparisons with an Other far away. Not only mass media images, but improved transportation and the rise of literacy alter the contact and movement of peoples.

William Loker's introductory chapter to this volume notes also the scale of change as part of the power and threat of globalization. In the ecological sphere, exponential growth challenges our human capacities for response. It is difficult, for example, to comprehend the scale of deforestation and its consequences, the pace of population growth and its implications for sewage treatment or water supply. The rapid expansion and withdrawal of global industries or threats to build mines or to withdraw investment hamper both the perception of change and effective response to it.

How, then, do we begin to comprehend the historical present, attending to the bitter lot of the rural poor and joining our voices to calls for greater environmental sustainability, economic prosperity, and social justice? One of the challenges of a situation of rapid change is that patterns of life in flux are very difficult to apprehend and describe. A sociologist who spent time in Nicaragua shortly after the Sandinista revolution reported that so many different aspects of society were changing that it was too soon to be able to know what was happening. The emergence of new patterns that can be apprehended by the viewer or articulated by the actor take time. The powerful contribution of anthropology to the study of global processes is to provide a picture of the local, as it responds to and constitutes the global. Our fine-grained ethnographies, particularly when they involve many years of contact with a particular locality, can contribute an unmatched opportunity to test and refine generalizations that can illuminate ways that the present circumstances diverge from or echo the patterns of the past.

Latin America is a particularly appropriate focus of attention for anthropologists from the United States. For over a century, U.S. political power has exerted a major force in the region. Latin American elites in many countries have shifted their cultural and educational attention from Europe to the United States. Mass media have placed images of North American life in all parts of the region—even to the point that CNN has brought Atlanta baseball to the farming village of Paso, in Costa Rica, where I did research in the 1970s. Nor has interaction been one-sided. The migration of workers from many countries in Latin America to the United States has changed the face of many industries and communities, from meatpacking plants in the Midwestern heartland to the tobacco farms of Kentucky. Even our national condiment, ketchup, has been surpassed by sales of salsa, a gustatory marker of cultural borrowing.

Globalization involves contradictory processes, and we sometimes neglect the positive aspects of globalization. Global trade in fertilizer may present farmers with difficult choices about the risks of credit, but it may also guarantee improved yields. The vagaries of the marketplace may expand the uncertainties in the production of melons or cassava, but is the global trade in penicillin equally problematic? Or the decline in goiter through the spread of iodized salt? How have declines in illiteracy and infant mortality affected local change? Though we can see that poverty levels as measured by income and gross national product are appalling, and that health and educational improvements are far from what they might have been, there are many ways in which the past half century has brought new choices and new dignity to some groups of rural people. Rigid boundaries of ethnic and racial groups have begun to shift, and new demands for respect by indigenous traditions—from the Guatemalan highlands to the Amazonian lowlands—are supported now by international allies. The textured analysis of the ethnographer, reflecting interaction with multiple actors in the local drama, can go far to unravel these contradictory processes. Further, our work contributes the vibrant melding of the perspective of the outside observer and the views of those whose lives make up regional statistics.

As the authors of this volume explore global processes in the local contexts of their studies, five dimensions of development consistently emerge and intertwine: economic organization of production; household dimensions of consumption and investment; ecological aspects of sustainability; political processes of power, control, and resistance; and the subjective dimensions of how people make ideological sense in the midst of these changes. I will explore briefly two clusters of these issues.

Production, Consumption, and Ecological Change

As a region, Latin America has always been vulnerable to boom-and-bust cycles of international trade, and the globalization process of the present era is in some ways simply a new version of that linkage. Communities sprang up to serve international demands for indigo, sugar, and henequen, and later for coffee and bananas. In colonial Mexico, grazing cattle destroyed ecosystems, and timber harvesting depleted forests. Especially in South America, silver was mined for export, and all through the Americas, millions of indigenous people died and were replaced by Africans and Europeans. Even in the local subsistence sector, households were challenged by the extractions of *mita* and *repartimiento,* new political forms were created in the cargo system, and wholesale ideological transformation was attempted in the establishment of Christianity. Current economic aspects of globalization bear a strong resemblance to the "crisis" periods of the past.

Loker eloquently draws our attention to the ways in which rural people seek to participate in positive aspects of today's changing production systems, to *sacar algun provecho*. Barbara Dilly's analysis presents the sharp trade-offs for indigenous villagers in Amazonian Guyana of strategies to produce peanuts for trade, foodstuffs for local use, or vegetables for tourists. Each alternative for the household economy is weighed against the advantages of ready cash from wage labor in logging or mining activities. The conditions of wage labor for the Ngóbe of Panama are much less attractive, but Philip Young and John Bort document the population pressure and land scarcity that drive the Ngóbe to seek work on plantations and coffee *fincas*.

Globalization brings new standards of the desirable life, new wants, and new definitions of success. Several authors note that clothing styles, especially of the young, imitate fashion trends set far away. Ronald Waterbury's analysis of San Antonino, in Oaxaca, Mexico, documents the rising affluence of truck crop producers, who in turn have invested some of their profits in burro carts. This response to transportation needs, adopted while neighboring states see surges in trucks, buses, and cars, reminds us that responses to globalization are not homogeneous and that some localities seek appropriate technologies that are also ecologically more sustainable. Liliana Goldin also shows us that whereas some Guatemalan indigenous clothing is now produced for export and for tourists, it can also remain an important marker of ethnic identity. Indigenous Guatemalan rural women may become familiar with fashion styles from elsewhere as part of their work in the *maquiladora* industry, but they adopt traditional clothing when back in the village as part of their commitment to one of several dimensions of being "Maya." Both as a continuity with the past and as an act of resistance within the ethnic struggles of the present, clothing and other consumption items become expressions of complex ideological and political positions. One wonders, however, was not La Malinche enmeshed in a similar cultural complexity?

The pace of change in production systems raises uncertainties on many levels. Goldin documents the hundreds of new assembly plants in Guatemala, while hundreds more draw workers to several "development poles" in Mexico. Questions surround the long-term viability of these urban agglomerations. Simultaneously, many new "nontraditional" agricultural exports are financed and exported long before any accurate ecological evidence can assess the sustainability or even the negative consequences of these new production systems. Waterbury's Oaxacan case again provides an example. Families that adopted new technologies, especially irrigation pumps, were able to exploit the aquifer's water, improve labor efficiency, and expand vegetable production in a profitable way. Some families used their profits to improve housing, invest in education for their children, and move into commerce. For a percentage of the population, the depletion of the aquifer's resources will find them well established in a new, less vulnerable place in the social order. As with the fortunes made by felling the pine forests of Georgia and the timber of the U.S. Great Lakes region, the depletion of a resource does not always imply devastation to those left behind; some actually benefit, despite the wastefulness of the extraction process.

Several authors note the emergence in rural Latin America of household strategies combining small-scale agriculture with other activities, most commonly wage labor. Unlike the plantation labor or urban servitude of the past that may have been directly coerced, today's peasant family bricolage sometimes resembles the rural strategies common throughout the more marginal agricultural zones of the industrialized countries. To sustain healthy rural communities in all but the most favorable of agricultural regions of the United States, Europe, and Japan, families have turned to multiple job-holding or multiple sources of income. Whether by long-distance commuting (and remittances) or by short-distance jobs at nearby towns, rural families have often employed complex strategies to take advantage of local opportunities and family labor resources. Questions arise in assessing the current dilemmas of globalization: to what extent are these changes advantageous to the rural family and for which gender and generation? What increased dangers are presented by the necessity to seek supplementary income for farm families? Manuel Vargas's account of the Deep South region of the Dominican Republic notes the mixed consequences of migration in search of wage labor; Goldin's review of trends in Guatemala finds that the greater potential for exploitation in wage labor and the loss of cultural continuity make an argument in favor of supporting agrarian livelihoods.

Studies in Europe show that pluriactivity can sustain agricultural lifeways and support a higher quality of life than full-time industrial employment. However, conditions of wage labor in Latin America have far to go to match those of the European Economic Community. Our cross-cultural comparisons lead us to ask in what ways the out-migration for wage labor depletes and erodes local cultures and in what ways it enriches them, from improved incomes, new skills, and reduced land pressure. It is a loss to our current understandings that there were no anthropologists to document the similar processes of international out-migration in the last century in Poland, Italy, India, or China. The chapters here contribute to an understanding of what factors create more satisfactory economic outcomes in agriculturally marginal regions.

Power, Politics, and Inequality

Globalization and the new international division of labor have brought to the boardrooms of a few large corporations immense power over the daily lives of rural people. Dimensions of intrusion into local control are amply illustrated in this volume. Vargas shows us the consequences of becoming "hooked with the bank" for Dominican farmers who followed governmental incentives to plant mechanized sorghum. Preceding the small farmer loan program that was to bring prosperity to this disadvantaged area was the rising demand for chicken in the urban diet, the spread of a particular industrial poultry production system that required sorghum for processed feed, and the decision on the national level to meet this need by stimulating production of sorghum in a new region. Dietary patterns, ideologies of "modern production," market competition, national agricultural policy, and technological packages of agricultural innovations all combine in the globalization story of the Dominican Republic. Each piece of the narrative has a critical international dimension, but the local consequences of financial and dietary hardship are not internationally shared.

Another example of the international flow of policy prescription is David Guillet's review of irrigation laws and the new trend toward demand control rather than farmer-regulated irrigation systems in Latin America. Though many of the claims of efficiency and improved productivity have not been substantiated, national-level bureaucracies in Peru and other countries have been pushed and drawn to imitate the Chilean and Mexican examples. This is, in a sense, an international fashion trend in economic policy. Once again, however, the negative consequences of risk are not evenly shared.

The expansion of structural adjustment accords that Loker examines is far more than a fashion, however; it forms a massive pressure to shift power to new classes and new configurations of economic control. Once imposed on a nation, structural adjustments have such far-reaching consequences for everything from the price of food to the availability of health care that their sheer massiveness makes them difficult to document and understand. Local-level research that documents "la crisis" can provide an important counter to the obfuscations of national statistics of reduced inflation and investor incentives.

Within these dimensions of international power, many authors are concerned to explore changing relations of inequality on the local level. Goldin notes that the trends of increasing local inequality have been fed by international trade in crafts and foodstuffs in the Guatemalan highlands. The same stratification seems not to have occurred in the Oaxacan community studied by Waterbury, though the processes are well under way in the milk-producing regions studied by James McDonald. A history of relatively egalitarian landholdings and freedom from exploitative class relations provides important clues to why some communities have fared better in this regard than others.

Anthropologists often teach the importance of cultural preservation, as part of the international cultural "gene pool" that expands our known options in resolving the crises of the future. Several of the chapters provide vivid illustrations of the ways in which local inequality has been deterred. Guillet notes that in addition to providing for sustainable agricultural systems in many areas of highland Peru, traditional water management policies also inhibit the emergence of rural inequality. We might ask which of these practices might be transferable to other irrigation locales.

Gender is another dimension of changing power and family roles. Vargas notes that Dominican women in the Deep South lost some of their centrality to the household economic enterprise with the advent of mechanized agricultural production. As some Dominican families resist the negative consequences of agricultural modernization by strengthening traditional forms of labor-intensive production and pooled labor through *convite,* the question arises whether these organizational forms hold some potential for other situations of gendered disempowerment. Dilly notes the importance of Guyanese Amerindian women's work in vegetable and fruit production for ecotourism, but she also notes that such economic power for women may have negative consequences for a stable family partnership. Goldin additionally hints at changes within Guatemalan households, as young women earn scarce cash in the *maquiladora* plants. The gain to women of new economic clout may include a decline in traditional forms of gendered inequality, but it also may bring new strains in marital partnerships, a pattern seen in many parts of the world.

As globalization challenges local adaptations and lifeways, at times pauperizing the many while enriching the few, forms of resistance are an important part of the accounts presented in this volume. To illustrate forms of resistance to globalization, anthropologists often turn to collective efforts, such as *maquila*-inspired organized labor movements, peasant pressures for land reform, and urban consumer movements to protest rising prices in the aftermath of structural adjustments. Both organized efforts and individual acts of resistance are part of the fabric of response to global change. Forms of political organization, identities, beliefs, and migration patterns can all be dimensions of resistance.

Production cooperatives are an interesting example of political forms that empower small farmers. McDonald's account of milk producers in two areas of Mexico details the benefits to one community of a new producer co-op. The co-op provides stable transport and financing, through its linkage to a Dannon yogurt plant nearby. An educated, savvy co-op leader follows industry trends by surfing the Internet. Small dairy producers have improved their production efficiency through new farm investments, which in turn have improved sanitation and milk quality. Though favorable to small producers, the co-op is hardly a form of resistance because its establishment was encouraged by the large multinational corporation that benefits from the secure supply and reliable quality it provides. McDonald contrasts this favorable outcome of global contact with the case of another less-favored region in which small independent milk producers are vulnerable to market swings and seem to be declining in their ability to compete. In this area, there has been no coherent state policy to establish "stable regional milksheds." Technological and capital resources are lacking, and local self-sufficiency is declining. Local reliance on imported milk presents policy dilemmas for any nation, but this is acutely so in the context of international sales of tainted milk powder from the Chernobyl region of the former Soviet Union. The anthropological comparison of two milk-producing regions highlights these "glocal" paradoxes.

Resistance also takes the form of new ideological commitments. Young and Bort demonstrate that the Mama Chi religious movement served to revitalize Ngóbe culture in western Panama and encouraged political organization with positive consequences for Ngóbe struggles for territorial rights and ethnic identity. Goldin notes that the multiple identities of the highland Guatemalans provide a way to articulate different systems of production and the social worlds that contextualize them. Protestantism is another direction of resistance, a new Christian ideology that supports a rejection of older forms of convivial expense in alcohol consumption, embeddedness in obligations to community, and gender roles that inhibit entrepreneurial success. An individual's shift to jeans and a new haircut may also be a form of resistance, not to international power but to generational power. Migration to work in a factory may be a reluctant journey to help out a family in dire straits, or an adventure into a future with more options. For the same individual, migration can embody dimensions of duty, personal aspiration, and resistance to parental authority.

In the end, the most valuable contribution of the anthropologist is the rich detail of the ethnographic method. Combining the voices of the Guatemalan migrant and her parents, the Oaxacan vegetable producers and their educated children, the rain forest Amerindian villagers, and the indebted Dominican farmer, we can begin to discern the many meanings of globalization. As we understand poverty over the life cycle and the changing integration of local ecosystems with national patterns of production, we can contribute to the global vision that is necessary for the empowered citizen and the enlightened decisionmaker.

1

Grit in the Prosperity Machine: Globalization and the Rural Poor in Latin America

William M. Loker

Is it possible for the rural poor in Latin America to engage the globalizing economy and *sacar algun provecho*—to reap some benefit—from this engagement? The answer to this question is critical for the future of millions of people and their communities, and it reverberates across the globe as hundreds of millions of people in rural areas face similar crises and challenges, similar economic imperatives and ecological disequilibria.[1] Yet the answer to this question is not self-evident, and analysts and participants in public policy debates disagree quite sharply on the consequences of economic globalization for the rural poor (for a review of various positions in the globalization debate, see Power 1997). To a large extent, the answer depends on the ideological lens with which one views the processes of globalization and of rural communities. Also, the answer is contingent on the local context and circumstances of the meeting between the global and the local.

This book explores this meeting of the global and the local in a variety of contexts in rural Latin America, from Mexico to Peru. Through the detailed examination of case studies, we hope to begin the process of specifying under what conditions rural residents can engage the forces of globalization creatively and with some degree of success in material and social terms. The chapters that follow are rich documents recounting the experience of local actors—in this case, rural residents from diverse contexts in Latin America—as they struggle to come to terms with, adapt to, *sacar algun provecho* from, and defend their interests in a world of emerging market forces. These experiences have been recorded and analyzed by scholars with the expressed intent of understanding the interplay of global-local forces of change. There is no other way to understand this interplay

9

of global and local forces than to be on the ground, to record and observe, to analyze and consult with local people in an effort to comprehend their current circumstances.

We view this effort as a (small) step in the construction of general statements regarding the shape of the interplay of local and global forces in rural Latin America. We need to analyze the collection of cases presented here (and many others), from a variety of theoretical perspectives, in order to come to even tentative conclusions regarding what factors and circumstances shape the outcome of the intersection of the global and the local. Our goal should be to define critical variables that influence the ability of the rural poor to *sacar algun provecho* from this changing relationship. Doing this will require a creative interplay among theory, empirical case studies, and an openness to transdisciplinary investigation.

Before embarking on an analysis of these case studies, this introductory chapter presents a brief overview of the macropolitical context in which rural communities in Latin America are operating today. My remarks will focus on several areas: the ideologies of global change, the position of Latin America in the global context, and the role of anthropology in analyzing and informing debates on globalization.

Latin America, Neoliberalism, Structural Adjustment, and Globalization

Latin America has experienced a number of significant changes in recent years that force us to rethink our approaches to understanding people and their livelihoods in the region.[2] These forces include urbanization, liberalization, and democratization. These three terms capture a complex series of events, policy measures, and social forces that are transforming the Latin American social, political, and economic landscape. Despite these sweeping changes, the problem of mass poverty persists and is once again rising to the forefront of the political agenda. The number of poor has increased both in percentage terms and in absolute numbers compared to 25 years ago (see Table 1.1). Poverty remains concentrated in rural areas; a higher percentage of rural dwellers live in poverty compared to urban areas. But as Table 1.1 indicates, in terms of absolute numbers, for the first time in history, there are now more poor people living in urban than in rural areas of Latin America.

These changes come in the aftermath of the lost decade of the 1980s (the height of the debt crisis), with its frustrated economic expectations. One pervasive lesson of the debt crisis was the vulnerability of Latin America economies to external economic events and their subordination in the global political economic context to the demands of international

Table 1.1   Changes in the Magnitude of Poverty in Latin America, 1970–1990

Year	Poor			Absolute Poor		
	Total	Urban	Rural	Total	Urban	Rural
	(percent of total population)					
1970	45	29	67	24	13	40
1980	41	30	60	19	11	33
1990	46	39	61	22	15	37
	(in millions of people)					
1970	119.8	44.2	75.6	63.7	19.9	43.8
1980	135.9	62.9	73.0	62.4	22.5	39.9
1990	195.9	115.5	80.4	93.5	44.9	48.6
	(Absolute poor as percentage of poor)					
1970	53	45	58			
1980	46	36	55			
1990	48	39	60			

Source: IFPRI 1995.

Note: "Poor" individuals have incomes inadequate to meet minimum daily nutritional requirements, as well as other needs such as hygiene, clothing, education, and transportation. "Absolute poor" have incomes inadequate to supply minimum daily nutritional needs even if other basic needs are forgone.

institutions and creditors. The example of Peru's economic disaster, when populist president Alan Garcia pursued a "heterodox" economic strategy including unilateral limits set on debt repayments (in defiance of international creditors), has not been lost on other Latin leaders (see Pastor and Wise 1992 for a review of the Peruvian heterodox experience). If poor countries require access to foreign capital as a prerequisite for the economic growth that is the necessary, but not the sufficient, condition for reducing poverty, then Latin American governments realized as never before that they either had to play the economic development game by rules set in Washington, D.C., Paris, Berlin, and Tokyo or risk dramatic economic declines.

These rules generally followed from an economic philosophy termed "neoliberalism." Neoliberalism can be defined as a theory of political economy that claims that the market is the most efficient mechanism for the distribution of goods and services in society, that private property and capitalist economic principles are the most efficient means for the production of goods, and that state interference with the workings of the market and capitalist production should be minimized. Policy prescriptions that flow from the neoliberal approach include (1) fiscal adjustment: measures designed to reduce fiscal deficits by national governments; (2) privatization:

the selling off of state enterprises that had emerged in sectors such as heavy manufacturing, oil and mineral development, public utilities, and consumer goods; (3) decontrolling prices: including the elimination of subsidies and liberalizing exchange rate policies; (4) decontrolling fiscal policies such as exchange rates and interest rates; (5) trade liberalization: reducing or removing tariffs, quotas, and other measures designed to protect national economies from international competition; and (6) investment liberalization: removing barriers to foreign investment generally and in specific sectors of national economies. The neoliberal philosophy was generally implemented initially through the mechanism of structural adjustment programs, in response to the debt crisis and other economic problems affecting Latin America from the late 1970s onward.

Structural adjustment programs have been implemented across Latin America from the late 1970s to the present. The result has been a series of measures including the "downsizing" of government via a dramatic wave of privatizations, a reduction in the state's role in economic planning and policymaking, and often dramatic cuts in government-supplied social services in accordance with the dictates of structural adjustment packages. These measures have been adopted with varying degrees of enthusiasm and consistency in countries from Chile to Mexico, sometimes externally imposed, sometimes eagerly generated by national governments. Analyzing the social effects of structural adjustment has been a major topic for scholars, and an important literature on this subject has emerged (see Zuvekas 1997 for a recent review of this literature). The fact that these events were played out against the backdrop of the collapse of communism and the breakup of the Soviet Union only served to drive home the dictates of capitalist development with greater force. The result is that Latin American countries are now inserted in the world economy in new ways that directly affect the livelihoods and survival strategies of the rural poor.

The collapse of the Soviet Union also removed the most important practical justification for foreign aid and development assistance: the superpower rivalry and its accompanying competition for political-military alliances and access to resources and markets in the developing world. Furthermore, it greatly weakened socialism as an ideological counterweight to capitalism. Although the vast majority of projects and initiatives funded through multilateral and bilateral development assistance over the years were capitalist in nature, the viability of socialist ideologies and political parties placed pressure on the architects of development to incorporate social concerns into development, to present capitalism with a human face. At least in theory, attention to such issues as social equity was necessary to avoid revolution and to counteract the appeal of socialism. The end of the Cold War has marked the decline of socialism and the rise of neoliberalism as the predominant ideology guiding international development. Increasingly, development is seen not as something to be accomplished by "projects," but as a series of broader changes centered on global economic relationships.

Neoliberalism was on the ascendant even before the collapse of the former Soviet Union in the policies of Ronald Reagan and Margaret Thatcher in the 1980s. Many analysts (e.g., McMichael 1996) see the debt crisis of the 1980s as a critical turning point in global economic relations. Philip McMichael argues that the debt crisis created the objective conditions, institutional basis, political instruments, and ideas necessary to steamroller the poorer countries into accepting the neoliberal consensus on the value of trade liberalization and fiscal discipline. Neoliberalism thus provides the ideological basis for globalization, while structural adjustment programs provide the policy mechanisms for creating an economic context at the national level conducive to globalization.

These policies form the basis for the "globalization project" in which the forces of global capitalism, assisted by advances in telecommunications and computer technologies, have increasingly and rapidly changed the nature of the global economy. Yet globalization refers to a series of interrelated processes that are much broader than structural adjustment. These processes of globalization have been noted by many analysts and include:

- the globalization of finance and capital so that flows of money and investment occur at a greater scale and an increasingly accelerated pace;
- the rise of international institutions and frameworks such as the General Agreement on Tariffs and Trade (GATT) and the World Trade Organization (WTO) (joining the UN, the World Bank, and the International Monetary Fund [IMF]) to supervise the integration of states into the global economy, subordinating states to global economic discipline in the process;
- the "hollowing out" of the state as it loses important economic functions such as exchange rate policies, policies on tariffs and trade, and even fundamental decisions about taxation and patterns of government spending to global institutions;
- the move toward the "privatization" of state enterprises in many countries, further weakening the power of the state to influence internal economic conditions and introducing powerful economic actors—transnational corporations—ever more forcefully into the national affairs of these countries;
- the increased differentiation of the Third World, which has lost any remaining coherence as an analytical construct as some countries emerge as "winners" in the globalizing economy (newly industrialized countries [NICs], "Asian tigers," "big emerging markets") and other regions (sub-Saharan Africa, Central America) fall further behind as they are cut off from global financial flows (aid and investment);

- the variety of local responses to the weakening of the state, including the rise of new social movements such as nongovernmental organizations (NGOs) as participants in local struggles to create viable livelihoods in an increasingly destabilized and uncertain social and economic environment (Escobar and Alvarez 1992);
- the increase in transnational migration as one form of new social movements in response to conditions of hardship and uncertainty in the new global economy, accompanied by the rapid diffusion of cultural images and ideas around the world (see Schiller, Basch, and Blanc-Szanton 1992);
- and the rise of fundamentalisms and other nativist reactions to the social and cultural destabilizations of globalization, especially the transnational migration mentioned above, as well as growing numbers of political refugees crossing all kinds of borders.

One of the most important implications of all of these changes is that development as a concept can no longer be conceived of as something that happens in the Third World. As globalization increasingly comes to replace the idea of development, we understand that these changes—social and political, economic and cultural—affect everyone on the planet. This is true of global environmental threats, such as greenhouse warming, the proliferation of toxic waste, or the reduction of biodiversity; it is also true of the social and economic dark side of globalization as increasing competition pits workers and localities (in both developed and developing countries) against one another in a race to the bottom to provide inexpensive and compliant labor, tax breaks, and other aspects of a favorable business climate in an atmosphere of relentless competition to attract investment (Brecher and Costello 1994; Peck and Tickell 1994). People and communities throughout the world feel the effects of these changes, though unevenly and in different ways.

The list of general trends and their ramifications associated with globalization could be extended indefinitely. Overall, one has the impression that we are living in a period of sweeping social, economic, and political change. As social scientists, we are busy playing analytical catch-up with rapid change. That these trends come at a time of great intellectual ferment—some would say weakness—in the social sciences has perhaps undermined our abilities to come to analytical grips with these phenomena.

Globalization: New Wine in Old Bottles?

The phrase "old wine in new bottles" refers to an attempt to dress up old ideas in new packaging, without any fundamental change in the intellectual offering. The emerging discussion of globalization has been accused of just this problem (Petras and Vieux 1992b). However, it can be argued that, despite obvious historic continuities with colonialism, imperialism, and the economic neocolonialism of the second half of the twentieth century, the current set of forces summarized under the term "globalization" represents a radical shift that we are busy trying to fit into old, exhausted paradigms—new wine in old bottles.

Globalization represents such a major leap in the reach, penetration, and power of global capitalism that is qualitatively different in terms of the scale, scope, and intensity of its effects. As stated by Francisco Sagasti,

> The worldwide expansion of productive and service activities, the diminishing importance of national frontiers, and the extensive exchange of information and knowledge, all coexist with the concentration of "global" activities in certain countries, regions, cities and even neighbourhoods, and also with the marginalization of many local productive and service activities and of the people engaged in them. (1995:591)

Globalization and "Development"

Perhaps the first major conceptual victim of globalization is the very notion of development, a notion that has been under siege from all sides in recent years. Development has been criticized on environmental grounds as encouraging an unsustainable relationship between a burgeoning population and the earth, modeled after wasteful patterns of industrial overconsumption in the rich countries. Environmental critics claim that the earth cannot support six billion Western-style consumers and urge changing lifestyles in the rich countries as well as a new model fulfilling needs in the poorer countries (Goodland, Daly, and el Serafy 1992). The outlines of this new social model are usually left unspecified. Development has been criticized on the right as a bureaucratic, wasteful process, the primary effect of which has been to serve entrenched elite interests in aid-receiving countries and create an entrenched "aid industry" wasteful of tax money and other resources in the donor countries. Critics from the right, following the neoliberal paradigm, would prefer to see private investment play a much larger role in "developing" the poorer countries. How societies are to cope with the social dislocations of "savage capitalism" is usually a question that is not even entertained.

Development has also been subject to radical critiques from the perspective of intellectually trendy postmodernism. (The postmodern critique has been summarized by Martin Hopenhayn [1993].) Postmodernists have critiqued development as totalizing, meta-narrative reflecting a misplaced belief in progress and one that promotes a vision of society that is imitative, culturally derivative, and politically oppressive (Sachs 1992). Although such critiques of development are not groundless, postmodernism tends toward a fascination with aesthetics and a rejection of historical determinism. This leads to an ahistoric present orientation that rejects all conceptual models as totalizing and views plans for the future as coercive and utopian. The emphasis is on atomistic individualism, privileging agency to the neglect of structure. The rejection of metanarrative and totalizing discourse leads to an extreme relativism that trivializes conventional indicators of development such as access to health care and education.

As Hopenhayn (1993) points out, the postmodern critique can intentionally or unintentionally serve the interests of those who deny the responsibility of the rich countries for some measure of the underdevelopment of the less-developed countries and who argue for the elimination or reduction of assistance to the poor in developing countries. The exaltation of diversity leads to the exaltation of the market as the only social institution capable of bringing order without coercion, while the critique of intellectual and political vanguards and metanarratives leads to a critique of the transformational function of politics and of social planning. Postmodernism denies the existence of a value frame that stands apart from culturally situated discourse (such as some notion of "progress" or "emancipatory" activity); hence it is impossible to question the waste, alienation, and growing inequality of modern industrial society. The postmodernist critique of ideologies includes a critique of Marxism and more humanistic socialist variants that are considered examples of utopian thought (and, therefore, not to be trusted), as are their agendas of redistributing wealth and reducing inequality. In short, to the extent that postmodernism claims that there is no enduring value frame from which we can base our criticism of the status quo, it represents a dangerous path of intellectual disengagement from the pressing problems of mass poverty and exploitation.

These critiques, whether green or red, right or left, modern or postmodern, should not blind us to the fact that people do have demonstrable needs and rights and that these needs are not being filled and rights are being violated in the current global system. It should not lead us to ignore the demand for development that is indeed present among the world's people. Perhaps the most telling attribute in the current moment is the paucity of "big ideas" to pose as alternatives to neoliberalism. Many observers are dismayed with the fraying of the social fabric created by global capitalism. Many can see its obvious negative effects in terms of income inequality, loss of a sense of community, and the feeling that control over important decisions is being passed to a global elite beyond the reach of the vast majority of the world's citizens (see, e.g., Korten 1995). Yet there is a notable lack of compelling, generalizable alternatives to the current market triumphalism.

Neoliberalism Redux

It is easy to condemn the development policies of the last decade for their cruelty and indifference to suffering of the poor majority. Even the bankers who have imposed structural adjustment packages recognize their negative consequences (Morley 1992). Yet it is difficult to imagine an alternative cure to the bloated bureaucracies, lack of fiscal discipline, and corruption that characterized state-led development in so many countries. For example, it is truly wrenching to see Costa Rica go through the pain associated with structural adjustment. Yet it is equally difficult to imagine how Costa Rica's political economy could be sustained when one of every six jobs was generated by a creaky government bureaucracy (Rohter 1996). Costa Rica clearly did not have the local economic base to sustain the admirable social welfare system that is currently being so painfully dismantled. The alternative to this dismantling is for Costa Rica to be dependent on external revenue streams to maintain this system—that is, some sort of permanent international welfare system for the redistribution of wealth. Although there may be many who would support such an institutionalized system of international redistribution of wealth, such a system of redistribution is ultimately dependent on the noblesse oblige of the rich countries. This is a weak reed on which to stake any country's future.

Mainstream analysts of global political economy have always proposed only two alternatives for "development" globally, where development is seen as synonymous with reducing poverty: economic growth or income redistribution. Regarding redistribution, there has never been a consensus within the wealthy countries for a massive redistribution of wealth to help poor countries reduce poverty. There probably never will be such a consensus. Redistribution would have to be massive to have a real impact on global poverty. It is difficult to foresee such a process ever occurring voluntarily. Foreign aid represents a tiny effort at wealth redistribution, and even that effort is politically unpopular.

This leaves economic growth as the primary means of achieving development, that is, reducing poverty. Much of the debate in development economics since 1947 has centered on how best to encourage growth. Much of this debate has also focused on the role of the state in creating the conditions for growth through mechanisms such as tax and trade policies, laws governing foreign investment, public investment in infrastructure and education, and other initiatives at the level of government to influence economic performance. With the rise of Reaganism and Thatcherism in the 1980s, the fall of communism, the experience of the debt crisis, and the (transitory?) economic success of the NICs of East Asia, a consensus of sorts emerged. This consensus focused on export-led development, the reduction of the state, private enterprise as the primary motor of economic growth, the free flow of capital, and the doctrine of "comparative advantage" as guiding principles in inducing economic growth and development.

The neoliberal consensus is far from unanimous, however. There is a substantial body of empirical data, as well as strong theoretical arguments, that points to the weakness of neoliberalism as a development strategy. For instance, there is considerable debate and doubt as to whether the Asian NICs, such as South Korea and Taiwan, followed the minimal state strategy currently being promoted (McMichael 1996:41). The financial crisis of several of the Asian tigers (Thailand, Malaysia, Indonesia, South Korea) in 1997 further calls into question the neoliberal model. Sorting through the published literature evaluating neoliberalism is a difficult task, however, because many of the attacks on neoliberalism are tendentious and so ideologically loaded as to be of little practical utility in countering neoliberal arguments. But there are good empirical studies that document the effects of neoliberal development on particular villages, regions, and countries. Recent critiques of neoliberalism generally focus on its lack of sensitivity to local social and historical contexts, its negative effects on social equity, and its inability to incorporate environmental sustainability concerns.

Neoliberalism as Ahistorical and Ethnocentric

Neoliberalism, for all its faults, has very well-developed theoretical underpinnings based in neoclassical economics. For this reason, proponents of neoliberalism analyze the problem of development with a "cookbook approach": if a series of macroeconomic adjustments are successfully implemented, then economic growth will be restored. Since economic growth is a necessary precondition for poverty reduction, the neoliberal formula promises to achieve development. To the extent that results fall short of those predicted in the model, the fault is assumed to lie in implementation, not in the model. One commentator remarks on the irony of these "recipes" for former socialist nations:

> The economic transformations envisaged in these countries ironically mirror the communist project. They implement an intellectual blueprint . . . drawn up within the walls of American academia and shaped by international institutions. . . . They offer a panacea, a magic elixir which, once taken, will cure all ills. Replace nationalization of the means of production with private property and plan with market, and you can leave the structure of the ideology intact. . . . Facing . . . the gravest economic crises in their history, countries all around the globe are told to plunge in and persevere. (Przeworski 1992:45)

Neoliberal formulas take little account of the existing and historical institutional and social contexts in which reforms are implemented. Neoliberalism is generally "econocentric," "technocentric," and "commodocentric" (to use

Michael Cernea's terminology [1996:15]). The narrow focus of neoliberalism on a limited range of economic variables, as well as a focus on technology and commodities, abstracted from the social context in which technologies and commodities operate, is a fatal weakness of the approach.

Neoliberalism treats the state as the neutral arbiter of contending social forces. The state is seen as a disinterested manager of society and the economy, which will implement structural adjustment measures following the prescribed recipe. In reality, the state itself is one of the resources in play in the process of development. The political power that inheres in the state is a valued resource in and of itself. Those in power during periods of structural adjustment are not disinterested managers of the economy, but instead are actively pursuing advantage in the context of the new regimes being created. An example of this is the enormous corruption of Carlos Salinas's regime in Mexico, now coming to light. Clearly, the Salinas government was not a neutral arbiter of contending economic forces, but an economic actor itself. Although Mexico may be an extreme example, it is not an isolated one. Corruption scandals in Honduras (the government of Rafael Leonardo Callejas), Colombia (Ernesto Samper Pizano), Brazil (Fernando Collor de Mello), and Peru (Alberto Fujimori) indicate that states implementing structural adjustment cannot be expected to be isolated from class interests. The wave of privatization associated with neoliberal structural adjustment presents a particularly rich field for corruption.

Another weakness of neoliberalism in relationship to the state is its uncritical acceptance of the state as a unit of action with little or no regard for the importance of transnational economic actors, especially corporations. It is one of the true ironies of neoliberalism that the process places increased emphasis on and faith in the state as a manager of the economy, while at the same time reducing the power of the state to take autonomous decisions in the political economy. The state is expected to efficiently and effectively implement a series of economic policies, but the content of those policies is dictated from without by the IMF, the World Bank, the WTO, and other supranational organizations. This problem is particularly acute for small nation-states like those in Central America and the Caribbean. Can we truly expect such states to have any degree of autonomy in the face of overwhelmingly powerful external economic forces, including transnational corporations whose scale of productive activities dwarfs those of many states?

Neoliberalism and Social Equity

The fundamental dictum of neoliberalism is represented in a slogan: a rising tide lifts all boats. Economic growth is seen as enlarging the economic pie, so that the competition for wealth and goods in society is not a zero-sum game. When critics of neoliberalism point to cases of regressive effects of laissez-faire capitalism on income distribution, proponents of the approach claim that this problem is either temporary (the Kuznets phenomenon) or irrelevant. Income distribution may worsen, but if the economic pie expands rapidly enough, the lot of the poor is still improved. (See Baer and Maloney 1997 for a review of income distribution effects of neoliberalism in Latin America.)

The reality in Latin America is quite distinct. Against a backdrop of a declining gross domestic product (GDP) in many Latin American countries in the last decade, most have experienced regressive trends in income distribution as well (CEPAL 1994). Most of the countries lost a great deal of ground in terms of social equity during the crisis of the 1980s and subsequent structural adjustment processes. Consequently, income distribution in the early 1990s was even worse than in the late 1970s. Some countries saw a slight decline in income inequality in the early 1990s (the success of neoliberalism?). However, in no case were these improvements enough to make up for the worsening trends experienced in the 1980s (CEPAL 1994: 2). The only exception to this rule was Chile, where the period 1987–1990 was marked by a downturn in social equity in rural areas coupled with a sharp rise in average household income. The poorest 25 percent of households maintained a virtually constant level of income, while the poorest 40 percent registered a modest 9 percent gain. The deterioration of social equity permitted the richest 10 percent to register a gain of over 90 percent in their household income: their real income nearly doubled (CEPAL 1994:3).

The critics of neoliberalism who wish to demonstrate worsening levels of relative and/or absolute poverty have to be very careful in their selection of cases, however. We must examine instances when the application of the neoliberal development model has been thorough and sustained. Otherwise, criticisms can simply be deflected as representing incomplete applications of the approach, or situations where the full effects of these reforms have not yet worked their magic (see Pastor and Wise 1992 for a discussion of incomplete neoliberal development in Peru of the 1980s; see also Baer and Maloney 1997). Mexico is an absolutely critical case in this regard, as its commitment to structural adjustment and a neoliberal model has been quite firm for over a decade.

The figures for trends at the national level in Mexico are not encouraging. Comisión Económico para América Latina (CEPAL) data for Mexico indicates that in urban areas, income distribution became significantly more skewed from 1987 to 1990. The share of income for the richest 10 percent increased from about 33 percent to over 40 percent, whereas that of the poorest 40 percent declined from 15 percent to 12 percent (CEPAL 1994:3). A recent analysis of the incidence of poverty in rural Mexico in the 1980s demonstrates that there was a clear increase in the extent, depth, and severity of extreme poverty in Mexico from 1984 to 1989 and that most of this increase was concentrated in rural areas (McKinley and Alarcón

1995:1575). Terry McKinley and D. Alarcón place the blame for this trend squarely on "the policies of structural adjustment implemented in the late 1980s [that] imposed a heavy cost on low-income households and a disproportionately high cost on rural households in particular" (1995:1575). Using a slightly different methodology, a CEPAL/Instituto Nacional de Estadística, Geografía, e Informática (INEGI) study (1993) indicates a slight amelioration in poverty from 1989 to 1992 in percentage terms, though the number of poor people in rural areas increased in absolute terms from 6.7 million in 1984 to 8.4 million in 1989 and 8.8 million in 1993 (as cited in McKinley and Alarcón 1995:1576).

Another important test case for the effects of neoliberal development models is Peru, where the Fujimori government applied a radical program of economic shock therapy with his election in 1990 (and subsequent autogolpe [self-coup]). The effects of the initial shock are well known to Peruvianists (and Peruvians!). A recent summary article by Janet Tanski (1994) documents the immediate devastating impact of economic shock therapy in its initial years (1990–1991) on the urban poor, women in particular. The published literature on subsequent events is more sparse. Since that time, however, Peru has become one of the economic success stories of Latin America. The disaster of the economic crisis of the late 1980s and the economic shock of the early nineties left Peru with per capita income levels approaching those of 1966. Growth of GDP in 1994 was over 13 percent and continued at 7 percent in 1995, before slowing to 2.6 percent in 1996 (see Table 1.2). This restored per capita income figures to those prevailing in 1986, before the most recent economic crisis.

Yet it is doubtful that the macroeconomic success of Fujimori's neoliberal approach has "lifted all boats." Peru's population stands at approximately 23 million. Of those, 12.3 million are considered to live in poverty, of whom 4.5 million live in extreme poverty. It is estimated that 40 percent of the population lacks access to basic services (potable water, electricity) and 20 percent earns less than the equivalent of U.S.$1.00 per day (*Avance Económico* 1996). Fujimori has pledged to make poverty reduction the centerpiece of his political and economic strategy for the rest of his term, with the target of halving poverty by the year 2000. Whether this goal is compatible with other aspects of the neoliberal program remains to be seen. Clearly, the Fuji-shock was implemented with little attention to cushioning its blow on the poorest sectors. Can neoliberalism be given a "human face" in this phase of Fujimori's policies?

Environmental Sustainability Issues

Sustainability is perhaps the strongest alternative discourse contesting the development terrain with neoliberalism. Spurred by concerns over global environmental change, sustainability has attempted to give environmental

**Table 1.2   Change in GDP and the Consumer Price Index (CPI)
in Peru, 1980–1997**

	GDP Growth (%)	GDP/Capita Growth (%)	GDP/Capita (1993 U.S.$)	CPI Growth (%)
1980–1985	–4.2	n.d.	n.d.	102
1986	9.2	6.9	2,191	200
1987	8.5	6.2	2,363	67
1988	–8.3	–10.2	2,099	660
1989	–11.7	–13.5	1,791	3371
1990	–5.4	–7.3	1,670	7481
1991	2.8	0.7	1,688	409
1992	–1.4	–3.4	1,641	73
1993	6.4	4.2	1,698	48
1994	13.1	0.8	1,900	23
1995	7.0	4.9	1,996	11
1996	2.6	1.0	2,196	12
1997 (est)	5.5	2.0	2,240	9

Sources: Dornbusch 1988 (1980–1985 figures); IDB, 1996 (1986–1997 figures).
Note: In the above columns, "n.d." indicates no data available.

concerns central importance in development theory. Sustainability started as a radical critique of conventional development theory, but the broadness and lack of precision in the term has made it susceptible to co-optation by a variety of mainstream development actors. Sustainability began by posing a question: what kind of development is compatible with (a) reducing poverty globally in a situation of rapid population growth, (b) the finite nature of the earth's resources, and (c) the ability of ecosystems to absorb the by-products of industrial society?

This perspective has the potential to (and actually did) lead to some fundamental rethinking of the notion of development, as well as the realization that "sustainable development" was a concept that applied to the rich countries as well as the poor; that is, sustainable development was simply not occurring in the rich countries, given their rate of resource use and pollution. This reinforced the notion, already vaguely present in development discourse, that the rich countries are not appropriate models for the poorer countries. In fact, they are probably not models of sustainability for their own future development. However, the term "sustainability" has also been interpreted as indicating the necessity of sustaining economic growth, which will allow poorer countries to deal with environmental problems (World Bank 1992).

Environmental issues basically do not fit within the neoliberal paradigm; they are an epistemological blind spot. Environmental problems in neoliberalism are basically handled under the same assumptions as those in neoclassical economics: as externalities, as examples of market failures, or as questions of eventual substitution of scarce resources by (as yet undiscovered) cheaper alternatives. Neoliberalism finesses the environmental question by positing that we simply grow our way out of these problems. "Government and business leaders assure us that the solution of these problems lies in pursuing even more single-mindedly the liberalization policies that produced these problems" (Power 1997:77). Neoliberals ignore fundamental questions regarding sustainable levels of consumption and production, and the need to control human wants and requirements in a finite world (Bennett 1988).

Latin America and Globalization: Old Wine, New Wine, or Whining?

Among Latin Americanists, attitudes toward the globalization discourse vary from a strong feeling of déjà vu to excitement and concern regarding what they view as a sea change in human society, which is affecting Latin America in fundamental ways. All of the trends associated with globalization are present with a vengeance in Latin America: the dramatic advances in telecommunications technologies and the attendant explosion of information (via, e.g., the Internet, World Wide Web); the globalization of cultural images, including a continued or accelerating trend toward urbanization and the rise of an urban-based culture of consumption of these images; the trend toward political democratization; the increasingly global scale of all aspects of economic activity, especially finance, accompanied by increasing power of multinational corporations; the strong influence of international mechanisms of governance such as the North American Free Trade Agreement (NAFTA), GATT, the WTO, and the UN; new political relationships shaped at least partially by the end of the bipolar world order that characterized international relations after World War II; and the internationalization of such social problems as global environmental change, burgeoning refugee populations, uncontrolled transnational migration, and the rise of global criminal syndicates (such as the Mexican and Colombian cartels) (see Sagasti 1995 for a recent review). Taken together, these trends amount to more than old wine in new bottles, though the resulting new wine may, in fact, be more bitter than the colonial vintage it replaces. Where do these changes leave Latin America? More specifically, what are the implications of these trends for the rural poor in Latin America?

Latin America, Globalization, and Social Change

Globalization has political, economic, and cultural implications for Latin America. These can be only briefly outlined here. One of the most positive trends in Latin America has been the establishment of electoral democracies

throughout the hemisphere, with the exception of Cuba. This has been accompanied by the resolution or reduction in intensity of internal guerrilla
wars in Central America and Peru. The latter trend is clearly linked to the
breakup of the Soviet Union, though how one explicates the causal links
here depends largely on ideological orientation. Although far from achieving societies that are models of social justice, it is definitely the case that
most counties of the region have more participatory, pluralistic, and open
political systems in place than they had a decade ago. This creates the possibility of open political organizing by vulnerable sectors in Latin America, including the rural poor, with the human costs generated by government repression much reduced.

At the same time, the challenges to governance have become immense.
There is a clear disjunction between the capabilities of the state to meet social demands and the scale of those demands. The fiscal discipline imposed
on countries of the region (structural adjustment) has left states weakened
and with little room for maneuver in terms of social programs to reduce unemployment and provide basic services. Although democracy has triumphed,
the proponents of democracy find they have inherited a "hollowed out"
state, as many of the functions formerly exercised by the state have passed
to the market (exchange rates), corporations (privatization of many state-run
industries), or newly emerging international institutions (GATT, WTO).

Meanwhile, the demands on the part of those social sectors that have
suffered under structural adjustment grow. Added to this growing need for
economic redress is the rapid growth in the economically active population, due both to the baby boom of the 1960s–1970s (see Table 1.3) and
to increasing participation of women in the workforce. It is entirely unclear if the postmodern industrial/service/information economy can absorb
workers at the rate necessary given the growth of the workforce, even if
economic growth remains robust. Many of these jobs are currently located
in the overburdened, rapidly growing urban areas. This is a good reason
for prioritizing development in rural areas (Loker 1996).

As mentioned, one of the most significant aspects of globalization is
the revolution in telecommunications that has facilitated the rapid transfer
of information and financial resources around the globe. Perhaps equally
significant, yet understudied, is the transfer of cultural (largely U.S.) images around the world. The impact of radio and television on the attitudes,
values, and aspirations of Latin Americans, both rural and urban, is well
known, but it has not been explored systematically. Given the flood of
U.S. cultural images and products in Latin America, the cumulative effect
is probably enormous: urban poverty coexists in the shadow of U.S. fast-
food outlets, and villagers retire at night with images of *Miami Vice* and
Beverly Hills 90210 in their minds. In reality, Latin American identity
itself is under assault.

The impact of global computer networks as a medium of communication on rural Latin America has been much less direct (with the notable

Table 1.3 Total Population and Population of Working Age in Selected Latin American Countries, 1960–1990 (in thousands)

	1960			1980			1990			Average Annual Growth Rate		
	Total Pop.	% Working-Age Pop.	Working-Age Pop.[a]	Total Pop.	% Working-Age Pop.	Working-Age Pop.	Total Pop.	% Working-Age Pop.	Working-Age Pop.	Total Pop. 1980–1990	Working-Age Pop. 1960–1980	Working-Age Pop. 1980–1990
Argentina	20,878	64	13,362	28,624	63	18,033	32,322	61	19,716	1.3	1.51	0.09
Bolivia	3,428	55	1,885	5,570	53	2,952	7,314	54	3,950	2.5	2.27	2.96
Brazil	72,594	54	39,201	121,286	55	66,707	150,368	60	90,221	2.2	2.69	3.07
Chile	7,614	57	4,340	11,145	62	6,910	13,173	64	8,431	1.7	2.35	2.01
Colombia	15,538	50	7,769	25,794	60	15,476	32,978	61	20,117	2.0	3.51	2.66
Costa Rica	1,236	50	618	2,284	59	1,348	3,015	60	1,809	2.4	3.98	2.99
Dominican Republic	3,231	49	1,583	5,697	53	3,019	7,170	59	4,230	2.2	3.28	3.43
Ecuador	4,413	52	2,295	8,123	52	4,224	10,587	57	6,035	2.4	3.10	3.63
El Salvador	2,570	52	1,336	4,525	52	2,353	5,252	53	2,784	1.4	2.87	1.70
Guatemala	3,964	51	2,022	6,917	54	3,735	9,197	52	4,782	2.9	3.12	2.50
Haiti	3,675	55	2,021	5,413	53	2,869	6,513	56	3,647	1.9	1.77	2.43
Honduras	1,935	52	1,006	3,662	50	1,831	5,138	52	2,672	3.4	3.04	3.85
Mexico	38,020	51	19,390	70,416	52	36,616	88,598	59	52,273	2.0	3.23	3.62
Nicaragua	1,493	50	746	2,771	50	1,385	3,871	52	2,013	3.4	3.14	3.81
Paraguay	1,773	51	904	3,147	53	1,668	4,277	55	2,352	3.2	3.11	3.50
Peru	9,931	52	5,164	17,295	54	9,339	21,550	58	12,499	2.3	3.01	2.96
Venezuela	7,502	51	3,826	15,024	55	8,263	19,735	58	11,446	2.7	3.92	3.31

Sources: Wilkie 1993: tables 626, 1306; World Bank 1992: table 26; author's calculations.
Note: a. Working-age population includes those aged 15–64.

exception of the Zapatista use of the Internet). Although computer networks may not have penetrated most of rural Latin America, they have drawn the intellectuals of many countries into a closer dialogue with counterparts around the world. Sagasti has suggested that we now speak of two civilizations in the world, with the great divide being those with the capacity to "generate, acquire, disseminate and utilize knowledge, both traditional and scientific" (1995:600) and those without this capacity. Globalization as a process is driven by knowledge, especially scientific knowledge that drives technological innovation. To the old divisions between rich and poor countries, industrialized and less industrialized, we now must add knowledge-producing versus knowledge-consuming countries. The role of that knowledge in globalization is so critical that participation in globalization is largely defined in terms of knowledge makers versus knowledge takers. The role of traditional knowledge in this mix is unclear, but the realm of indigenous technical knowledge is one area where Latin America is particularly rich.[3] In the realm of scientific knowledge, Latin American countries find themselves at a disadvantage, though the spread of computer-based networks is linking Latin intellectuals with the global knowledge community. Although this is positive, it represents another deep divide, one that follows the already deep divisions of class throughout the region. Arguably, this trend draws Latin American intellectuals farther away from the concerns of their own society, reproducing the global divide at the national level.

The Condition of the Rural Poor in Latin America: Grit in the Prosperity Machine

The main reasons to pay attention to the rural poor are their numbers and their poverty. Sources vary in their estimates of poverty in Latin America, but most agree that the number of poor is growing in absolute terms. Table 1.1 indicates that over 45 percent of the Latin American population is poor and that the number of poor has increased from 120 million in 1970 to around 200 million today. Rates of rural poverty are extremely high in most Latin American countries (Table 1.4), ranging from an astonishing 95 percent of the rural population classified as poor in Haiti to over 75 percent of the rural population in Central America and Bolivia and over half of the rural population in all but five countries.[4] For example, Marielouise Harrell, Cutberto Parillon, and Ralph Franklin documented the extent of malnutrition in Peru and concluded that about 38 percent of children there suffered from some degree of malnutrition and that 70 percent of the most serious cases were found in children residing in households dependent on agriculture for production or wage work (1989:326). A recent report on

Table 1.4 Estimated Rural Poverty in Latin America, 1980

	Poor (%)	Destitute (%)	Total Rural Pop. (in thousands)	Total Rural Poor (in thousands)	Total Rural Destitute (in thousands)	Rural Poor as % of Total Pop.
Mexico	68	26	23,348	15,877	6,070	21
Central America	75	52	13,014	9,773	6,712	
Guatemala	84	52	4,253	3,573	2,212	46
Honduras	80	70	2,359	1,887	1,651	47
El Salvador	76	55	2,913	2,213	1,602	44
Nicaragua	80	50	1,291	1,033	646	36
Panama	67	38	967	648	367	32
Costa Rica	34	19	1,231	419	234	19
Andean Region	69	31	24,778	17,809	7,725	
Colombia	67	23	9,226	6,181	2,112	23
Ecuador	65	20	4,279	2,781	856	31
Peru	68	39	5,720	3,890	2,231	21
Bolivia	86	74	3,102	2,668	2,295	48
Venezuela	64	9	2,451	1,569	221	11
Brazil	73	43	39,398	28,761	16,941	23
Southern Cone	31	9	9,313	2,879	836	
Paraguay	63	29	1,847	1,164	536	34
Chile	56	11	2,106	1,179	232	10
Argentina	10	1	4,890	489	49	2
Uruguay	10	4	470	47	19	2
Caribbean	78	41	9,266	7,217	3,777	
Haiti	95	86	4,381	4,162	3,768	80
Jamaica	51	n.d.	1,090	556	n.d.	25
Dominican Rep.	75	n.d.	2,751	2,063	n.d.	36
Trinidad & Tobago	40	n.d.	940	410	n.d.	34
Grenada	25	9	140	26	9	24

Source: FAO 1988.
Note: In above columns, "n.d." indicates no data available.

rural poverty projects that, if current trends continue, the number of rural poor will increase from an estimated 126 million in 1988 to 153 million by the end of the century (FAO 1988:2).[5]

While the number of rural poor is increasing, so is the number of urban poor and the incidence of urban malnutrition (Solomons and Gross 1987). "Between 1950 and 1980, there was a marked displacement in marginality away from the agricultural sector toward the urban economy in all 17 countries where data are available, except Uruguay" (de Janvry, Sadoulet, and Young 1989:402). Rural people are drawn to the city by the expectation of higher wages and improved access to services. One trend of the past 35 years is a growing gap in rural versus urban wages, with the rural sector losing ground (FAO 1988). Yet economic growth and industrialization are not going to absorb rural people. According to Alain de Janvry and colleagues (1989:400–404), economic growth appears to be increasingly *less* labor absorbing over time, presaging the continued existence of large marginal sectors in the countryside and the city unless steps are taken to directly address this issue.

The notion that agriculture should shed labor to supply workers for industry is obsolete. Instead of shedding labor for the nonagricultural economy, agriculture should be viewed as a sector to *absorb* labor, either directly in productive activities or through linkages to agriculturally related activities such as processing, marketing, and other services. Agriculture must provide sustainable, satisfying livelihoods for more, not less, people. There are already too many people in the city and not enough jobs, as illustrated by the explosive growth of the informal sector, squatter settlements, and additional indicators of urban economic marginality. Where is it easier to deal with poverty: in the city or in the countryside? Until recently, it was thought that addressing poverty was easier in the city. But now, cities are so swamped, this is questionable. Yet, to staunch the flow of rural-to-urban migration, the countryside must be something more than a place to "warehouse" the poor, or the natural and social environments in rural areas will also be overwhelmed. This will have drastic consequences for the design of the "social infrastructure" necessary for sustainable development (discussed below).

Latin American rural communities are also important as test cases for the new global economy. In what way can large rural populations throughout the poorer countries be effectively incorporated in the global economy? A global economy/society that cannot create productive roles and meet the needs of the rural poor is unrealistic and dangerous. The challenge is to take care of poverty in situ—in the countryside—rather than exporting it to cities or internationally. Transnational migration is real and growing, and it will continue to grow. This is the ultimate logic of globalization. As other factors of production—financial capital and technology—

have become internationally mobile, we can expect labor to become more internationalized too. The flaw in this logic is, of course, that human beings are not simply "production factors," and their mobility can lead to serious social problems in terms of stress, alienation, and crime: the antithesis of development. To quote Karl Polanyi:

> To allow the market mechanism to be the sole director of the fate of human beings and their environment . . . would result in the demolition of society. For the alleged commodity of "labour power" can not be shoved about, used indiscriminately, or even left unused, without affecting also the human individual who happens to be the bearer of this peculiar commodity. (1944:73)[6]

What roles will rural people play in the global economy? Will they serve as producers of basic grains for consumption and sale? If so, their role in food security at the regional and national levels looms large. Will they serve as producers of specialty, labor-intensive export crops for the winter market of North America and Europe? This has been shown to be a development path fraught with difficulty, especially in the absence of strong local and national institutions to guide this process (Barham et al. 1992; Carter and Barham 1997; Conroy, Murray, and Rosset 1996). What is certain is that the historical neglect and current moment have not been favorable to most of the rural poor.

Rural Communities in Crisis

The nature of the current crisis of rural communities varies by country and by region within countries and even from community to community. But there are common elements to this crisis associated with the structural position of the rural poor within national economies. This crisis is linked to the changing overall economic context of Latin American countries briefly described above, which ramifies throughout the national economies of these countries. Rural communities are directly affected by, and respond to, these changes. The basic outlines of these forces have been sketched by de Janvry and colleagues:

> The Latin American peasantry has been the victim of a "double (under-) development squeeze." . . . On the one side, the peasantry has been unable to protect access to land and average farm size has been declining, forcing peasant households to seek sources of income outside the farm. . . . At the same time, employment opportunities . . . have grown slowly, permanent workers have been increasingly replaced by seasonal workers . . . , scholars of peasantry have heatedly debated whether peasants would increase in numbers by successfully competing with family farms . . . or would decrease in numbers [and] . . . be transformed into landless

proletarian workers. . . . Neither position is correct. Peasants do increase
in numbers—but as a sign of systemic failure in providing them with sufficient employment. . . . Peasants become increasingly dependent on
wage earnings as a component of household income—but without becoming landless as they maintain continued access to a plot of land, however small. With peasants thus existing as a residual category, with insufficient access to either land or employment . . . , they account for the
bulk of poverty in Latin America. (1989:396–397)

This "double underdevelopment squeeze" has had a number of consequences for individuals, households, and communities trying to survive
this crisis. These consequences have been documented by a number of researchers in the region (see, e.g., Durham 1995; Stonich 1993; Murray
1994).

These researchers agree substantially in their views of the main causes
of this crisis:

1. a dualistic pattern of agricultural production into commercial/ex-
   port sectors and subsistence/basic grain sectors, linked by the wage
   labor of subsistence/grain farmers in the export sector;
2. the highly inequitable distribution of resources in the two sectors,
   with the export sector expanding its land base at the expense of
   smaller producers and the natural environment;
3. preferential treatment by the government of both urban sectors
   (Michael Lipton's "urban bias" [1977]) and the export-agriculture
   sector;
4. a growing population and a stagnant or declining resource base
   (land);
5. efforts by smallholders to intensify (adopt chemical inputs) or ex-
   tensify (expand into previously uncultivated areas), either of which
   often leads to environmental degradation.

The end result is that the rural poor resort to increasingly disparate
and desperate livelihood strategies. These include local agricultural labor
within the community or region, migrant agricultural labor in the export-
agriculture sector, and cyclical urban and international migration—all of
which divert productive labor from agriculture, making efforts at sustainable intensification of agricultural production more problematic. The
households of the rural poor seeking to diversify income sources are often
fragmented, with members of the household living in various places at different times and coming together on rare occasions. The traditional view
of rural households as a co-resident, cooperative group sharing a common
labor pool oriented largely to agricultural production is increasingly a
myth. For example, the growing *maquiladora* sector in Central America

draws heavily on young women from the countryside as a source of cheap labor. These women and girls eagerly seek these employment opportunities, despite difficult working conditions and low wages, to escape the economic and social constraints of the countryside. They often work for extended periods in factories, sending a portion of wages home to subsidize the (rural) household. Periodically, they leave the wage labor sector and return to the countryside for extended periods of time, reincorporating themselves in the household labor pool (based on personal observations in the El Cajón region of Honduras; see also Stonich 1993). Central America is thus following the Mexican pattern of increased importance of remittance income for the survival of rural households and communities (see Durand and Massey 1992:25ff. for a review of the importance of remittances in rural Mexico).

The double squeeze on the rural poor also leads a significant portion of households to colonize "frontier" zones of agricultural expansion, inducing deforestation and often ephemeral productivity gains in these fragile ecosystems and causing social conflict among colonists, indigenous inhabitants, and large landowners. This process may be combined with retaining residence in the home community, as documented by Jane Collins (1988) in southern Peru, or it may be permanent, as observed in numerous colonization efforts in Amazonia. Carlos Aramburú (1984:163) estimates that of every five migrants who leave the Peruvian Sierra, four go to the coast (mostly to urban areas), and one goes to the tropical forest region. Jeffery Jones (1990) and Susan Stonich (1993) discuss links between highland poverty and lowland colonization in Honduras. John Vandermeer and Ivette Perfecto (1995) document a similar pattern in Costa Rica. Thus the crisis in long-standing and relatively densely settled highland regions is indirectly responsible for environmental degradation in the lowland humid tropics.

Increased population pressure, land shortage, and an acute shortage of capital often induce unsustainable intensification of agricultural practices in rural communities. The well-known process of shortening fallows in low-input agricultural systems leads to a downward cycle of lower yields, loss of agricultural fertility, soil erosion, and other negative consequences (Trenbath, Conway, and Craig 1990). Small farmers may attempt to reverse this process by the adoption of chemical inputs, but these are often inappropriately used and handled in an unsafe manner, causing further environmental deterioration and creating health problems among those handling these products. Marketing channels and dispersed, unorganized buying patterns lead to high costs of inputs to the rural poor and high middleman profits.

The increased "rationalization" of production among larger farmers, including mechanization (often subsidized by government policies such as fuel subsidies, input subsidies, and imports of agricultural machinery), leads to a decline in wage labor opportunities in agriculture, as well as a decline in the personalistic bonds that formed an important social component of the survival strategies of the rural poor: patron-client relationships, *compadrazgo* (godparenthood), and other social mechanisms that blunted the severity of gross income inequality and assisted the survival of vulnerable groups in the countryside. The drive toward economic efficiency undermines long-standing cultural precedents of social solidarity, however hierarchical and paternalistic these may have been. The end result is the breaking of the traditional social contract and increased vulnerability among marginal households, groups, and individuals.

The double squeeze of declining land and employment opportunities is occurring in a context of shrinking government resources to cope with the social problems generated by these multiple, interlocking social, economic, and ecological crises. The responses of the rural poor to this failure of the state to guarantee the basic conditions for earning a livelihood vary, ranging from migration and diversification to the seeking of alliances with NGOs that have sprung up to fill the vacuum left by the withdrawal of the state.

The Historical Marginalization of the Rural Poor

The current crisis in rural communities has its origins in the historical neglect of the rural poor by national governments. There are numerous reasons why the rural poor have been neglected in Latin American development and why, despite their evident persistence, they are expected to—and in many cases it is hoped that they will—disappear. Perhaps foremost among these reasons is the industrial bias in development: industrialization has been seen as the sine qua non of development. Rich countries are industrialized. Industrialization increases labor productivity. Industrialization has been viewed by many as the escape from the trap of dependency on export of primary goods. In this view, agriculture's role in development is viewed solely as the sector that contributes to industrialization through transfer of resources (capital and labor) to industrialization (Lewis 1954; cf. Johnston and Mellor 1961). The industrial bias is reinforced by an urban bias in development (see Lipton 1977): political leaders are from cities, and urban life is more highly valued by most of those who hold positions of power and influence. Also, the concentration of population in cities has made it politically imperative and expedient to serve urban interests. This is compounded by the historically weak grassroots development of political parties due to urban origins and structural barriers to participation of rural people (e.g., dispersion, lack of skills and education). There is also an export/capital-intensive bias in agricultural development:

when attention has turned to the countryside, the focus has been on larger, more heavily capitalized production units because this approach fits in with developed world models (export-led development, "tractorism"). It is also easier to work with resource-rich farmers who are fewer in number and are more accessible, educated, wealthy, and influential. Furthermore, the export sector contributes foreign exchange for industrialization and the payment of foreign debt obligations. Many of these biases simply reflect prevailing class and power biases in development; in fact, some would see class and power relations as the basic factor underlying the biases enumerated above. What is interesting is that so-called revolutionary governments have seldom favored the rural poor or sought "campesino-led" development. In nonrevolutionary situations (by far the majority), class and power interests tend to channel development resources to ruling elites, such as urban industrialists and export agriculturalists (often the same individuals), not to the rural poor. In revolutionary situations, campesinos are not understood or trusted, are seen as "lacking revolutionary potential," and are generally grouped as a "backward sector" that should ultimately disappear. Writing of smallholders, Robert Netting comments that

> it is intriguing that for both the socialists . . . of the left and the free-market capitalists of the right, the agreed-upon path to agricultural development has been the large-scale, mechanized, energy-dependent, scientific, industrialized farm. Smallholders have been universally stigmatized as unproductive, regardless of their yields per unit of land, on the grounds that (1) they use too much labor; (2) they do not produce a large surplus for the market; and (3) they do not make rational economic, scientific decisions about production and innovation. (1993:21)

With the recent "environmental turn" in development discourse, the rural poor have been further demonized as destroyers of land, degraders, deforesters, shortsighted abusers of biological resources, and otherwise enemies of sustainable development due to either ignorance or desperation or both. All these factors lead to a conceptualization of the rural poor as a residual category, as "surplus population" and "obstacles to development"—as if development were something that can occur outside of efforts to realize the human potential of millions of people.

In summary, the prevailing development model sees the rural poor as antimodern—the antithesis of development—not as human beings whose basic needs require attention. If the rest of the program is followed, the needs of the rural poor will somehow be taken care of, almost in passing, as a by-product of development of other sectors of the economy (e.g., industry, capital-intensive export agriculture). This seems true whether we are talking about the modernization paradigm of the 1950s or the neoliberal development paradigm of the 1990s. Campesinos are seen as having no comparative advantage and no constructive role in the national economy or the global division of labor. The rural poor simply do not fit into the predominant development paradigm; they are grit in the prosperity machine. Yet, there they are.

In examining the case studies presented in the chapters that follow, there are generalizations that can be drawn about the meeting of the global and the local in rural Latin America.

1. *Local agroecology matters:* Taken collectively, the case studies communicate that the effects of globalization will vary sharply, depending on the local agroecological context. Some of the most important variables affecting the outcome of this process are:

    a. *Initial distribution of resources:* Access to land is particularly important. For example, the relatively egalitarian access to land in San Antonio, Oaxaca (see Chapter 2), and Almolonga in the Guatemalan highlands (see Chapter 4) enabled a more constructive response to market opportunities and "modernization" than, for instance, in the Dominican Republic's Deep South (see Chapter 8).

    b. *High agricultural potential:* Those with access to relatively fertile, well-watered land (e.g., San Antonio, Almolonga), as opposed to lower-potential lands that are less fertile (see the discussion of Amerindians in Guyana in Chapter 7 and the discussion of the Ngóbe in Chapter 5) or subject to unfavorable climatic conditions such as drought (e.g., the Dominican Deep South) or fluctuation (e.g., the Ngóbe), are better positioned to respond favorably to globalization.

    c. *Favorable market access:* Market access is one aspect of "high agricultural potential" just discussed. Ready access to markets confers numerous advantages on rural producers. For example, the people of San Antonio and Almolonga are relatively well placed to market high-value products, whereas those in the Dominican Deep South, the Ngóbe, and the Amerindians of Guyana face formidable barriers to market access.

2. *Demographic stress, intensification, and nonfarm employment:* Several of the chapters (those on Oaxaca, the Ngóbe, the Guatemalan highlands, the Dominican Deep South, and the Amerinidans in Guyana) directly or indirectly address the issues of population growth and intensification of agriculture. The potential for intensification is linked to the agroecological factors mentioned above, as well as to available technology and skills/knowledge on the part of local producers. Again, the contrasts between the situation in the Guatemalan highlands and Oaxaca

with that of the Ngóbe, the Dominican Deep South, and Amerindian Guyana are instructive in this regard. Virtually everywhere, the viability of rural communities is increasingly dependent not only on an effective agricultural system, but on nonfarm employment as well. This frequently takes the form of petty commerce (Oaxaca, Almolonga), though Chapter 7 explores the interesting case of ecotourism as a source of farm and nonfarm income. The explosion of *maquiladora* employment (discussed in Chapter 4) is a decidedly mixed blessing for rural people in desperate need of employment, as it is vulnerable to exploitative working conditions.

3. *Fragmented social identity:* One of the effects of globalization that appears in several of the case studies is the fragmentation of social identity, frequently along generational lines. In their respective studies of the Guatemalan highlands and the Dominican Deep South, Liliana Goldin and Manuel Vargas explicitly recognize that globalization is leading to a generation gap in terms of people's identification with agriculture as a way of life. Although not surprising given the portrait sketched above of the rural crisis and growing importance of wage labor among the rural poor, this may presage a more fundamental shift away from identification with rural life in general. Also, as people are drawn into more varied spheres of social interaction, either vicariously through mass communications or existentially through periodic migration (either locally, nationally, or internationally), individuals experience this fragmentation on a personal as well as a group level (see Goldin's discussion of the effects of *maquiladora* employment). This topic has been explored theoretically by Michael Kearney (1996) from a postmodern and Marxian perspective.

4. *Collective organization and action:* Several of the case studies (those by James McDonald, David Guillet, and Philip Young and John Bort) emphasize the importance of collective action for rural survival. McDonald, in his discussion of the dairy sector in Mexico, analyzes the circumstances under which collective responses on the part of rural producers emerge and effectively articulate rural demands and potentials. Guillet discusses the importance and value of what can be termed "indigenous social knowledge," that is, the organizational capacity of rural indigenous people that has emerged over the long term to manage resources (in this case, water), to resolve conflicts, and to articulate collective concerns. Arguably, indigenous social knowledge is one of the most important, and underrecognized, factors affecting the articulation of local people with global forces. Young and Bort document the emergence of self-conscious ethnicity (another frequent "identity response" to globalization) and the use of this as a means of collective organization among the Ngóbe in Panama. In the Ngóbe case, we are witnessing the attempt, under considerable pressure, of a group of people to create indigenous social knowledge in the form of collective institutions based on ethnic identity.

5. *The value of community:* The cases that document the importance of collective action (and those that highlight its importance through its absence) suggest that collective action is much easier to construct in relatively stable, enduring communities where reciprocity can be expected. These conditions still prevail in many rural communities in Latin America. But these conditions are clearly on the wane due to such forces as the fragmentation of identity, the generation gap, and migration. Once lost, a sense of community is difficult to recapture. One of the most disturbing aspects of globalization is the tendency of emerging market forces to undermine community social stability and solidarity. Families and communities are split. Members migrate seasonally or permanently, to urban areas or internationally. The moral consensus and reciprocal altruism that hold communities together are eroded by extended absence in the desperate search for centavos. The ideological basis of community that gives meaning and common purpose to collective action and reciprocal altruism likewise is eroded as new ideas, aspirations, and goals intrude in rural Latin America. Just as we discover the importance of community to livelihood, personal well-being, and sustainability, it disappears before our eyes. To the extent that residential stability, ideological conformity, face-to-face relations, and reciprocal altruism characterize rural communities more than anonymous, anomic urban communities, it may be more feasible to construct community and appropriate social institutions to realize sustainable development in stable rural communities rather than urban areas.

6. *Sustainability:* Closely related to all the issues raised above is the problem of sustainability. Sustainability issues loom large even in relatively "successful" globalization. The depletion of the aquifer in San Antonio, Oaxaca; the overuse of pesticides in San Antonio and the Guatemalan highlands; the prospects of land degradation in Guyana associated with intensified cassava production (and less directly with ecotourism); the lack of clear technological alternatives for growing numbers of Ngóbe in western Panama; and the nutritional, economic, and emotional dependency on the (unreliable) state created by agricultural "modernization" in the Dominican Deep South are all examples of the failure to generate sustainable livelihoods for rural people in the context of globalization. One of the bright spots in this regard is the persistence of farmer-managed irrigation systems in Andean Peru (see Chapter 6). Yet, according to Guillet, these sustainable systems are under assault by proponents of globalization, with their drive to privatize water resources. The case studies thus reinforce the vocal and persistent critique of globalization on environmental grounds. The inability of neoliberalism to incorporate environmental concerns (its aforementioned epistemological "blind spot") may be its greatest vulnerability. This is small consolation to the rural people and others who suffer the consequences of nonsustainable development (see Johnston 1994 and 1997 for further discussion of these critical issues).

Earlier, this chapter drew attention to the symmetries between social-ist prescriptions for development and the prescriptions of neoliberalism. The resistance of neoliberalism to empirical data that counters its top-down, cookbook approach to development is a characteristic it shares with other failed ideologies. In the context of discussing rural life in Romania in the 1960s, Cernea remarks on the restrictions placed on empirical research:

> In that period, rife with distorting dominant ideology, the top-down pre-scription for research was to ascribe to reality the image of how it was supposed to be, but wasn't. Genuine fieldwork was ostracized, *as it im-plied a threat to the establishment: the threat of deflating the ideological balloon with reported empirical evidence.* (1996:7; emphasis added)

One can only hope that neoliberalism will not prove as impervious to em-pirical evidence as Romanian communism. But it is incumbent upon social scientists to uncover and provide the empirical evidence necessary to "de-flate the ideological balloon" of neoliberal capitalist development and to pragmatically and emphatically communicate these findings to policymak-ers. In addition to calling the crowd's attention to the emperor's neolib-eral clothes, we must also seek out the examples of successful engagement with the market, determine the appropriate conditions for the creation of dignified livelihoods, and identify creative responses on the part of rural communities to the changes associated with the global and the local. The chapters in this book represent efforts along this line.

Conclusion

Latin America is actively involved in the forces of globalization in all its aspects. Democratization, urbanization, and the insertion of Latin America into institutional mechanisms for the organization of a global political economy (e.g., GATT, NAFTA, and the Caribbean Basin Initiative) are all predominant, if uneven, trends in the region. As we have seen in the re-view above of the trends guided by neoliberalism and globalization, these forces do not add up to an automatic improvement in human welfare for the majority of Latin Americans. Yet, undeniably, these trends open up new political and economic spaces for marginalized groups within the re-gion. The main purpose of this book is to explore how these spaces are being perceived, occupied, and exploited by the rural poor in the region.

Forty years of development discourse, projects, and theory have not changed one fundamental fact: Latin America is dependent on the United States in ways that are entirely asymmetrical. The region remains in a po-sition of dependency economically and politically. When the United States calls the neoliberal tune, the Latin American countries must learn to dance. Unfortunately, there are few other partners available (Europe and Japan), and they, by and large, are calling similar tunes.

This is the macrocontext in which Latin American countries must function. Globalization and neoliberalism are, at present, the only games in town. There are clear dangers for Latin American countries in entering into open competition ("free trade") with the "overdeveloped" countries. In the scramble for resources and markets of the current era, the poorer countries—and the poor within those countries—are ill-prepared to compete. Although the flow of private investment into Latin America has increased in recent years, the vast majority of this investment is concentrated in Mexico and Brazil. Globalization is producing an increased differentiation within the former Third World generally and within Latin America in particular. Within the poorer countries, the rural poor, due to their historical neglect and marginalization, are at a further competitive disadvantage. Just as Latin American countries must determine under what circumstances they can compete, rural people must figure out how to *sacar algun provecho* from this competitive environment as well. What strategies are available? Under what circumstances can smallholders find a niche? The panorama is decidedly mixed. Many of the trends of globalization are unremittingly negative for Latin American countries and especially for the rural poor. But globalization with democratization opens up opportunities for the rural poor as well as for other social actors. The chapters in this book explore how the rural poor are struggling to find economically and culturally satisfying roles in this rapidly globalizing context.

I will always remember graffiti I saw emblazoned on a wall in 1988 in Peru, during the crash of Alan Garcia's populist experiment. It read, *No se come discursos* (You can't eat speeches). Nor can you eat books or chapters like this one. It is incumbent upon anthropologists who work in campesino communities to apply their knowledge and to help people, individually and collectively, find alternatives that allow them to fulfill their basic needs. We must document their successes as well as the failures and contribute to the formation of policies and institutions that create dignified, satisfying lives for men and women in rural Latin America.

Notes

1. This chapter focuses on rural areas, though it is clear that the fates of rural and urban regions are inextricably linked. To the extent that solutions to meaningful livelihood are not found in rural areas, the problem will be transferred to urban areas. There are reasons to believe (discussed in this chapter) that the problem of meaningful livelihood may be more difficult to resolve in urban areas.

2. Latin America is a heterogeneous region. This chapter (and the book as a whole) focuses mostly on Mexico, Central America, and tropical South America.

Even within this group of countries, there is significant variation in terms of the structure of agriculture, the number and percentage of rural poor, the role of agriculture in the economy, and other relevant variables. The chapter attempts to discuss general trends, using a number of country-specific examples.

3. Indigenous technical knowledge and indigenous social knowledge are areas where Latin America displays considerable wealth. Knowledge of species, ecosystems, and agroecological management strategies—and the social institutions that sustain them—is an important human resource of the region. How these fields of knowledge will weather globalization is problematic, as discussed in several chapters in this volume.

4. Data in Table 1.4 are from 1980, as published by the Food and Agricultural Organization (FAO) in 1988. More recent comprehensive data is difficult to obtain, but according to Alberto Valdés and Tom Wiens (1996), rates of rural poverty have not changed substantially in recent years. Their data indicate continued high rural poverty rates in Latin America (over 50 percent) for the countries for which they have data and a continued "exporting of poverty" to urban areas.

5. FAO data in Table 1.4 and International Food Policy Research Institute (IFPRI) estimates cited in Table 1.1 differ due to differing methodologies for identifying poor and rural people.

6. The criticisms of migration expressed here do not imply that all migration, whether rural to urban, national, or international, is bad. Many individuals benefit from migration. But it is clearly the case that cities in Latin America are overwhelmed in terms of provisioning basic services and suffer many human and ecological problems as a result (see Hardoy, Mitlin, and Satterwaite 1992 for a review of these problems). Also, it is unclear whether international migration is sustainable either in terms of solving the problems of sending communities or in terms of the growing political backlash in receiving countries (e.g., Proposition 187 and similar initiatives in the United States).

2

Commercial Family Farmers and Collective Action: Dairy Farming Strategies in Mexico

James H. McDonald

En México comemos queso y yogurt, en ocasiones hasta de leche.[1]

The recently exposed "milk scandal" involving Raúl Salinas (former director of CONASUPO, the National Company for Popular Subsistence, and brother of former President Carlos Salinas de Gortari [1988–1994]) highlighted one dimension of Mexico's dependence on foreign basic foods. It is claimed that in 1987, Salinas was responsible for importing thousands of tons of Irish powdered milk contaminated with radioactive residue that was a by-product of the Chernobyl nuclear accident in the Ukraine of the former Soviet Union in April 1986. This tainted powdered milk was then allegedly processed and sold to the Mexican public by a variety of large commercial dairies (cf. Zamora 1997). The scandal threw fresh attention onto one of Mexico's smaller agricultural sectors and raised questions about Mexico's ability to provide this important basic food in a country where 50 percent of the population experiences some level of malnutrition (*Siglo 21* 1996). The overall devastation of Mexico's agricultural economy after the implementation of the North American Free Trade Agreement (NAFTA) on January 1, 1994, has forced the Mexican government to re-focus its attention on agricultural development.

The opening of the Mexican economy with the General Agreement on Tariffs and Trade and its more specific regional version embodied in NAFTA created a large-scale, integrated trading bloc. The move toward the opening of the Mexican economy can be traced back to the crash of the global oil market in 1982, which left Mexico deeply indebted and virtually bankrupt. Due to the failure of its economic protectionist policies and state-centered model of economic development, Mexico became an important test case for neoliberalism, with its emphasis on economic globalization, free trade, and privatization. The participating NAFTA nations—Mexico, Canada, and the United States—are mandated to drop tariff barriers impeding free trade over a period ranging from the agreement's implementation to 15 years, depending upon the commodity in question. Many argue that trade barriers were already minimal by world standards, averaging 23 percent in 1985 and only 6.5 percent in 1990 (Arsen 1996:37). Proponents of free trade contend that under conditions of international competition, the production of commodities will shift to countries that can produce them most cheaply and efficiently. Mexican dairy farmers, for example, are not efficient when compared with their U.S. counterparts. The U.S. yield per cow is about five times that produced by Mexican dairy farmers (McDonald 1997). With the implementation of NAFTA, the new tariff rate quota for U.S. powdered milk imports was set at 40,000 tons, roughly the previous five-year average. Although structural and policy changes were occurring prior to NAFTA, the implementation of the agreement sped up the process for Mexico's dairy farmers, who found themselves in immediate competition with U.S. dairymen. Neoliberals would argue that Mexico would be better off purchasing nonfat powdered milk at international market prices, and its inefficient dairy farmers could produce other commodities in which they have a competitive advantage. This perhaps sounds reasonable when framed in the impersonal systems perspective of the policy analyst, but it raises a number of serious questions about the effects of globalization on the well-being of rural peoples, who may have few viable alternatives to their agrarian way of life.

This chapter will explore in comparative perspective the experiences of small commercial dairy farmers in the Mexican states of Michoacán and Guanajuato as they seek to find new competitive alternatives. To achieve greater economies of scale and better integration with the market, groups of farmers in both areas have begun to form cooperatives. One objective of this chapter is to consider the internal and external conditions that support collective action of this sort. As T. White and C. Ford Runge observe, "despite [a] strong theoretical base, and advances in understanding the correlates of success, we still do not fully understand why and how collective action institutions emerge in the first place—and survive in the long run. . . . [E]mpirical analyses can help to improve our understanding of institutional emergence and evolution" (1995:1684). A second objective of this chapter is to consider the effects of transnational dairy processors on local dairy producers. Unlike the majority of research on Mexican globalization that is critical of the role of transnational corporations (TNCs), the case of Danone de México[2] in Guanajuato is an example of how a large TNC is playing a constructive role by providing a secure market for quality milk that, in turn, provides an economic environment in which farmers are willing to invest in the modernization of their farm enterprises.

Specifically, I will examine different regional contexts and strategies adopted by farmers in Mexico's dairy sector as they engage and cope with a new economic reality in which farmers must produce higher-quality milk at a lower cost. Small- and medium-scale commercial dairy farmers that dominate dairy production in the northwestern highlands of Michoacán and the central mesa of Guanajuato (north of the lowland Bajío region) will be compared and contrasted as they struggle to meet the demands of a rapidly globalizing economy. This research centers on the areas of San José de Gracia-Cotija, Michoacán, and San Miguel de Allende-Dolores Hidalgo, Guanajuato (see Map 2.1). Both regions are noteworthy in that they are the largest milk-producing districts within their respective states. And in both regions, there are instances in which farmers have organized into cooperatives with greater or lesser success, while others have remained independent. Also in both cases, microregional variation is as striking as are differences between regions. A major factor driving this variation is the nature of local and regional markets as they intersect with specific historical and environmental factors that give structure to local farming communities.

Research was conducted during the summer and fall of 1996 in Michoacán, in which 48 interviews were obtained across four farmer categories: small (1–19 head of cattle), small-medium (20–49 head), medium-large (50–99 head), and large-scale farmers (more than 100 head). Other interviews were conducted with local political leaders, owners of dairy processing plants, local- and state-level agricultural officials (presidents of local dairymen's associations and officials with the Secretariat of Agriculture, Livestock, and Rural Development [SAGAR]), and others working in the agriculture sector in the study area. Additional fieldwork was also undertaken in Guanajuato as part of ongoing research I have been conducting there since 1987 that has followed the changes in the dairy sector in pre- and post-NAFTA contexts.

Ironies of Mexican Dairy Organizations and Dairy Policy

"Organization" is a current catchword being used by the Mexican government when it talks about agricultural development in the post-NAFTA economy. Farmers formerly protected by tariff barriers and subsidized in a closed economic system now have to compete in the international market. One irony of Mexico's dairy industry is its long history of organization at the local and state level through dairymen's associations. Yet these associations typically provide little more than tax receipts and the health certificates necessary for transporting and selling cattle. In other words, their main function has been a bureaucratic rather than an economic one, in which they provide an organizational infrastructure to contribute to the

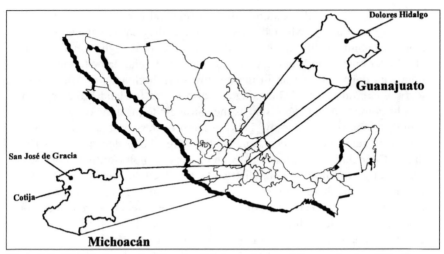

Map 2.1 Field research sites in Michoacán and Guanajuato, Mexico

development and transformation of the production and marketing of milk.[3] This is particularly noteworthy since Mexico has never been self-sufficient in milk production and is also the world's largest importer of powdered milk. Another irony of the Mexican dairy industry has to do with the government's role in shaping the industry through agrarian policy. On the one hand, the government has always had a strong presence through price controls placed on milk at the wholesale and retail levels. On the other hand, the government has done little to help farmers modernize their operations so that they can produce more milk, of better quality, more efficiently.

On the eve of NAFTA in late 1993, the vast majority of Mexico's dairy farmers were both unorganized and underdeveloped. NAFTA provided Mexican dairy farmers with little phase-in time so that, at the very least, the more capitalized dairy sectors could respond to the new market demands being placed upon them. The farmers that will be compared and contrasted in the following sections reflect the diversity of producers, markets, and environmental constraints as they vary across, as well as within, regions. Farmers who continue producing milk using "traditional methods,"[4] such as those in Michoacán, are finding that they cannot compete on a national level, let alone an international one. Perhaps less intuitively obvious are the problems faced by farmers in states, such as Guanajuato, where commercial farming methods are often intensive and mechanized[5] and the state's economy as a whole is comparatively robust. Yet far from being preadapted to Mexico's new economic order, these farmers are also struggling to successfully compete in Mexico's newly opened economy. Once-prosperous farmers are considering selling out altogether, and others are trying to find new ways to organize and lower their costs in a hostile economy marked by inflation, the removal of agricultural subsidies, scarce and expensive credit, a major monetary devaluation, and intensifying international competition.

Dairying in the Michoacán Highlands

Northwestern Michoacán is characterized by scarce agricultural land in mountainous terrain that has been historically isolated from the dynamic Central Mexican economy (Friedrich 1977). Irrigation is equally scarce, and most farmers in the region rely on seasonal rains and dry farming methods to cultivate poor-quality land that yields relatively small amounts of maize. Given the limitations on crop agriculture and the presence of abundant rangeland, the region has historically been a ranching economy oriented toward dairy production, especially cheese making (González 1972). Today, the San José de Gracia-Cotija area remains dominated by small-scale producers utilizing little or no mechanization (milking is commonly done by hand in the farmer's fields or in rudimentary stalls near the rangeland on which the animals are kept). Cattle are a hearty Cebu-Holstein mix that are well adapted to the rough, mountainous terrain.

During interviews for my research, both insiders and outsiders claimed that it is a unified region. I typically heard statements such as, "What you find in San José de Gracia and Cotija is all the same: small-scale farmers with little or no technology and low production. Farmers are all traditional." However, after conducting fieldwork in both communities, it became clear that although farmers in both locales were struggling to survive, a combination of local ecology, local market forces, and the level of farmer organization made them very different places.

San José de Gracia

The dairymen's associations in each community claim the majority of the municipality's farmers on their rosters. In San José de Gracia, the membership list shows that 82.9 percent (N = 340) have less than 20 head of cattle, 11.2 percent (N = 46) have between 20 and 49 head, 5.1 percent have 50–99 head, and only 0.7 percent have over 100 head.[6] The 410 members own a total of 6,113 head of cattle (an average of 15 head per member, a figure consistent with my general experience in the area). The vast majority of the association's members in the municipality of Marcos Castellanos, within which San José is located, own their land (82.4 percent [N = 338]); 6.3 percent (N = 26) rent land; and 11.2 percent (N = 46) are *ejidatarios* (peasant producers who work on land where the title is held by the state) or *comuneros*. As Luis González (1972) points out, land reform never really arrived in this corner of Michoacán. The largest *ejido* (agrarian community where title is held by the state) in the area is El Sabino, with a total of 51 members. As a consequence, *ejidos* figure minimally into the local economic and political topography.

Dairying is based on the production of maize as the main forage crop supplemented with open rangeland grazing during the summer rainy season. Farmers typically own 7–10 hectares of unirrigated agricultural land that render small yields of 3 or 4 tons of maize per hectare on average, while allocating about 1 hectare of poor rangeland per head of cattle that acts as a food source during the summer rainy season. Only the largest farmers in the region had access to irrigation or had groomed pastureland sown with improved grasses. Because of the inadequacy of the land to support agriculture and even modest dairy herds, all farmers were dependent on the purchase of expensive feed for their cattle in the form of *forrajes* (a mixture of forage crops) and *concentrados* (processed commercial feed). In fact, this dependence can be traced back to their earliest attempts in the 1950s to milk cattle year-round (González 1972). The cost of *forrajes* in 1996 was 74–78 pesos (about U.S.$10.00) per 40-kilo sack, but it had been only about half that cost the year before. The typical path by which farmers decapitalize is through the sale of their animals to pay off their debt to *forrajeros* (forage crop vendors). Indeed, this may be the way that farmers are most likely to lose their herds and go out of business.

The high cost of feed is painfully counterbalanced by the low local wholesale price of milk. The price of milk ranged from 1.70 to 2.10 pesos per liter (U.S.$0.23–0.28), with an average of 1.80 per liter (U.S.$0.24). All farmers sold their milk to one of the many small- to medium-sized milk processors in town. (Estimates ranged from 60 to 100 dairy processors in the municipality, referred to locally as *cremerias*, or creameries. Most of the town's creameries were small, family-operated enterprises.) A few farmers sold milk to the large milk processors. However, these large processors (e.g., RicoLacteos, which makes Nutrigurt brand yogurt, and El Sabino) primarily used fresh milk brought in by tanker truck from the Altos de Jalisco. The owner of RicoLacteos argued that he did so because the quality of the local milk was not up to the standards he required and that in the Altos he could work with organized dairy farmers equipped with milk refrigeration tanks holding 5,000 or more liters. He therefore could avoid working with individual local farmers who produce only 150–300 liters per day. In all other cases, fresh milk arrives at creameries warm and sloshing in cans lashed to the backs of burros or rattling in the back of pickups. Larger creameries might place the milk in refrigeration tanks, whereas the smaller ones simply process the day's milk immediately. So there is a convenient market for milk in San José, and farmers rarely had trouble selling their product to a local creamery. (The flow of milk in this system is illustrated in Figure 2.1).[7] But as one farmer noted, "As long as there are local creameries willing to buy poor-quality milk, farmers here won't organize and they won't modernize their operations."

A secure market, however, does not necessarily mean a profit for farmers. A local veterinarian provided me with a cost-benefit analysis for four ranches that underscored the severity of what farmers referred to as "the crisis." Each analysis was carried out in July 1996.[8] When comparing feed costs with milk income, all farmers examined were losing money daily, and in some cases, the amounts were significant. The smallest farm had only three cattle in production and six calves, which resulted in a loss of 45 pesos per day (U.S.$6.00). Another small farm with a herd of 16 cattle in production, 15 dry cattle, and 20 calves experienced a loss of almost 400 pesos per day ($53.33). A small-medium farm with 20 head in production along with five dry cattle and 30 calves had a loss of 203 pesos per day ($27.11). Finally, a medium-large farm with 90 cows in production, 30 dry cattle, and 50 calves was losing 719 pesos per day ($95.87).[9] In general, the data suggest that the larger the farm (and hence the more dependent on purchased feeds), the greater the daily financial loss. Farmers would recover somewhat from these losses during the rainy season when their cattle consume wild grasses on rangeland, but the rainy season provides relief for five months at best (June–October), and then only when rains are abundant. The price of milk also drops during the rainy season because production rises and the market is literally flooded with milk.[10]

In the face of the dairy crisis in San José, how are farmers responding and attempting to adapt to rapid change? Most keep working as they always have. Farmers espoused a kind of radical individualism that was consistent with the National Action Party (PAN) politics of the town. PAN had recently won municipal elections, and its pro-business message is consistent with the neoliberal entrepreneurial discourse of the federal government. Farmers had not responded by searching for innovative solutions to their problems, such as collective organization. When questioned further about this, they typically said that the formation of cooperatives would help them lower their high production costs (feed, seed, fertilizer, medicines, etc.) but that collective action was nevertheless "impossible" in San José because the farmers did not have the "mentality," were mistrustful of one another, or were simply accustomed to working only for themselves. Others noted that previous attempts to organize had failed when greedy and corrupt cooperative members took advantage of any benefits for themselves and their networks, at the expense of others. Twice in the 1970s farmers attempted to form cooperatives. In the most impressive attempt, a group installed a large milk refrigeration tank, milk dehydrator, and pasteurizer. They eventually sold their venture. Currently, no farmers have refrigeration tanks or are otherwise organized to sell their milk to a large

Figure 2.1 Flow of milk in San José de Gracia, Michoacán

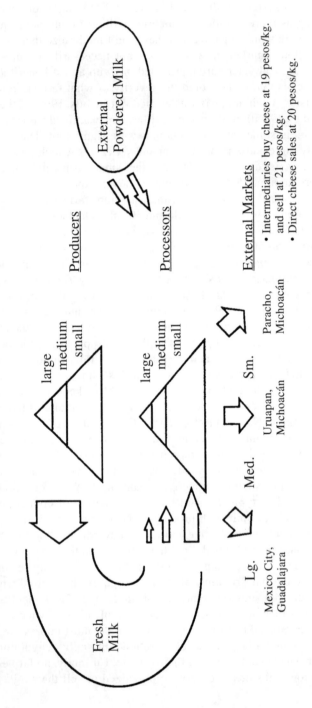

Producers

External
Powdered Milk

Processors

large
medium
small

large
medium
small

Fresh
Milk

Lg.
Mexico City,
Guadalajara

Med.
Uruapan,
Michoacán

Sm.
Paracho,
Michoacán

External Markets
• Intermediaries buy cheese at 19 pesos/kg.
  and sell at 21 pesos/kg.
• Direct cheese sales at 20 pesos/kg.

client. In sum, farmers were very suspicious of organizing, and felt they had enough empirical evidence to back up their general misgivings about such activity.[11] Yet most felt that they could gain advantages from such organization in terms of lowering their costs of production. Interestingly, they did not see organizing as a strategy to market their milk.

Most farmers recognized their precarious position and said that they would like to modernize their farms, but at the same time, they also realized that there was no possibility of doing so given a whole host of constraints: the high cost of scarce credit, the unstable economy and low price of milk, the lack of long-term and predictable agrarian policies by the state and federal governments, the seemingly unregulated importation of powdered milk, and the lack of a stable and viable market for their milk. Many also remarked that given the small size of their farms, the frequent lack of such basic resources as electricity, the poor quality of their land and cattle, and so on, it was impractical to invest in expensive efforts to mechanize and otherwise modernize their operations. It simply was not cost-effective. Thus in San José, farmers stumbled forward into an uncertain future with the knowledge of their disadvantageous position in the larger economy, yet without viable strategies for attempting to deal with their problems.

Although farmers' lack of confidence in government projects and mistrust of corrupt leaders who had taken advantage of them in the past are strong rationales for avoiding such entanglements, it was nonetheless striking how little farmers knew of government projects that were currently available to dairymen. It seems that a critical information gap characterizes San José. We will see in the following section that farmers in Cotija have access to more information through an active local dairymen's association cooperative.

Cotija

Cotija is located 60 kilometers south of San José and is situated at the juncture of the highland cold country and a more temperate zone that is lower in elevation, making this area slightly better for agriculture. As a marker of its temperate climate, Cotija is located on the northern edge of the avocado and sugarcane zones in Michoacán (Moreno García 1981). Whereas the overall organization of milk production is similar to that of San José, some farmers had diversified into avocado, a few had access to some limited irrigation water, and others had transformed a bit of their rangeland into pastures, albeit sown with wild grasses, but superior to anything in the cold country to the immediate north. The local dairymen's association of Cotija claims 856 members with 19,948 head of cattle (an average of 23 head of cattle per farmer). Small farmers with less than 20 head comprised 61.5 percent (N = 527) of the dairy farmers in the area, small-medium farmers with 21–49 head accounted for 27.5 percent (N = 236), medium-large farmers with 50–100 head accounted for 9.2 percent (N = 79), and large farmers with more than 100 cattle accounted for 1.6 percent (N = 14).[12]

Four things differentiate Cotija from San José: (1) milk prices were the lowest recorded in the greater region (including Jalisco, Guanajuato, and Michoacán) at 1.5 pesos per liter (U.S.$0.20); (2) because of the low milk prices, many farmers sold their milk on the street for 3.0 pesos per liter (U.S.$0.40);[13] (3) the dairymen's association not only provided basic services, but also operated as a cooperative, purchasing members' milk, selling them discounted cattle feed, fertilizers, seed, and medicine, and providing veterinary services;[14] and (4) the municipal government and dairymen's association were controlled by the center-left Party of the Democratic Revolution (PRD).

Furthermore, Cotija is shaped by the regional market in different ways than is San José. First, farmers have a more limited market. They can sell to a medium-sized cheese-manufacturing plant, smaller creameries, or to the dairymen's association. Although no formal census exists, the dairymen's association estimated that there were only 20–30 small creameries in town. As one of its projects, the Cotija dairymen's association successfully applied for a state program to help it purchase a bulk milk refrigeration tank. The project was completed in January 1996 at approximately the same time that milk prices began to drop. Association members, in turn, began selling milk on the street, rather than to the dairymen's association, in order to make a profit. Since Cotija has a more diversified economy than San José, it is possible for farmers to sell much of what they produce on the street. Consequently, members sold far less of their milk to the dairymen's association than might otherwise be expected. Additionally, the dairymen's association has been unable to find a viable market for its refrigerated milk, despite combing the entire region for a client (going as far as San José). The only outlet for refrigerated milk was the government-run Liconsa plant in Jiquilpan, 35 kilometers to the north, which was willing to pay only 1.82 pesos per liter (U.S.$0.24), an additional profit of $0.04 over the price of warm fresh milk. This was not enough to cover the costs of running and maintaining the tank and transporting the milk to Jiquilpan. As a consequence, the tank had yet to receive a drop of milk. Ironically, even though Cotija had a less robust market than San José, farmers were surviving by selling on the street for a reasonable price, and their cost of production was slightly lower because of the dairymen's cooperative.

Cotija's farmers had a list of prioritized problems similar to that of the farmers in San José, with the further inclusion of a lack of commercialization of milk in their region that would provide them with a stable market. To attempt to counteract the weak local market for their milk, their long-term goal is to mount a project through the dairymen's cooperative that would install a pasteurizer to process their own milk products. They recognize, however, the cost of such a project and realize that it is not feasible under current economic conditions.

Unlike their counterparts in San José, most Cotijenses felt they were well organized, and they perceived benefits to having organized. They explained their ability to organize in simple terms: they had a structure similar to that of the dairymen's association in San José until 1989, when the association was taken over by the current president, who has shown solid leadership and honest management so that the benefits of organizing are realized by the membership. And unlike San José, which is politically oriented toward the conservative PAN, the association president in Cotija extolled the social justice, grassroots message, and group-oriented approach of the PRD. When disunity or lack of organization was noted among farmers in Cotija, they were not talking about the relative organizational success of the dairymen's association, but about the relationship of Cotija's farmers to the market: farmers were not organized to sell their milk as a group to a client; instead, everyone sold individually to a number of outlets (local creameries, a local medium-sized cheese-making plant, the dairymen's association, or on the street).

In both areas of Michoacán, farmers identified the following critical problems:

1. The high cost of purchased cattle feed
2. The low price they received for their milk
3. The poor quality of their cattle
3. Lack of commercialization of dairy products
4. Importation of cheap powdered milk
5. Severe ecological limitations (e.g., lack of water and agricultural land)

The Central Mesa of Guanajuato

Guanajuato presents a striking contrast to Michoacán in terms of the nature of dairy production. In the region of San Miguel de Allende-Dolores Hidalgo, farmers typically farm intensively (most often with irrigation) to support large herds of high-quality cattle. Elsewhere, I have detailed the transformation of the Guanajuato dairy industry as it is becoming increasingly centralized on farms employing capital-intensive technology (McDonald 1996). Farmers in this region make no use of open rangeland and maintain their animals in corrals that are adjacent to milking salons equipped with milking machines. Their predominately Holstein herds give an average of 15–18 liters per day in many cases. Since 1987, I have been working with dairy farmers in the region who were all formerly independent and sold warm fresh milk to a middleman who pooled the milk in a refrigeration tank bulk resale to one of the large dairy processing plants in the area. With the implementation of NAFTA, however, some of these farmers recognized the need to organize to better integrate themselves into the market and cut out the middleman to enhance their profits. Since the late 1980s, the price of milk has been dropping while the costs of production have been rising. Organization was thus viewed as the only means to increase profits. In 1994, the farmers formed a marketing cooperative. Many others in the area remained independent. What was striking to me upon my return to the area in 1996 was that the Dolores Hidalgo Milk Producers' Union had survived the 1994 peso devaluation, was making a profit, and was in the process of expanding (the group's president went to Montreal to purchase Canadian cattle to distribute among the membership). The cooperative had access to information about various state government projects and actively took advantage of them, while its highly mechanized but still independent counterparts had no idea that any government projects existed. At least in the short run, this suggests that there are institutional solutions to Mexico's agrarian economic crisis.

The Dolores Hidalgo Milk Producers' Union

Formed in 1994, this group of now 30 farmers represents what has become one of the state's model cooperatives.[15] Formation of the group grew out of a grassroots movement among farmers to find a solution to their growing problems as costs of production rose while milk prices dropped (a U.S.$0.10 per liter drop from 1989 to 1994, almost a 30 percent decline). As the president of the group recounted, farmers in the region understood that they were losing money by selling to a middleman rather than as a group directly to a dairy processor. Profits had eroded to the point where farmers were motivated into collective action and began to research the possibility of forming a cooperative and finding a large client for their milk.

But simply being organized and having a high-quality product are not guarantees of success without a buyer. The other critical piece of the equation thus came with the construction of the Danone de México yogurt plant in Irapuato, Guanajuato, which must use fresh milk to make its product, and that milk must meet basic quality requirements. Here the market is driving change. As one dairyman noted, "If you don't have quality, then the plant will drop you fast. From here to Irapuato is not close. It's two or two and a half hours." The farmers were contacted by Danone representatives who had been purchasing their milk through middlemen. The quality of

Dolores farmers' milk was good, but Danone was having trouble with middlemen adulterating the milk. Thus, they approached the farmers in the Dolores region with a proposition: organize, produce a high-quality product, and they would have a stable market for their product that would assure them a fair price. It was with this knowledge that Dolores dairyman organized and invested in the cooperative. They received a government loan for U.S.$85,000 for their plant, two milk refrigeration tanks, and pickup trucks to collect members' milk. They were responsible for repaying approximately half of that money through the Fideicomiso Instituidos en Relación con la Agricultura (FIRA)[16] and through BANRURAL, the government's rural development bank. Unlike many FIRA projects that target only wealthy farmers, this project's members range from large farmers with over 100 head of cattle to very small ones with 10–15 head.

Not only have these farmers achieved better vertical integration with the market, they have also achieved better horizontal integration among farmers in their region. In the latter case, co-op members have lowered their costs by purchasing commercial cattle feed in bulk, as well as medicines and fertilizers. Members who formerly milked by hand were able to purchase gas-powered milking machines through the co-op for just over U.S.$500 (this is half the cost of the machine; the other half was again paid through a state government program). The machines not only speed up the milking process so that farmers can expand their herds, but they also enhance milk sanitation and, therefore, its quality.

The keys to their investment confidence in an otherwise unstable and volatile economy are a stable client and a just price for their product. The co-op has a written contract that specifies the obligations of both parties, as well as price.[17] In the summer of 1996, the co-op received 2.10 pesos per liter (U.S.$0.28), plus an additional bonus for meeting or exceeding a basic standard for bacteria and milk solids (e.g., fat and protein), which bumped up the price per liter to 2.45 pesos ($0.33). (This represents a significant increase in profits over their independent counterparts discussed below.) Should they not meet those standards, these farmers have a ready outlet in the form of a small cheese maker who will purchase their milk. In the first two years of its operation, however, the co-op had needed to pursue this avenue only a few times. Additionally, the key to the co-op's success has been access to information. The co-op president is young, educated, and well known in the region. He is aware of different government programs, and he is adept at figuring out and translating their financial risks and benefits to his membership. He told me that he frequently visits the SAGAR office in Dolores Hidalgo, where he "surfs the Net" and is provided with current commodity prices on the international market. His leadership role is as much one of brokering information as it is of organizing farmers on the ground.

Although this group has both taken advantage of government programs and accessed a stable market, the members recognize that theirs is a
very special situation. In response to my comments about lack of commercialization of milk in Michoacán, for example, one farmer replied,
"But here we don't have plants either. The Danone plant is new, it's not
more than a couple of years old. The original Danone plant is in Mexico
City." I asked about other plants in the area—El Sauz, La Esmeralda, or
Leche LaLa. In response, he said, "El Sauz buys from small producers.
Why? They don't use much milk. They use lots of other things . . . powdered milk, whey, vegetable fat, and the like to make their products."

Independent Farmers in La Perla de Chipilo

On the other side of the valley near San Miguel de Allende is the dairy
farming community of La Perla de Chipilo (the Pearl of Chipilo). Farmers
here are mechanized, have high-quality cattle, and farm intensively with
motorized tube-well irrigation. Farms of 50 hectares support herds of up to
75 cattle (though most farmers today are dependent on commercial feed
and purchased alfalfa to supplement their own forage crops). These farmers have remained independent, and many in the summer of 1996 were ex-
asperated by the faltering economy. All farms had reduced their herds and
complained of losing money.

One farmer working with his family outlined how their operation was
slowly decapitalizing:

> We have 85 cows in production, 20 are dry, and another 33 are calves.
> [Five years ago,] we had 250 animals. We have to sell them to pay our
> electric bill [for our well]. Like yesterday, we sold two in order to pay the
> bill for the electricity. Now those cows are older, give a bit less milk.
> . . . Once, yes, we did have to sell; [one year ago and again two years
> ago] we sold 15 young cows to pay the bank because the interest rates
> were extremely high. Now we're debt free. Few cows, but . . . I tell you,
> we've sold cows because if you want to keep your operation, you have to
> sell [some] to maintain the ones remaining. Now there's not enough
> money. Before, you could put some away to fix a problem, say, with the
> well. But now if you have a problem and the well breaks down or you
> have an expensive electric bill, you have to sell cows to pay [for them].

He went on to detail the level of his losses: "I've done a budget including
the cost of medicine, wage laborers, commercial feed, and . . . you lose. Or
rather, to produce a liter of milk costs you $2.50 [pesos] and they are giv-
ing you $1.70 [pesos]. How much do you lose? 80 centavos."

This turned out to be something of an overstatement. His daily production was 1,300 liters for a gross profit of U.S.$8,610 per month. If his
estimated cost of production per liter was correct, then he was losing an

amazing U.S.$4,052 per month. This was an impossibility. When he de-tailed his major monthly costs (electricity, alfalfa purchases, medicine, commercial feed, workers' salaries), a clearer picture emerged.[18] They to-taled U.S.$6,033, leaving $2,577 in net profit. Each of the two brothers makes about $500 per month, and the father takes home the other $1,500. But there is nothing left over for repairs and other unforeseen disasters. So although the family members make excellent money by Mexican stan-dards—certainly placing them among the Mexican middle class—they see their standard of living in peril of slipping away.

Others, however, were less fortunate. A neighboring farm with ap-proximately the same sized herd of cattle was clearing only U.S.$100–200 per month after expenses. These middle-class farmers were struggling, and the future looked bleak. What this underscored was the wide range of vari-ability in the profitability of these independent small commercial capital-ist farms.

Conclusion

Given the different cases discussed in this chapter, what can be concluded about successful dairy farmer collective action, as well as farmer resis-tance or inaction? White and Runge (1995) find that the presence of the following factors are both necessary and sufficient to predict the emer-gence of farmer collective action: previous experience with collective ac-tion, knowledge of potential benefits or gains, and the potential of farm-ers to personally gain from collective action. The case of San José de Gracia is characterized by few of these factors. Farmers there know little about the possible benefits of collective action, and many noted that po-tential gains from such activity were questionable. Indeed, many farmers questioned the value of investing in the modernization of their farms when confronted with a lack of commercialization of dairy products in their re-gion. There is no stable outlet for their milk other than the local cream-eries, which neither demand quality nor pay for it. But, clearly, the most important factor in the course of San José dairy farming is previous expe-rience with collective institutions that had failed (the two attempts to form dairy cooperatives) or were seen as weak and corrupt (the dairymen's association).

Cotija provides an interesting contrast. In many ways, it is a place that is even more economically marginal that San José, yet it shows some com-mitment toward collective action. Although farmers there had no previous experience with collective organization, a critical difference is that they had more trusted leadership in combination with an undergirding social justice/communitarian ideological orientation associated with the PRD. As noted, both the president of the dairymen's association and the town's mayor were PRD members. So Cotija farmers understand the possible benefits of collective action; but as White and Runge (1995) argue, sustaining collective action hinges upon continued gains. Following their logic, the investment burden placed on co-op members through the purchase of their milk refrigeration tank, coupled with its disuse for lack of a viable market, could easily undermine their activities.

It is the Dolores Hidalgo case that best clarifies the factors that contribute to successful organization. Much like the Cotija case, these farmers had no previous experience with collective action but had a competent and trusted leader who could articulate the risks and benefits of such action. The presence of a stable, predictable market willing to pay a just price is equally important so that farmers could envision the likelihood of long-term gain.

Unlike White and Runge (1995), who found in their Haitian study that no external incentives were necessary to stimulate collective action, the critical exogenous factor that emerges in all the cases outlined in this chapter is the need for a stable market willing to pay a just price for milk. Given the presence of strong, trusted leadership and the absence of negative experiences with collective organization, farmers appear willing to organize, take risks, and modernize their farms. In the case of San José de Gracia, not only would farmers need the incentive of a strong commercial market, but given their previous history and mistrust, they would also need neutral and knowledgeable outside intervention to help them organize.

Of these exogenous factors, it is the market that bears further comment. The state is faced with a paradox: it wants farmers to organize and to achieve economies of scale and better market integration, but at the same time, Mexico lacks the commercial dairy infrastructure throughout most of its regions to support such activity. In a European example, Robert Ulin observes that in a highly competitive and globalizing market in the early part of this century, small winegrowers in France formed cooperatives and, through these, gained access to expensive technology (harvesting machines, large storage and bottling facilities, and a fleet of trucks for shipment) and better vertical integration with markets, and thus survived and even flourished. He argues that the formation of cooperatives allowed small growers to maintain their private, smallholder property relations while accommodating to their insertion in a global capitalist economy (Ulin 1988:253).

The case of the Dolores Hidalgo cooperative suggests a similar scenario. If small- and medium-scale dairy farmers, as well as their larger counterparts, have access to stable markets that will pay them a just price, they will innovate institutionally and invest in the modernization of their enterprises. The alternative is increasingly clear for many farmers in this study: abandon dairying and perhaps leave the countryside in search of urban wage labor. The farmers of Dolores Hidalgo are not a lone example. In the state of Jalisco, large dairy processors such as Nestlé and Sello Rojo (Red Seal) have successfully organized farmers into cooperatives equipped with milk refrigeration tanks, and they in turn sell their milk in bulk to those processors. Farmers, in fact, were given little option. They either organized collectively, or those dairy processors would not buy their product. By 1995, 330 tank projects had been undertaken in Jalisco (as opposed to only five projects in Michoacán) (Rodríguez Gómez 1995:8). It is worth noting that Jalisco is Mexico's leading dairy-producing state. This does not mean, however, that it is an area that is ecologically better suited for dairying than Michoacán or Guanajuato. Rather, it represents a well-organized commercial milkshed with companies that are committed to buying milk produced in that region. Prices, though, remain similar to what we have seen for independent producers in Michoacán and Guanajuato, rather than moving in the direction of the Danone plant in Guanajuato.

In both Guanajuato and Jalisco, it appears that much-denigrated TNCs are providing a much-needed market for farmers willing to organize, who, in turn, are able to take advantage of greater vertical integration with those large dairy processors. Especially in the case of the Dolores Hidalgo cooperative, it appears to be a mutually beneficial relationship in which farmers have a reliable market and receive a reasonable price while processors are assured of predictable amounts of a quality product. In this case, the bonus paid for meeting minimum quality standards is further incentive for farmers to do everything in their power to meet or exceed them. The market is clearly driving change.

It could be argued that what is evolving is little more than a variant of contract farming. Gina Porter and Kevin Phillips-Howard (1997:228) characterize contract farming as a situation where farmers supply land, labor, and tools while contractors supply various inputs, such as seed and fertilizer, and often extension services to help ensure the quality of the crop being produced. Crops are then either centrally processed or exported by the contractor. With only a little bit of tinkering, we could apply their definition to the relationship between dairymen and dairy processors. In the case of dairy, however, the criticism leveled at contract farming—environmental degradation, self-exploitation, and the increased use of child labor—does not necessarily hold. At least for the moment, the Guanajuato dairymen retain control over the production process in contrast to contract farmers, who are often characterized as wage laborers on their own farms. Here we have farmers using contractual relations to better organize production and marketing. It provides them with stability and predictability where none had previously existed.

There are, however, potential downsides to this uneven process of modernization. The data from Michoacán shows that many small farmers, even under the best of circumstances, are not competitive and will most likely be squeezed out of business. The case of independent farmers in Guanajuato is even more telling and reveals the haphazard nature of co-operative formation in Guanajuato, where there is no widespread industry and state-based initiative to get farmers organized, as in Jalisco. Processes of change are occurring so rapidly that these once profitable farmers may also wind up as economic casualties before they can react. This calls into question the role of the state in encouraging the creation of stable regional milksheds. An important step in that direction would be the marked reduction of powdered milk and milk derivative imports by Mexico, thus forcing dairy processors to work with dairy farmers. Neoliberals might now interrupt and say, "Look, the Mexican dairy industry just can't compete with more efficient international competition and consequently should be out of business. Any suggestion of slowing or stopping powdered milk imports in fact supports our position." I would counter this with the following arguments. First, much of the international competition producing cheap powdered milk is itself heavily subsidized. Second, Mexico needs to give its farmers a chance to become more efficient. To do so, it needs to stimulate the expansion of dairy commercialization. Without such interventions, the dairy industry will develop very unevenly and, in some places, will most likely collapse altogether. The stakes are high as Mexico loses the ability to remain self-sufficient in yet another of its agricultural sectors and becomes increasingly dependent on foreign sources of food.

Notes

The Michoacán portion of this research was carried out under the auspices of a research project entitled Mejoramiento de la Calidad de Leche: Problemática y Alternativas en Jalisco y Michoacán (Enhancing the Quality of Milk: Problems and Alternatives in Jalisco and Michoacán, Mexico). This was a collaborative, interdisciplinary project between the Centro de Investigaciones y Estudios Superiores en Antropología Social de Occidente (CIESAS-Occidente) and the Centro de Investigación y Asistencia en Tecnología y Diseño del Estado de Jalisco (CIATEJ) designed to examine the changing sociocultural, economic, and technological conditions experienced by dairy farmers in Jalisco and Michoacán as a result of globalization and the opening of the Mexican economy. Funding for the project was provided by the Consejo Nacional de Ciencia y Tecnología. The University of Texas at San Antonio (UTSA) provided additional funding for this research, as well as support for ongoing work in Guanajuato. Although many people have contributed to this research, I would especially like to thank Guadalupe Rodríguez Gómez at CIESAS, who was the investigator for the Calidad de Leche project; Fernando Durazo and Patricia Chombo at CIATEJ; and Armando Cortez, who was my graduate research assistant from UTSA. Additionally, I would like to acknowledge the support of historian Luis González, whose insights into San José de Gracia were invaluable. Finally, I would also like to thank William Loker for his helpful comments and suggestions on an earlier draft of this chapter, as well as those of an anonymous reviewer.

1. This quotation—translated as "In Mexico we eat cheese and yogurt, and on occasion it's made from milk"—is from a humorous commentary on the Mexican dairy crisis that I heard from a farmer in Cotija, Michoacán (July 1996).

2. Danone de México is a part of Groupe Danone, a large TNC headquartered in France. Groupe Danone is best known worldwide for its dairy products and bottled water, including such familiar U.S. brands as Dannon yogurt and Evian springwater.

3. Local offices tend to be weak institutions. A common complaint from local leaders is that they retain very little of the revenue generated through their activities (in addition to the services noted in the body of the text, they also issue letters of recommendation and letters authorizing the movement of cattle across municipal boundaries, and they occasionally mediate the implementation of government programs), for which a nominal fee is charged. The majority of their revenue is forwarded to the main dairymen's association office in the state capital.

4. By "traditional methods," I mean a combination of dry farming to produce maize for animal forage, hand milking animals once per day often in the fields, maintaining small herds of low-productivity cattle (usually Cebu-Holstein mixes) that are well adapted to the local environment but may produce as little as 5–7 liters of milk per day, and the sale of warm fluid milk. It is a labor-intensive, low-technology, low-productivity regime.

5. These farms, in contrast, commonly have access to irrigation, sow hybrid maize and alfalfa crops, milk twice per day using milking machines, and maintain high-quality dairy stock that produce 15–20 liters per day. Many farmers still sell warm fluid milk to middlemen. Whereas dairying remains a labor-intensive activity, mechanization has made it somewhat less so, and it has also permitted farmers to expand herd size.

6. The presidents of both dairymen's associations noted that these figures are probably low since many farmers (especially large farmers) underreport herd size. Nevertheless, given the lack of any other dairy census, these figures provide a good starting point and underscore the smallholder nature of the region.

7. Processed milk products from small- to medium-sized processors still enjoyed a fairly robust regional market in the summer of 1996. For example, small processors of cheese in the El Sabino *ejido* near San José de Gracia sell their cheeses in Uruapan and Paracho, Michoacán. One cheese maker I interviewed processes about 1,200 liters of milk per day. On Saturday he goes to Paracho and sells approximately 1 ton of cheese to stores and people who sell in the local market, at a rate of 20 pesos per kilo (U.S.$2.67). Another resident of El Sabino who makes his living as an intermediary selling cheese in Uruapan buys about 800 kilos of cheese per week at 19 pesos per kilo ($2.53) and sells it for 21 pesos ($2.80), a profit of 1,600 pesos ($213.33) per week before expenses. Medium-sized operations in San José reported a regional and national market for their product. Large operations have a national market for their product.

8. It is important to note that these surveys do not account for costs (e.g., medicines, workers' wages, electricity, fuel, transportation of milk to market) other than that for cattle feed that was purchased and/or produced by each farm. It should also be noted that they were conducted at the start of the rainy season. During this period, farmers' stocks of feed are completely depleted and their rangeland has not yet recovered, so they are dependent on purchased feeds to maintain their herds. Consequently, the losses recorded by these surveys are high relative to the rest of the year.

9. In this final case, however, the cattle were *doble proposito,* or dual purpose (raised for beef and milk production)—a Cebu-Holstein mix that gives less
milk but produces high-quality beef and is well adapted to open rangeland. Consequently, a considerable amount of the daily loss is ultimately made up by sale of
these cattle. But in the summer of 1996, beef prices were also down, so we can
only assume that this farm would not recuperate all of its losses.

10. This underscores the inefficiency of local markets under conditions where
overall demand is not met by domestic production levels.

11. Farmers also expressed little knowledge of government programs, and
many believed that none existed. Others were aware of a few programs but felt that
they had been denied access to them by corrupt administrations in the local dairymen's association who had not informed the membership of these programs and
had monopolized resources for themselves and their followers. As a consequence,
most farmers expressed little interest in government programs because they felt
that they would never get legitimate access to them. Additionally, they felt that
government programs are poorly administered and are expensive for farmers, and
that government "experts" failed to understand the reality of the problems faced by
farmers in rural Mexico. In sum, they were very skeptical of such aid.

12. Cotija's somewhat more even distribution of farmers across categories in
comparison with San José is in part attributable to the fact that Cotija has more
beef cattle production (characterized by larger herds). They were not distinguished
from dairy producers in the dairymen's association membership list.

13. Although it might seem logical that all farmers would try to sell their
product directly to a clientele, it should be remembered that such activity is time-
consuming and costly (e.g., transportation of milk if the farmer has a delivery
route, time and added work if the farmer sells the milk himself, or wages paid to a
worker who delivers the product).

14. For example, a 40-kilo sack of commercial cattle feed in Cotija cost 72
pesos versus the cost in San José of 74–78.

15. The cooperative started with 22 original members.

16. FIRA operates out of the Banco de México, which oversees loans to commercial capitalist farmers.

17. Colleagues in Jalisco (Mexico's number-one dairy-producing state, which
is also experiencing demands to organize and produce a quality product) report no
similar move toward formal contracts. Rather, in Jalisco, "contracts" are at best
verbal (M. Guadalupe Rodríguez Gómez, personal communication, 1996).

18. It should be noted that these monthly costs do not include other inciden-
tals such as gas or diesel fuel or costs for any maintenance.

3

"Lo Que Dice el Mercado": Development Without Developers in a Oaxacan Peasant Community

Ronald Waterbury

On a warm and cloudless day in 1970, while walking through a farmer's fields with him in the peasant community of San Antonino in the valley of Oaxaca, I queried my informant routinely. Why, I asked, was he going to plant this particular crop at this particular time? For a moment he appeared perplexed by the stupidity of a question like that coming repeatedly from an educated person like me. Being the good friend and *compadre* that he was, however, he suppressed his annoyance and answered patiently, "Es lo que dice el mercado" (That's what the market demands). It is in the spirit of that response that I present in this chapter a case history of something approaching a naturally occurring test of the neoliberal model of agricultural modernization: development without developers. Following a very brief overview of the march of economic liberalism (classical and neo) through the Mexican countryside, I will describe the largely spontaneous, market-driven adoption of new agricultural production techniques in a peasant community in the valley of Oaxaca during the 1960s and 1970s. More specifically, I will recount the events related to the adoption of new technology, describe the adjustments in labor processes that accompanied it, and detail the resulting increases in labor productivity.[1] I will then assess some of the socioeconomic ramifications of those changes and conclude with questions concerning the economic and ecological sustainability of the new production techniques and assess whether globalization—the theme of this anthology—had anything to do with it.

The nineteenth-century liberal agrarian model was embodied by the yeoman family farmer working his privately owned land in a free market

61

economy. In Mexico, by means of the Lerdo law, the Liberal Reform government hoped to facilitate the transformation of the country's large class of peasantry into a yeomanry by outlawing communal land tenure. However, the modernization policies of the Porfiriato—the period from 1877 to 1911 when the nation was controlled by Porfirio Díaz—engendered quite different results for the peasantry. In most of Mexico, rather than being transformed into yeomen, the peasantry was either displaced or converted into a labor reserve for the expanding hacienda system. In some regions, mostly in the south, where hacienda expansion was less voracious or where traditional peasant communities were useful to—or at least not a hindrance to—the interests of the regional elites, a communitarian peasantry persisted.

Consequences of the ensuing Mexican Revolution were contradictory for the countryside. Whereas agrarian reform restored legal protections for the peasantry's land base through the communal and *ejido* land provisions of Article 27 of the 1917 Constitution,[2] it also cleared away the political and economic deadwood of the remaining traditional hacendado class, opening up space for a more modern-oriented landed class. Furthermore, following the high point of pro-peasant agrarian populism during the administration of President Lázaro Cárdenas (1934–1940), the Mexican government has resolutely pursued developmentalist policies that have favored capitalist agriculture over peasant agriculture, resulting in the bulk of the government's infrastructure investments, technical assistance, and economic subsidies benefiting large-scale capitalist enterprises, mostly in central and northern Mexico, where a peasant sector had never been extensive or had been largely eradicated. In what some scholars termed "neolatifundismo," Article 27 was circumvented in a variety of extralegal ways in order to cobble together the large tracts of land considered necessary for capitalist agriculture (Carlos 1981; Cordera and Tello 1984; Esteva 1980; Gledhill 1991; Hewitt de Alcántara 1976; Reyes Osorio et al. 1974; Sanderson 1981, 1986; Stavenhagen et al. 1968; Young, Freebairn, and Snipper 1979). The recent counterreform of Article 27 has simply consummated the de jure removal of nearly all encumbrances on the free market in land (Calva 1993; Cornelius and Myhre 1998; DeWalt and Rees 1994; Tellez 1993).

Although the peasant sector in recent decades has received a much smaller share of the government's agricultural development support, it has not been abandoned altogether. One important reason for this is that the material misery and political repression—and ethnic deprecation, since a substantial proportion of the peassants are also Indians—experienced by this sector have spawned cycles of civil unrest.[3] For Oaxaca, one of the nation's poorest and most rural states, this has resulted in a parade of much-ballyhooed programs, partially or wholly funded by international development agencies.

The focus of most of the programs has been on attempts to improve living conditions through education, medical clinics, and public works projects such as roads, electrification, and potable water systems. However, several programs have been at least partially directed toward modernizing agricultural production and marketing. Among the programs and agencies active in Oaxaca during the period covered by this chapter were the Cultural Missions of the Secretariat of Public Education, Plan Oaxaca (an expansive UN-funded operation), CONASUPO (the federal government's agency that buys and sells basic subsistence crops and goods), the secretariats responsible for agriculture and water resources (which went through several reorganizations and name changes over the years of this study), the Integrated Program for Rural Development (PIDER), the Commission for Marginal Areas, the national rural development bank (which has also experienced several reorganizations and name changes), and the Sistema Alimenticio Mexicano (SAM), or the Mexican Food System. Recently, of course, there has been the National Solidarity Program, the high-profile antipoverty program instituted by President Carlos Salinas de Gortari but now being modified to carry the stamp of the current president, Ernesto Zedillo. Given the large proportion of indigenous communities among Oaxaca's rural poor, the National Indigenist Institute (INI) has been a major player in development efforts, either on its own or in conjunction with other programs (Appendini 1992; Cornelius, Craig, and Fox 1994; Fox 1993, 1994; Fox and Aranda 1996; Fox and Moguel 1995; Gates 1993; Grammont 1995; Grammont and Tejera Gaona 1996; Moguel 1994; Otero 1996; Prud'homme 1995; Randall 1996).

The overall effect of these governmental development efforts in Oaxaca, judging by the continued high indices of poverty and emigration, has been minimal (Aguilar 1995; COESPO 1993; Embriz et al. 1993; Ramales 1996). According to advocates of government intervention and responsibility, the failures in Oaxaca and elsewhere stem from underfunding, poor design, and mismanagement of the programs. For neoliberal purists, however, the failures derive from the very notion of government intervention. From this perspective, agricultural development—even for poor peasants—is best left to the unfettered private initiative of farmers rationally allocating their factors of production in response to the free market.

The Setting

The site of this study, San Antonino Castillo Velasco, is one of the numerous corporate peasant villages that dot the countryside of the valley of Oaxaca in southern Mexico. (See Map 3.1.) It is a large bilingual Zapotec- and Spanish-speaking community (population in 1970 was c. 4,000; in

Map 3.1 General research area, Oaxaca

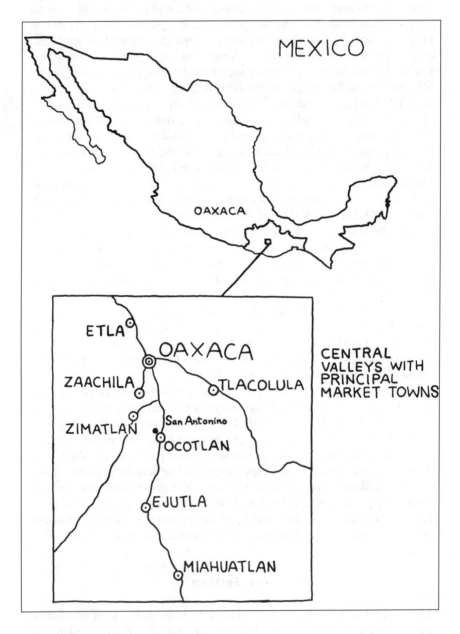

1990, 4,400) located some 30 kilometers south of the state capital, Oaxaca City (1970 population, 116,000; 1990, 300,000). The community is predominantly agricultural, with most households (84 percent) engaged in farming directly as cultivators on their own land and/or as sharecroppers of fields belonging to other villagers. Only an insignificant number of households (2.5 percent) rely upon agricultural wage labor as their major source of income.

Farming is not the village's sole occupation. The majority of households engage in complex economic strategies that combine agriculture with other remunerative activities. Trading in the regional market system leads the list of secondary occupations; but many other activities are pursued, including storekeeping, bread making, butchering, tailoring, dressmaking, milling, and the embroidering and trading of "peasant" blouses and dresses for the national and international crafts market. For some households, such nonagricultural activities provide the principal source of income, with farming only a secondary pursuit. In fact, most of the wealthiest people in the community are not full-time cultivators, but rather butchers, storekeepers, and wholesale traders (Waterbury and Turkenik 1976; Waterbury 1989).

The distribution of land in San Antonino is not equal, but the skew is not extreme and ownership of village land by outsiders is insignificant. Smallholdings are the rule: 90 percent of landowning households possess less than 2 hectares, and 63 percent own less than 1 hectare. Approximately 20 percent of households have no land, but the majority of those are female-headed or at the extremes of the socioeconomic developmental cycle, that is, recently marrieds or the elderly who have sold or given out their land to their heirs. Most land is privately owned and freely bought and sold. Although an area of communal land exists, it is parcelized and bought and sold as if it were private.[4] There is no *ejido*.[5]

San Antonino's habitat is favorable for agriculture. The terrain is nearly flat, temperatures are always suitable for cultivation, and the soil is relatively fertile alluvium. The major limiting factor is water, as the climate is semiarid (mean annual rainfall of 730 millimeters for the years 1970–1979) and no perennial streams pass through or near the community. However, precipitation, which is concentrated in late spring and summer, is usually sufficient for seasonal rainfall farming; and the aquifer underlying nearly all of the community's domain is close to the surface, making well irrigation possible. (For a survey of geography, land, and water use in the valley of Oaxaca to c. 1970, see Kirkby 1973.)

Reliance on rainfall or irrigation is intrinsic to the two production strategies that have long characterized San Antonino's agriculture: truck gardening and corn farming. The villagers themselves distinguish between these two strategies and label them *hortaliza* and *labranza*. The first refers to the intensive, irrigated cultivation of cash crops such as onions, garlic, cabbage, lettuce, radishes, herbs, and flowers. The second is the growing of milpa, principally maize, often associated with squash and occasionally with beans (all primarily subsistence crops) and sometimes intercropped with castor beans (a cash crop). Farmers employ one or a combination of these two strategies depending upon a complex set of considerations including size of household labor force; labor opportunity costs (other non-agricultural remunerative activities to which household labor might reasonably be allocated); the amount, quality, and location of fields; and projections of comparative returns. The vast majority of San Antonino farmers are *hortelanos* (practitioners of *hortaliza*); in 1970, they accounted for 78 percent of households with agriculture as their primary occupation; in 1978, the figure was 81 percent.

It must be made clear that the adoption of modern technology beginning in the 1950s did not initiate cash crop production in San Antonino. Historical sources indicate that *hortaliza* has been practiced in San Antonino for at least a century and likely longer, albeit to a much lesser degree; and Tonineros (as persons from San Antonino are often called) have long had a reputation as marketplace traders. Furthermore, although modernized production techniques have recently given great impetus to the predominance of *hortaliza* over milpa, the trend appears to have begun years earlier in response to expanded market opportunities made possible by improved transportation.

Moreover, to reiterate a main point of this chapter, it is important to underline that the changes I will describe below are not the result of direct intervention by outside development agencies.[6] With two exceptions, San Antonino has had minimal contact with government officials involved in agricultural development. For a short while in 1965, a Cultural Mission team of the federal Secretariat of Public Education (see Hughes 1950), including an "agronomic technician," resided in the village. The technician, however, was minimally trained and, according to my informants, knew less about farming than they did. In fact, villagers complained that he learned techniques from them that he then disseminated to neighboring communities the team was also serving.[7] For its part, the Cultural Mission group, feeling that it had been poorly received and that Tonineros were unalterably resistant to "modern culture," departed San Antonino after only a few months' stay. The other intrusion, a short-term government gift of motor pumps, will be discussed below.

Contact with agricultural extension services has been practically nonexistent. In 1969, two extension agents from the federal Secretariat of Agriculture set up a table in the weekly market in Ocotlán, the district head town, where they offered consultations. However, they admitted to me that they received very few requests for advice—to my knowledge no Tonineros were even aware of their existence—and the practice was soon abandoned. In 1972, according to the head of the extension office in Oaxaca, there were but eight agricultural agents in the state (excluding the Isthmus of Tehuantepec, which formed part of another administrative zone), only two of whom were assigned to the entire valley of Oaxaca, one based in Tlacolula, 70 kilometers from San Antonino by road, and the other in Etla, 45 kilometers distant. By summer 1980, there had been no observable improvement. In 1976, a joint endeavor of two government agencies, the INI and PIDER, established a demonstration plot on the outskirts of Ocotlán. But again, its presence was never publicized in San Antonino, and, as far as I could ascertain, nobody from the village ever visited it. Also in 1976, the National Agricultural University at Chapingo (located in the valley of Mexico) sent occasional busloads of students to the community. However, these were not extension team visits, but rather educational field excursions for the students with no benefits to the villagers. Another ambitious-sounding program, SAM, was initiated during the López Portillo presidency with the aim of making Mexico self-sufficient in food by 1982 (the end of López Portillo's term in office). Although one of SAM's stated goals was assistance to peasant farmers, like other programs it actually devoted the preponderance of its energies and resources to larger-scale commercial operations. Besides the fact that the program has been judged a failure nationally (Barkin 1987; Spalding 1984), as far as I know it had no effect on San Antonino.

The slighting of San Antonino by outside development agencies might, ironically, be a side effect of the community's success. The head of the regional office of the Secretariat of Agriculture confided to me that they expended their limited budget elsewhere because San Antonino's *hortelanos* were like "Japanese farmers" and thus less needy.

Traditional Technology and Techniques

To serve as a comparative baseline for the discussion of modernization, I will here provide a brief description of traditional *hortaliza* techniques. (Milpa techniques will not be described since they have been affected little by modernization.) Before doing that, however, a clarification of how I am using the terms "traditional" and "modern" is in order. I am aware that in common parlance—and as employed by some scholars—the terms carry substantial ideological or ethnocentric connotations. Emically, for some people (traditionalists), some ideas and behaviors are judged superior simply because "we" have "always" thought and acted this way. In this sense, traditionalism is an ideology that anoints present practice with legitimacy rooted in a group's past. (Etically, of course, it has been amply demonstrated that traditions are invented, reinvented, modified, and selected for their present utility.) On the other hand, for other people (modernists, or *progresistas* as they are called in San Antonino), some behaviors are judged superior simply because they are "new" and/or because they are associated with "others" judged to be more "advanced" or knowledgeable. This is legitimization deriving not from the time-honored past, but rather from the efficacy-honored present. Since efficacy prevails over tradition much more readily in the realm of technology than it does in other sociocultural domains—religion, for instance (for an example from San Antonino, see Waterbury 1996)—in this technology-focused paper, I will eschew a discussion of the semantic nuances of the terms "traditional" and "modern." Here I will simply use the terms in their more descriptive and ideologically neutral gloss of provenance and relative time. By "traditional," I mean relatively endogenous and old; by "modern," relatively exogenous and new. The qualifier "relative" is particularly critical for the concept of modern; a small, gasoline-powered pump and 50 meters of plastic tubing can hardly be called state-of-the-art modernity when compared with the irrigation technology employed by commercial vegetable growers in California's Central Valley.

So to move on to the specific issue at hand, traditional *hortaliza* techniques in San Antonino are those practiced prior to the mid-1950s, the derivation of which lies essentially in the colonial and even precolonial eras. They required a minimal tool kit: shovel, machete, *barretón* (a kind of hand trowel), rope and *cántaro* (watering pot), and a few cane baskets. Most *hortelanos* did not own their own plowing equipment (a team of draft animals and a metal-tipped wood plow), but rather hired a *labrador* (a milpa farmer) to till the soil.

The *cántaro* was a 10- to 12-liter pot with a distinctive conical shape. Its wide shoulder and narrow bottom facilitated self-tipping in the well, and its narrow outward-flared mouth enabled it to be grasped firmly and inhibited the sloshing out of water while the pot was being manually hoisted from the well and carried to the plants to be irrigated. Since at least colonial times, the *cántaro* was made of black pottery in the village of San Bartolo Coyotepec. By 1950, however, ceramics had been replaced by a tin version fabricated by cottage industries in Oaxaca City. The pot was used in conjunction with shallow wells (maximum 10 meters to the water surface) located in each field. These were dug with simple hand tools and were either unlined or, occasionally, reinforced with cylinders woven from split *carrizo* (cane).

Production techniques were highly labor intensive. The soil was first given several plowings, and any large clods that remained were pulverized using a crude wood mallet, usually fashioned from a tree limb. The furrows were then leveled by shovel, and precisely spaced rows of *cajetes* (shallow depressions) were dug over the entire plot. The seedlings were transplanted by hand into these depressions. To water the crop, the *cántaro* was lowered into the well by a rope, allowed to fill, and the water-filled pot was pulled up hand over hand, carried to the plants, and its contents poured into the *cajetes*. This process was repeated until the entire crop had been irrigated. To reduce the distance from well to watering area, several wells were usually dug in a single field. This irrigation technique, although exceedingly laborious, was highly efficient in its use of water. By concentrating the water directly on the plant roots, it attenuated the dispersion and evaporation of moisture and minimized weed growth in the interspaces.

Weeding, fertilizing, and pest control also were manual operations. Weeds were removed usually with the *barretón,* occasionally with a shovel, or sometimes simply by pulling out the unwanted growth with bare hands. Fertilizing most commonly consisted of applying manure directly to the *cajetes* during plant growth. Every few years, manure was worked into the soil during plowing.

Pest control, when attempted at all, was limited to crushing or stripping worms and insect larva off the leaves with the fingers, a task frequently assigned to children.

Finally, harvesting was carried out also using simple tools or bare hands. The produce was either packed immediately into sacks or baskets in the field and taken directly to market, or it was transported home in bulk for later packing and marketing. Transport among house, field, and the regional marketplace was primarily by burro back, human back, or, less frequently, the lumbering oxcart (which most *hortelanos* also had to rent from milpa farmers).

Prior to 1900, most of San Antonino's cash crops were sold in the marketplace of Ocotlán, with only a small portion transported by burro train or oxcart to other marketplaces in the valley or beyond by San Antonino traders. As transportation improved, Oaxaca City's marketplace gradually became the major outlet for the community's produce. A railroad spur line linking Ocotlán to Oaxaca City was built in the first decade of the twentieth century. Motor truck and bus service began in the 1930s, but initially it was sporadic due to the unreliability of the vehicles and the poor condition of the roads. However, with the paving of the highway between Oaxaca City and Ocotlán in the late 1940s, along with steady equipment improvements, motor transport has entirely replaced the slow and infrequent train service. San Antonino was connected directly to the highway by a 1-kilometer paved access road in the 1950s.

Modern Technology and Techniques

Soil Preparation

Use of tractors for plowing began on a limited basis in the 1950s when machines owned by residents of other towns first became available for hire

in San Antonino. Since then, demand for service has risen steadily to the
point that now almost all farmers rent tractors for initial tilling wherever
field size permits. The final furrowing, however, is still usually done by
the ox-drawn wood plow because villagers prefer the form of the furrow
it makes and because, as some informants contend, the tractor's weight
packs the soil too tightly. The first tractor owned by Tonineros was acquired in 1956 when three men jointly purchased a midsized machine for
both personal use and rental. But within a short time, dissension arose, and
one of the associates bought out the others and retained the tractor for his
own exclusive use. Rental of outside tractors thus continued until 1970
when two other villagers each bought a large tractor and made it available
for hire. By 1980, six Toninero households owned and hired out a total of
eight 80-horsepower diesel tractors (Fords and Massey-Fergusons).

The pulverizing of soil clods after plowing continued to be performed
in the traditional manner, as none of the village tractors were equipped
with harrows. However, in fields that are pump irrigated, the digging of
cajetes is no longer necessary. Depending upon the crop, planting is now
done directly in the furrows or in long *tablas* (beds) formed by leveling
every second or third furrow with a shovel.

Fertilization

The adoption of chemical fertilizers also began in the mid-1950s. According to informants, they were introduced by a salesman from an agricultural
supply house in Oaxaca City who visited the village and encouraged a few
farmers to try the new type of fertilizer by providing the initial sacks
gratis. Use spread steadily by emulation, perhaps reinforced at that time by
the rising price of manure. All *hortelanos* now rely heavily on chemical
fertilizers that are readily available for purchase right in the village. Manure continues to be utilized regularly only for radish crops and the raising
of seedlings; all other vegetables and flowers are grown almost exclusively
with chemical fertilizer. However, the practice of plowing in manure before planting has not died out completely. A few farmers believe it is beneficial to plow in an application of manure every few years because, in
their opinion, constant reliance on chemical fertilizers leads to deteriorat-
ing soil conditions.

Chemical fertilizer use has been uninformed by technical assistance.
Villagers experiment on their own or sometimes ask advice from salesclerks in the Oaxaca City supply houses. The one exception occurred in
1976 when a representative of Guanomex, the government-controlled fertilizer company, gave a brief public lecture in the community. The presen-
tation was well attended, and the Guanomex representative promised to
have an extension agent dispatched to provide further assistance. But no

follow-up person ever arrived. To date, as far as I know, no one has chosen specific fertilizers based on laboratory soil analysis. In 1960, engineers engaged in an irrigation study did take a few samples for testing. However, as one of the three farmers involved explained, the data from the analysis was never utilized because it arrived by mail in the form of a technical report using symbols he did not understand (although he was functionally literate). Moreover, the recommendations were geared to commercial farmers with stipulations of hundreds of kilograms of fertilizer per hectare, and he simply did not have enough cash to purchase such a large quantity at one time.

Consequently, the variety of chemical fertilizers employed has been limited. The type utilized exclusively for many years and still the predominant product is granulated ammonium sulfate, an inorganic fertilizer containing only nitrogen (25.5-0-0).[8] Recently, a few other fertilizers have gained favor, including two additional granulated products and a liquid. One of the granulated fertilizers is urea, a more concentrated form of nitrogen; the other is a product called P-K-Nitro, a balanced blend of nitrogen, phosphorus, and potassium. The liquid fertilizer goes by the trade name Gro-Green (villagers call it "Gro-Gringo"), which has a 20-30-10 formula.

Granulated fertilizers are applied by spooning or hand sprinkling a quantity on the ground near each plant prior to irrigation. Liquid fertilizer, like liquid insecticide, is sprayed from a manually pumped tank that is slung from the shoulder or carried in a backpack. Chemical fertilizers are almost always applied to growing plants, not incorporated into the soil during initial cultivation.

Pesticides

Insecticides were first adopted in the early 1960s shortly after the introduction of chemical fertilizers. Several village onion traders who regularly traveled to Puebla on buying trips observed their use there in conjunction with portable manual sprayers. They decided to try them in their own fields back in San Antonino. This technology also spread by emulation and had become common by the late 1960s. At the present time, the practice of eradicating insect pests by hand has completely died out; almost every *hortelano* now owns a sprayer and employs liquid insecticide.

Initially, only one or two brands of general-purpose insecticide were utilized on all types of garden crops. However, by 1980, several other products had come into use, and a few villagers had even begun applying fungicides. Some of these new varieties come in powder form and are applied by shaking a plastic net bag over the plants. Weed eradication remained a manual task into the 1980s, as no one by then had tried herbicides.

Pesticide application, like chemical fertilizer, was determined by trial and error supplemented by advice from salesclerks. The amounts applied vary greatly, with some farmers using quantities many times beyond manufacturers' recommendations. Similarly, although many of the products contain DDT and other dangerous substances, safety precautions printed on the containers are generally ignored. I know of numerous instances in which pesticides continued to be used right up to harvest and, in the case of a tomato crop, application proceeded through the actual picking period even though the label clearly admonished the farmer to cease usage weeks prior to harvest. This problem was exacerbated by the fact that a significant percentage of the adult population was functionally illiterate and thus unable to read the labels. And even those who could read had little or no understanding of the potential harmful effects of these new products.

Seed

Commercial seed was introduced in the late 1950s, brought back, as was insecticide, by village traders. Acceptance was relatively rapid, and since the mid-1960s, purchased seed has been in widespread use. These new varieties did not entirely displace homegrown (*criollo*) seed, but rather increased the variety of seed types available, thus giving *hortelanos* greater flexibility in dealing with seasonal shifts in climate, transport, and consumer preferences.

Irrigation

The first irrigation pump in San Antonino was purchased in the mid-1950s by a villager who had become familiar with them while working for a commercial farmer in another area. (In recognition of this man's preoccupation with horticultural techniques, Tonineros have bestowed upon him the nickname of "El Jardinero" [the gardener].) Without doubt, others in the community were also aware of mechanized irrigation by this time, especially those Tonineros who worked in the United States as braceros.[9] Nonetheless, compared with other new inputs, the process of pump adoption was slow. Over the next few years, the initial innovator was observed by others, but less than a half dozen followed his lead, probably because of unfamiliarity with the machinery and the accompanying alterations in planting techniques along with economic prudence—that is, uncertainty whether tooling-up and operating costs would be rewarded by substantially increased returns.

Then, in 1960, the process of pump adoption was affected by one of the few cases of government action in San Antonino. Norberto Aguirre Palencares, an Institutional Revolutionary Party (PRI) candidate for the

Federal Congress, visited San Antonino as part of his election campaign. Being an agronomist by training, Aguirre appreciated San Antonino's truck gardening potential and promised to provide the village with motor pumps. To determine the size and type of pump, he dispatched a team of technicians to carry out a preliminary study. However, the study itself engendered suspicion on the part of many villagers, who feared that it would result in higher taxes or, worse yet, an attempt by the government to expropriate their land. (Even though the largest landholding in San Antonino falls far below the limit set by the agrarian reform laws, the fear of expropriation is widespread among community members.) These trepidations were exacerbated by the fact that the arrangements for the pumps were being made with the village's PRI committee. The majority of Tonineros were leery of politicians of any stripe, and a small but vocal minority was vehemently anti-PRI.

As expected, the PRI candidate won the election. What was not expected was the delivery to the village of 32 1.5-inch motor pumps. They arrived, however, with no technical assistance as to their operation and little information—at least public information—as to their distribution. As a result, rumors and accusations propagated by leaders of the village's conservative faction and the parish priest circulated through the community. It was asserted that since the government never gives away anything for nothing, it would later demand payment for the pumps and, in the event of default, confiscate the land. At one extreme, it was rumored that the pumps were a gift from the Communists, who would not only take away one's land but also one's children. Consequently, few of the pumps were actually put to work, most of them remaining under the portico of the municipal building collecting dust and rust. All the pumps, including those in use, were eventually repossessed by the government.

This distribution of pumps by the government might at first glance appear to weaken my theme of development without (outside) developers. However, given that no technical assistance was provided with the pumps and that only a few of the pumps were actually used, I think it safe to say this particular intervention was minor. In fact, it could be argued that the political brouhaha generated by the donation may have actually set back the adoption processes.

Be that as it may, farmers later did begin to purchase their own pumps. In 1966, only about 25 households owned pumps; in 1970 the number had risen to 126, and by 1978, an estimated 440 households had purchased pumps. Presently, all *hortelanos* irrigate with pumps.

Until the early 1970s, gasoline-powered pumps were used exclusively. At that time, a few villagers with plots close to residential power lines bought electric pumps, a shift that has intensified since 1976, when electrical service began to be extended out to the fields (more about this below). All the pumps used are small, ranging in size from 1.5 to 3 inches in output diameter. The gasoline units are coupled to 4- to 8-horsepower motors and the electric models to 2-horsepower, three-phase motors. Since the majority of plots are small, and since many wells will not sustain rapid extraction of large volumes of water, most farmers prefer the 1.5- or 2-inch versions. These smaller machines have the added advantage of easier transportability, an important consideration as a single pump is frequently used in several scattered fields and the pumps are almost always taken home at night for safekeeping.

The adoption of motor pumps brought a related change in well construction. Wells are now considered permanent improvements, and only one is excavated per field. They are deeper than pot wells (15 meters and more) and are lined with brick-and-cement cylinders. Although most wells are still dug by hand using techniques similar to before, part-time specialists are now usually hired for their construction. By 1980 a few Tonineros were engaging well diggers from the nearby community of San Pablo Huixtepec, who employ a hand-powered mechanical contraption that can perforate 20 meters or a little more under ideal conditions. Such wells are lined with metal cylinders 30 to 40 centimeters in diameter. Water is conducted from the wells to the areas being irrigated by a combination of lightweight, flexible plastic tubing and shallow, shovel-dug ditches.

Harvesting, Marketing, and Transport

Harvesting and packing are still done entirely by hand. But marketing is now more direct. A large portion of the community's fields are presently reachable by dirt service roads, and produce is frequently packed and loaded onto rented trucks right in the field, from where it is shipped directly to the marketplace, most often in Oaxaca City.

Modes of transport within the village have changed also. Bicycles have become increasingly popular. Prior to 1960, only 5 percent of villagers owned a bicycle, whereas by 1978, almost half of all households owned at least one. The ownership of horse- or burro-drawn carts has shown a comparable proliferation, especially among *hortelanos*. As recently as 1970, only 5 percent of gardeners possessed a cart; by 1978, approximately half of them had bought one. Although it is perhaps difficult to conceive of horse or burro carts as modern, given the conditions extant in San Antonino, they are an economically and technologically appropriate advancement. They reduce travel time considerably and facilitate the transport of pumps and other equipment, two important considerations in a community where household fields are distant and scattered. Furthermore, carts cost but a fraction of what pickup trucks do—which are the closest motorized functional equivalent—and require no new operating or maintenance skills. The decade of the 1980s brought with it an explosion in the number of small trucks, but the bulk of them are operated for hire or are used in association with nonfarming occupations such as trading, baking, butchering, and storekeeping.

Labor Productivity

Since labor is the factor of production over which peasant households have the greatest control, changes affecting labor productivity take on signal significance. And in San Antonino, the adoption of these modern agricultural techniques has substantially augmented labor productivity by reducing the amount of labor time required to produce a given yield or, in spatial terms, by expanding the area cultivable by a given input of labor time.

The most far-reaching changes were in irrigation, traditionally the most arduous and time-consuming aspect of truck gardening. Figures 3.1 and 3.2 show the very substantial labor reduction between traditional and modern irrigation techniques for four crops that were selected because they are commonly planted and because they demonstrate a range of water requirements. For comparative purposes, the figures assume no precipitation. Real irrigation requirements, of course, vary with the amount and distribution of rainfall. Nonetheless, all these crops are planted year-round; hence, during the dry season, actual irrigation labor times equal the figures given in the graphs. Also for comparative purposes, the figures in these graphs were calculated on a per hectare basis. In reality, however, no household plants a hectare of radishes or cilantro with either traditional or modern irrigation techniques, and a full hectare of onions or cabbage is rare. Furthermore, aside from the labor requirements of such extensive plantings, many households do not possess a hectare of land, and even those that do are not likely to devote so extensive an area to a single crop because of the risk-spreading economic strategy that prevails among San Antonino farmers.

Other adjustments accompanying mechanized irrigation—bed preparation and planting methods—have also brought about considerable labor reductions. Cabbage planting time, for example, has been reduced threefold from the 46 man-days per hectare required to prepare and transplant in traditional *cajetes* to 15 man-days per hectare for the present simple furrow cultivation. Slightly less but still significant time savings result also from the shift from *cajete* to *tabla* planting.

Mechanized irrigation's effects on weeding time have been minor and offsetting. Although water flowing through ditches and over *tablas* encourages greater weed growth, weeds can often be cleared more easily wielding a shovel while standing rather than stooped using a small hand

Figure 3.1   Labor Input for Selected Crops, Pot vs. Pump

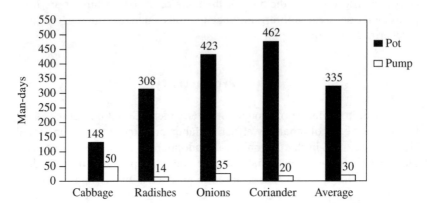

Figure 3.2   Percent Labor Reduction From Pot to Pump

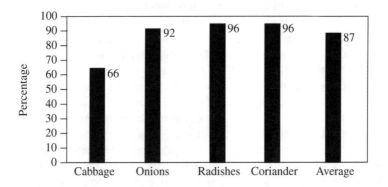

tool. And, more important, much weeding can now be performed while irrigating, that is, during the free minutes between the opening and closing of the ditches—time that was included within irrigation labor in my calculations. As I noted before, herbicides have not been adopted.

Other modern techniques such as tractoring, new seeds, chemical fertilizers, and pesticides have altered labor inputs only marginally (although they have increased yields). Granulated chemical fertilizers are applied manually, just as manure is. Although precise time input figures for traditional fertilization are not available, the greater ease of handling and the smaller volume of material needed would probably result in some time reduction for chemical fertilization. Similarly, there are no labor time figures

for traditional manual pest control. But since it was not routinely practiced, and when practiced was usually assigned to children, labor time inputs of the traditional and modern methods for insect control cannot be
meaningfully compared. To be conservative, I assume the application of
insecticides, and certainly that of fungicides, to be a wholly new time cost,
albeit a relatively minor one. In the case of cabbage, for example, it is 3.8
man-days per hectare; for onions, 4.8 man-days per hectare.

In short, then, the labor time effects of modernized *hortaliza* techniques for cultivation phases other than irrigation and bed preparation have
been insignificant. On the other hand, the mechanization of irrigation and
the adjustment of planting to it have substantially reduced labor inputs by
an average of almost 90 percent.

To restate these time savings in terms of the increased amount of land a
household can work, my data indicates that a household with one man devoted full-time to gardening using traditional techniques can work only 1,000
square meters (0.1 hectare). With modern techniques, this same production
unit can plant 3,000 square meters (0.3 hectare). Households with larger labor
forces can, of course, work proportionately greater areas. A household with
four men (e.g., a father and three sons) dedicating all their time to horticulture using traditional methods can cultivate 4,000 square meters (0.4 hectare),
whereas with modern methods, it can work approximately 1 hectare. One
might expect such large work teams to exhibit an even greater increase in
labor efficiency; however, this is usually not possible because almost all
households have fractionalized and dispersed holdings, and the majority of
plots are less than half a hectare in size. Hence, the augmented efficiency of
a multiple labor team is offset by the resultant increase in transportation and
setup times. Conservatively, then, it is estimated that the change from traditional to modern production techniques has meant a threefold increase in the
amount of land workable by the same size labor force.

Along with augmented labor productivity, the modernization of technology has also brought a considerable reduction in drudgery. Within the
confines of this chapter, I cannot present a Chayanovian analysis of the
drudgery factor (Chayanov 1966; Durrenberger 1980). However, it is safe
to say that although drudgery is not as objectively measurable as is time, it
nonetheless is a subjective-physical factor of considerable importance to
San Antonino farmers, who emphatically declare pump irrigation to be
much less strenuous than pot irrigation.

Commitment to Modernization and
Quest for Greater Efficiency

The combination of time and drudgery reduction has engendered an irre-
versible commitment to the modernization of *hortaliza* technology and

techniques. With rare exceptions, fledgling households will eschew truck gardening until they have acquired, by one means or another, the use of a pump and a serviceable well. And mature households that have adopted the new techniques will not, in the vast majority of cases, return to the old ways. If their own pump breaks down, they will borrow or rent one. Failing that, they will forgo gardening until they can repair or replace their pump rather than revert to pot irrigation. Furthermore, there is now a widespread desire on the part of San Antonino *hortelanos* to expand technical knowledge and to increase efficiency in order not just to save labor time, but also to maintain or improve upon net cash returns—a serious problem due to inflating input costs. This is illustrated primarily in the recent shift by some villagers from gasoline to electric motor pumps because the latter are cheaper to purchase and maintain, less troublesome to operate, and easier to transport and set up.

The motivation to shift to electric pumps was so great that it managed to overcome three strong and long-held aversions: the formation of inter-household economic cooperative ventures, willing involvement with an outside government agency, and the acceptance of bank loans. The electrification effort resulted in the establishment of the first successful cooperatives in the community's history. On the initiative of villagers, several associations were formed to contract with the Federal Electrical Commission (CFE) to extend power lines out to their fields and to obtain the necessary loans from the regional branch (BANCRISA) of the federal rural development bank (BANRURAL). The first cooperative, after many months of bureaucratic delay and intimidation that saw the membership dwindle from the initial 19 to six, inaugurated its new electrical grid in July 1976. The first group's success encouraged others to follow suit. By August 1980, four additional associations had been formed, and a combined total of some 70 wells electrified; furthermore, at least two other groups were in the process of formation.[10] These associations do not imply a major break with household economic autonomy since what is owned cooperatively is only the electrical infrastructure of wires, posts, and transformers. Wells, pumps, and plots continue to be individually controlled and worked and electricity consumption individually metered and paid for. However, in 1978, another association formed that did extend the degree of cooperative relationship somewhat further. This case—the only one first suggested by government representatives—involved the joint exploitation by 13 farmers of a single deep well (60 meters). The group not only cooperatively financed the venture (with the aid of a BANCRISA loan), but also jointly maintains the pump. Each farmer pumps water directly from the well to his field (the system does not employ a collection-distribution tank) on an informal rotational basis and is charged according to the amount of electricity consumed each usage as indicated on the meter.

The government's role in the deep-well enterprise was equivocal. True, government representatives suggested the project; the federal Secretariat of Agriculture and Hydraulic Resources "donated" the well (it had actually been drilled and capped three years earlier as part of a separately budgeted regional project to test the valley's aquifer); and BANCRISA provided the loan (secured by land deeds surrendered by each of the cooperative's members, and at 12 percent annual interest, the same rate charged by commercial banks at the time). On the other hand, red tape, unethical behavior by bank officials, and lack of coordination between agencies (both state and federal) led to lengthy delays and innumerable trips to Oaxaca and Mexico Cities, all of which most surely would have precipitated the abortion of the project were it not for the tenacity of one or two leaders of the cooperative. For example, one of the leaders not only had to brave the BANCRISA hierarchy, but also had to convince members of the cooperative to persist in the face of obstacles imposed by a bank loan officer who became disgruntled when the cooperative refused to pay for a truckload of gravel for the new house he was building.

Socioeconomic Implications

I turn now to some of the implications these changes in agricultural production techniques have had for land use and land pressure, socioeconomic stratification, and employment and migration.

Land Use and Pressure

Land use changed in three general ways. The proportion of land planted to vegetables and flowers as against milpa crops expanded, idle land was put back into production, and, to a minor degree, fields were being purchased by Tonineros in neighboring communities.

Hortaliza crops steadily replaced milpa through a twofold process. First, there was a shift away from corn farming. It is difficult to precisely quantify this assertion because modernization was already under way when I took my first census in 1970, and, as indicated earlier, from 1970 to 1978, the percentage of *hortelanos* rose only slightly. However, according to older informants, beginning in the late 1950s, many persons who previously were exclusively or primarily corn farmers began to plant more or even all of their land to vegetables and flowers. Second, and of greater impact, is the expansion of plantings by *hortelanos* themselves. Whereas previously *hortelanos* planted to corn (or left fallow) any land they possessed in excess of their household labor's gardening capacity, with the new techniques they began to plant most or all of their land to vegetables and flowers. Moreover, many *hortelano* households whose land would have been adequate to absorb their labor supply using traditional techniques now found themselves with an insufficiency and sought to sharecrop fields from others, land that previously would likely have been planted to corn.

The extension of *hortaliza* was also bringing about a return of idle land to production. As late as 1970, based on aerial photography and my own on-the-ground inspections, I estimate that approximately 20 to 25 percent of the community's arable land was covered with substantial overgrowth, evidence of several years' abandonment. By mid-1978, virtually all this land was in production, in the process of being cleared, or planned for clearance.

Finally, the purchase or renting of land by Tonineros in other communities, which has occurred on a small scale for several years, has recently been increasing, according to informants. However, it is likely that purchases will remain limited. Portions of the neighboring communities' lands are communal or *ejido* and thus were legally inalienable (at least prior to the counterreform of Article 27 in 1992). And although purchase of private land in other communities—if proper procedures are followed—is and was perfectly legal, many Tonineros nonetheless considered the tenure of such land to be insecure. Moreover, travel to fields yet more distant is very time-consuming without a motor vehicle. Thus, the acquisition of land outside San Antonino's boundaries was an insignificant factor, and for practical purposes, we can view the cultivable area available to Toninero farmers as a closed pie. Therefore, one definite result of enhanced labor productivity and changing cropping configurations has been augmented land pressure. However, since plantable area was only beginning to reach its limits by the late 1970s, and some further intensification of the use of available land was still possible, land pressure had not reached extreme proportions. One indicator of that is price. Although land values in San Antonino doubled between 1970 and 1978, that was below the inflation rate of many other producers' inputs, not to mention most consumer goods.

Stratification

Historically, increased demand for land and the concomitant rise in its price have often been accompanied by greater concentration of land in the hands of a few wealthy households. But, by 1980 at least, that had not occurred in San Antonino. The largest landowner in 1970, a baker and traditional-style corn farmer who possessed approximately 17 hectares of farmland, was still the largest in 1978 and had not increased his holdings. Even more indicative is the fact that in 1970, 1.6 percent of village households owned 8 hectares or more of agricultural land, with their total holdings representing 15 percent of all the community's farmland; whereas in 1978, only 1.2 percent of households owned 8 hectares or more, amounting to 13 percent of all agricultural land. Although this change cannot be said to demonstrate a definite trend toward an even more egalitarian distribution of land, the figures certainly show that stratification, at least in terms of landholdings, had not come about by the late 1970s.

This absence of increasing land-based stratification is attributable to several factors. As I already pointed out, land pressure itself, although clearly intensifying, had not yet become extreme, nor had land prices risen out of the reach of all but the very wealthiest. And modernization itself, ironically perhaps, was altering some circumstances, both economic and cultural, that had previously permitted or motivated land accumulation. Economically, assuming a given labor force, a household production strategy involving the modernization of *hortaliza* production is principally technology driven, whereas the traditional corn farming strategy is land driven. In other words, households striving to increase their income by modernizing *hortaliza* production did so primarily by increasing their labor productivity through the use of modern technology and techniques. On the other hand, households that sought to increase incomes by means of traditional corn farming did so principally by augmenting their landholdings. Furthermore, for modernizing *hortelano* households, the high cost of modern inputs was drawing off funds they might have otherwise used to purchase land.

Culturally, values associated with land were also changing. Traditional norms inveighed against ostentation in lifestyle (clothing, housing, furniture, etc.), leaving land acquisition about the only socially acceptable repository of surplus wealth, as well as the principal investment for future economic security. In addition, the ideal goal of honorable parents was to leave their children an inheritance of land, the promise of which—or the threat of disinheritance—provided material reinforcement for the traditional parent-children social roles, especially parental expectations of respect and care in old age. These values were under assault from several directions. Important among them was growing consumerism. Modernization in San Antonino was not limited to tools of production but was also substantially modifying the definition of a desirable lifestyle. A steadily growing number of families were building new brick houses (or upgrading old dwellings) and purchasing consumer goods such as gas stoves, television sets, stereos, electric blenders, and more citified clothing, all of which absorb funds that might otherwise go into land. At the same time, the goal of accumulating land for inheritance purposes, although still a value for some parents, was also losing sway. Parents were increasingly recognizing the importance of formal education, and some parents were sending their children to secondary (and some even to postsecondary) school explicitly in lieu of land inheritance, a practice that both costs money and reduces the household labor force. In addition, the real or threatened options of emigration and urban employment were weakening the economic dependence of children on parents, hence diminishing the social control efficacy of land inheritance.

As in the case of land, by 1980, the concentration of modern technology into the hands of a few wealthier farmers had not occurred either. Although the costs of the new inputs were substantial and rising, they remained within the means of all but the poorest households, as evidenced by their widespread adoption. Credit has played an important part in this. For example, Oaxaca City distributors readily sold motor pumps to villagers on credit (at interest rates between 20 and 40 percent per annum), secured only by the right of repossession; and members of the electricity cooperatives could obtain equipment on credit from BANCRISA or sometimes directly from the CFE. In addition, in many households, agricultural tooling-up costs were subsidized by income from nonagricultural occupations (Waterbury and Turkenik 1976; Waterbury 1989). This situation was threatened in the 1970s, however, by a rapidly accelerating rate of inflation of input costs, which was offset only in part by a rise in the prices *hortelanos* received for their products. For example, between 1970 and 1978, the price of gasoline motor pumps rose as much as 500 percent, and the price of gasoline itself climbed 3.5 times. Over the same period of time, the average wholesale price for cabbage rose only approximately 3.0 times, onions 3.5 times, radishes and lettuce 4.0 times, and coriander 4.5 times (see Figure 3.3).

Another constraint upon stratification is the very social organization of production itself. The peasant vegetable and flower growers of San

Figure 3.3   Price Rise for Selected Crops and Inputs, 1970–1978

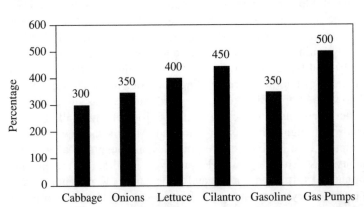

Antonino, like peasant artisans, are still precapitalist petty commodity producers (Cook and Binford 1990). The production unit is the household, which, in near-archetypal Chayanovian character, (a) is a family-integrated social group; (b) produces exclusively to meet the culturally defined consumption needs of its members; (c) is structurally undifferentiated as to ownership, management, and labor; (d) exercises control over its own inputs (in the case of land, either owned or sharecropped); and (e) relies upon its own membership for its permanent labor force (see Chayanov 1966). Three of these characteristics are particularly salient for this discussion: consumption orientation, household labor, and family structure.

Since no structural differentiation exists between producer and consumer—and, hence, between capital and consumption funds—the possibilities for substantial capital accumulation are severely limited. This should not be misconstrued to imply that Tonineros never save to acquire productive tools; they do. However, money allocated for production—from current sales or savings—requires reducing the share of their limited total income that can be allocated to consumption. Moreover, as I pointed out above, modernization is occurring not just in the tools and techniques of production, but also in the goods and styles of consumption, both of which are costly.

The continuation of the noncapitalistic household organization of production in San Antonino is evident in the labor factor. The traditional reliance on household labor has not changed. Although many San Antonino *hortelanos* hire day laborers—the number and frequency depending upon the amount of land and the plant cycle—virtually none employs permanent extrahousehold labor. Our informants explain this phenomenon in the pragmatic terms of diminishing returns. In their view, not only are the wages of hired workers high, but their productivity is low. Unless closely supervised, they are apt to be lazy, unreliable, and dishonest. It is difficult to corroborate my informants' qualitative assessment of hired labor, but my figures do confirm that wages have been escalating. Between 1970 and 1980, the cost of labor rose 900 percent.

Finally, since the social core (and corps) of the vast majority of households in San Antonino is the nuclear family, structural stratification—that is, intergenerational reproduction of strata—is inhibited by the cyclical nature of family composition, which, combined with particulate inheritance, renders intergenerational retention, let alone accumulation, of productive resources exceedingly problematic. (See also Chayanov 1966:53–69.)

In sum, for tangible stratification to occur, two interrelated developments would have to ensue. There would have to be a quantum leap in capital accumulation, permitting a substantially increased expenditure on productive inputs—land, technology, extrahousehold labor. And the social organization of production would have to become something more akin to a business enterprise, with greater structural differentiation of production roles and accounts from household roles and budgets. There is no evidence that either of these developments is taking place in San Antonino.

Employment and Migration

Unemployment and even underemployment are nonexistent in San Antonino and do not appear to be rising in spite of the increased labor productivity of truck gardening. And out-migration, which for many years had provided some safety-valve effect, has not increased since 1970, when the adoption of modern agricultural techniques began to accelerate. More specifically, the average annual emigration rate for the period 1970 through 1977 of 15.1 per thousand population shows no significant change from the decade 1960–1969, when the annual average was 15.9 per thousand.[11] Published rates for other Oaxaca communities are exceedingly scarce, but it would appear that emigration from San Antonino, though steady, has been and continues to be relatively moderate. By way of one comparison at least, Tilantongo in the Mixteca Alta region of Oaxaca experienced an annual average emigration rate for the period 1950–1960 of 41.3 per thousand population (Figure 3.4). Incidentally, this did not stem from modernization, but rather from economic stagnation (Butterworth 1975, 1977).[12] One factor explaining the relatively low emigration rate for San Antonino is, as discussed above, the lack of the kind of socioeconomic stratification that would displace large numbers of peasants from the land. Probably of even greater weight is the growing significance of nonagricultural occupations. As I said at the outset, San Antonino's households have long practiced complex economic strategies involving agricultural and nonagricultural activities. However, in recent years, reliance on nonagricultural occupations has acquired even greater importance. This reconfirms yet another component of A. V. Chayanov's theory of peasant economy: where market conditions permit, a household with agricultural resources insufficient to optimally absorb its labor supply will allocate labor to crafts and trades (Chayanov 1966:113; see also Cook and Binford 1990). The San Antonino case modifies Chayanov somewhat. There is also a matter of labor opportunity cost: even for households that possess sufficient agricultural resources to absorb family labor, if in the family's judgment its members can be employed in more remunerative activities (presuming the necessary capital and skills), it will not hesitate to do so. And even though San Antonino farmers take considerable pride in their agricultural proficiency—and a notable degree of aesthetic pleasure in a well laid out and tended field—I never once encountered a household whose economic strategies were encumbered by an all-consuming fondness for farming or a mystical attachment to the land, although I probed for such

Figure 3.4 Emigration from San Antonino and Tilantongo for Selected Periods

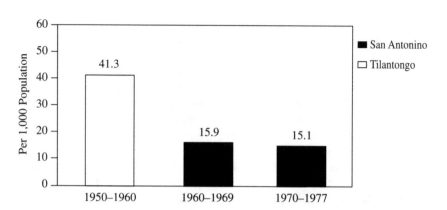

sentiments. Although a detailed exposition of San Antonino's nonagricultural occupations is beyond the scope of this chapter, suffice it to say here that such activities, by absorbing a substantial amount of labor time and by contributing to the maintenance—or even the improvement—of living standards, lessen the impetus for emigration.

Conclusion:
Questions of Sustainability and Globalizataion

I have presented a case history of a peasant community that has improved its material conditions substantially, and almost entirely on its own initiative. In the desire to improve their standard of living, individual peasant households have responded to the rising market demand for fresh vegetables and flowers by shifting production to those commodities and by investing their resources in new technology and production techniques. Furthermore, they have done so with minimal government economic or technical assistance. In most cases, credit to purchase the most costly new tools, the pumps, was supplied by the commercial distribution houses in Oaxaca City, not government agencies. Similarly, when tractors were needed, they were not supplied from an equipment pool managed by government-sponsored cooperatives or *ejidos,* as was true in some other parts of the state; rather, they were rented from village entrepreneurs who had also purchased their tractors on credit from commercial distributors. (The Ford distributor in Oaxaca City actually adjusted payment schedules in accordance with the agricultural cycle.) What little technical assistance farmers received also came from private sources: the sales personnel of commercial agricultural supply houses in Oaxaca City. Could we conclude, then, that the case described here provides a model of neoliberal agricultural development? Yes, for a while. But in the long run, probably not.

Even the short-term yes must be qualified, however, because what occurred in San Antonino did so under specific conditions that are not replicable for the vast majority of peasant communities. First, San Antonino enjoyed a favorable physical environment: soil, climate, and especially a high water table that permitted water extraction with small, relatively inexpensive motor pumps. Second, a number of preadaptive internal socioeconomic conditions prevailed, including (a) some previous experience with market-oriented farming, (b) heterogeneous household economic strategies that entailed nonagricultural activities that were capable of expanding to absorb labor displaced from agriculture by modern technology, and (c) the absence of a group of large landowners who could have taken unequal advantage of modern technology. Third, there were favorable external economic conditions, including (a) a regional and interregional system of marketplaces and trade networks that facilitated disposal of the community's produce, (b) constantly increasing urban demand for fresh vegetables and flowers, and (c) the absence in the region of a class of large commercial farmers who could compete with and/or displace peasant producers.[13] A fourth factor was the economic, technical, and social appropriateness of the technology adopted. It was economically appropriate because costs did not exceed the financial means of the majority of cultivators, technically appropriate because the equipment (most important, the motor pumps) could be operated and maintained by unschooled peasants and repaired by the few self-trained mechanics in the village, and socially appropriate because its operation did not require management or labor applications on a scale larger than could be provided by the peasant household.

However, there are several reasons to doubt the sustainability of this felicitous narrative. True, by 1980, increased productivity had not yet resulted in land pressures sufficient to engender the concentration of landholdings. But if the same levels of productivity were maintained much beyond 1980, I cannot see how significant land concentrations and land-based socioeconomic stratification would not be triggered. And if nonagricultural occupations were unable to absorb the labor of households displaced from agriculture, augmented emigration would be inevitable.[14] In addition to all of that are the vicissitudes of the market itself. Input costs have inflated precipitously in the last few years. Whether produce prices will keep pace is uncertain, especially in light of increasing competition from other peasant producers in the valley and particularly from imports from commercial farms outside the state.

The paramount threat to these market-oriented household farmers, however, derives from a factor external to the market itself: the ecological threat to sustainability, which renders moot the speculations in the previous two paragraphs. The quantum jump in water use for urban consumption, especially by Oaxaca City, by soft-drink and drinking-water bottlers, and for irrigation throughout the valley, coupled with several years of below-average rainfall, has steadily depleted the aquifer (Lees 1975; Santos Martínez 1992; Rodríguez Hernández 1994). This has spelled disaster for a substantial proportion of San Antonino *hortelanos* (Pasaran Jarquín 1998). The costs of deep wells and the irrigation equipment they require are well beyond the capital reach of individual Toninero households. For example, in 1978, the price of a 20-meter well excavated by the human-powered mechanical apparatus from San Pablo was already four times more expensive than a hand-dug 10-meter well; a 60-meter well perforated by a mechanized drilling rig cost 40 times as much. Furthermore, the option of forming additional deep-well cooperatives has been precluded by government conservation regulations prohibiting well drilling.[15] The depth of the water table also bars a return to traditional pot irrigation, although, as I said before, nobody would return to pot irrigation even if the water table were high enough to make it physically possible. Consequently, many fields have been returned to rainfall milpa cultivation, and some others are again being abandoned. Based on a brief and unsystematic survey, I would guess that as much as 10 percent of fields lay unused in 1993.

Has all of this spelled economic depression in San Antonino? No. On the contrary, my recent qualitative follow-up observations and interviews with key informants reveal even greater prosperity than before. In the diminished portion of the land where the water table is still reachable, *hortaliza* production continues full swing; and those fortunate *hortelano* households are doing well. The principal source of the community's relative prosperity, however, now derives not from agricultural production but from an even greater reliance on nonagricultural occupations, especially regional and interregional trading. These occupations, as I said earlier, have always been significant in San Antonino, but I suspect follow-up research will demonstrate that for a considerable segment of households since 1990, agricultural production has become a secondary activity. San Antonino fruit and vegetable traders range from Tapachula on the Guatemalan border to Mexico City, and they nearly monopolize supply to the coastal tourist resorts of Puerto Angel, Puerto Escondido, and Huatulco. In the late 1970s, one of my case history families lived in a small, humble, adobe-and-cane abode. The wife was a petty trader in the regional market system; the husband, with the help of his sons, toiled as a *hortelano*. A little over 20 years later, one of those sons built a large, brick, two-story

house with all the modern accoutrements. He supplies fresh produce to
Club Med in Huatulco.

The focus of this chapter, however, is not poverty or prosperity per se,
but rather agriculture. The hut-to-house accomplishment recounted above
derived not from tilling the soil, but from trade. In addition to building what
by village standards are opulent homes, produce traders have recently been
buying up fields as economic investments, which they either give out to
sharecroppers (mostly to corn farmers) or simply leave fallow. Trader wealth
therefore appears to be generating the kind of land pressure that modernizing farming has not done. According to an unconfirmed statement in 1995
by the president of San Antonino's communal lands committee, some traders
have accumulated over 20 hectares of land each, and consequently, more
cultivators have had to become sharecroppers.[16] So while San Antonino's
trading sector is booming, its agricultural sector appears to be stagnating.

And what about globalization? Extranational influences on Mexican
agriculture—whether truly global or simply hemispheric (especially from
the United States)—has existed for decades. The liberal modernization
program pursued by the Porfiriato government of the late nineteenth century had a strong globalizing dimension to it by welcoming foreign investment and favoring export over subsistence agricultural production. In
fact, the international marketing success of the Morelos sugar plantations
at the turn of the century so negatively impacted the peasants of the region
that it went on to become the epicenter of peasant participation in the
Mexican Revolution (Wolf 1969:3-50; Womack 1969). By comparison, at
that time, the valley of Oaxaca, other than as an importer of foreign-made
merchandise, remained largely peripheral to turn-of-the-century international markets, and for the valley's peasants, the revolution remained
largely something to be accommodated to rather than ardently joined (Waterbury 1975).

The recent neoliberal agricultural policies of the Mexican government
are more resolutely global than were their Porfiriato forebears. Based on
the theory of comparative advantage in international trade, many of the
policies were put in place even before the North American Free Trade
Agreement (NAFTA) went into effect on January 1, 1994. But Oaxaca's—
especially highland Oaxaca's—participation in all of this has been relatively negligible (Sorroza 1990). In an attempt to redress that, the current
state and national governments have been supporting efforts at increasing
the volume and kinds of agricultural exports from Oaxaca, and they are
having some successes with such products as organic coffee, *mezcal* (the
tequila-like alcoholic beverage distilled from local varieties of maguey),
and shiitake mushrooms. However, the overall economic impact of these
accomplishments has not extended broadly across the agricultural sector,
and this, coupled with the fact that support for local food crops remains in-
consequential, is contributing to another global phenomenon: the interna-

tional flow of labor. Between 1950 and 1981, Oaxaca rose from thirteenth to third place among states sending migrants to the United States (Rios Vásquez 1993). And the flow has become even greater since 1981. However, rather than invest heavily in peasant agriculture to stem the tide, the state of Oaxaca has turned to another global mechanism in an attempt to relieve rural poverty: *maquiladoras.*[17] As part of an industrial stimulus effort, the administration of Governor Diódoro Carrasco has provided tax concessions and made other contributions to encourage private companies to set up business in the state. In 1995, a plant was built on the Oaxaca-Ocotlán highway near San Antonino that was to process marigold petals into a natural food coloring and as an additive to chicken feed that would be exported internationally to commercial chicken producers. For reasons that were never publicized, the plant never went into operation. A year later, the building was emblazoned with the appellation "Ocotlán 2000," after the name of the governor's industrial development plan, Programa Oaxaca 2000, and, in a joint venture with Korean investors, was to serve as a garment assembly plant. However, the wage being offered in 1997 by the plant's potential operators was only 20 pesos per day (approximately U.S.$3.30 at the exchange rate extant at the time), an amount no Toninero (or rather Toninera, because the presumption was that it would attract women workers) would even consider accepting. Such a wage is below what even the poorest resident of the village makes in a day. In fact, agricultural day laborers in San Antonino at the time were earning 35 pesos per day, plus food. (Virtually all field hands come from other more impoverished villages since no Toninero will work for such low wages.) Apparently, other persons in the region were equally unimpressed with the wages the *maquiladora* planned to pay, because when I last observed the building in January 1998, it remained unused.

These two responses to global exigencies—migration and the "maquiladorization" of the Mexican economy—feed on rural poverty. Their influence on San Antonino has been minor because households have responded with considerable success to two other worldwide phenomena: urbanization and tourism, both of which augmented demand for fresh vegetables and flowers. San Antonino's households intensified their production of these products, and when stiff competition and the declining water table made that strategy less viable, many households shifted strategies again. For them, trading in the produce market is where the money is, not producing for it. *Es lo que dice el mercado.*

Notes

1. The modernization of production techniques can also affect other factors, such as yields per unit of land, net cash returns, the proportion of household

income allocated to capital equipment versus consumption goods, and so forth. However, I have chosen to concentrate here on the question of labor productivity (in terms of the amount of land workable by a given input of labor time) and leave these other issues for future analysis.

2. Article 27 restored the right of communal landownership and also provided for the formation of peasant landowning associations, called *ejidos,* which were granted lands confiscated from haciendas. *Ejido* land could be held in common or parceled. In either case, like communal land, it was inalienable.

3. The current actions of the Zapatista Army of National Liberation and the Popular Revolutionary Army are just the latest manifestation of the cycles of civil unrest.

4. The buying and selling of private and communal land are handled somewhat differently. Private land transactions are registered in the Ocotlán office of the state land registry, and owners pay an annual tax to the state. Communal land transferals are registered with the municipal treasurer, who charges a small fee.

5. In the 1930s, San Antonino was offered a piece of the small neighboring hacienda, La Chicuvica, as an *ejido.* Following the consensus arrived at during a village assembly, San Antonino's municipal authorities rejected the offer.

6. I am putting aside basic infrastructure improvements such as electrification and roads. After overcoming the resistance of a faction of traditionalists, the village's residential zone was electrified by the Federal Electrical Commission in the late 1960s—the costs of which were divided between the government and the villagers. The building and paving of the 1-kilometer access road that connects San Antonino to the main highway, which was also resisted by a group of traditionalists, was mostly paid for by the government.

7. It is not uncommon in the valley of Oaxaca for members of communities with agricultural or craft specializations to consider the skills associated with these specializations to be communal proprietary secrets and to resist their dissemination (e.g., see Stephen 1991). In this regard, local communities are functionally similar to medieval guilds.

8. Fertilizers are rated according to the proportion of three nutrients: nitrogen, phosphorus, and potassium.

9. It is interesting to note that, despite their exposure to modern commercial agriculture, participants in the bracero program did not play an appreciable role in pump adoption or in technological innovation generally. In fact, none of the ex-braceros in a sample I surveyed invested their foreign earnings in factors of production. Compared with many other communities in Oaxaca, relatively few Tonineros went to the United States as braceros, but those who did succumbed to the "migrant syndrome" (Reichert 1981) and spent their earnings for consumption purposes, including fiestas.

10. To qualify slightly my claim of no outside assistance in the development process, I am compelled to acknowledge my own role in the establishment of some of the electrification cooperatives. After the first cooperative had been successfully implemented, I offered my assistance to those intent on forming their own cooperatives. My help, however, was limited to drawing the maps demanded by the CFE, helping to draft and type up the necessary correspondence and legal documents, offering my own house for organizational meetings, driving committee members into the city and back, and accompanying them on some of their visits to the electrical commission and the government bank. To help reduce the risk of being robbed while carrying a large amount of money, I also drove one group from the government bank to the offices of the electrical commission to deliver the cash payment

demanded by the engineers in charge of the project. (Speculating about why they demanded cash rather than accepting a check from a government bank is beyond the scope of this chapter.) Perhaps my most significant intervention was when, a year after its founding, I was asked by the members of one cooperative to serve as an outside arbiter when the organization was on the point of disintegration due to accusations of malfeasance on the part of the executive committee. A special general assembly was convened so that I could listen to the accusers and the responses of the accused. The books were given to me for audit, and a few days later, I reported back that I had found no evidence of corruption. My judgment was unanimously accepted, even though the treasurer was my *compadre,* and the matter was closed.

It must be emphasized that my involvement had no effect on the overall process. The first cooperative was formed without my assistance (I wasn't even in residence at the time), the ones I helped would have been organized without me, and others were formed on their own afterward. Where I did intervene, my assistance only sped up the process and perhaps resulted in somewhat less arbitrary treatment from bank and electrical commission officials. As for the one case of my arbiter role, it is entirely possible they could have ironed out their differences without me. Furthermore, without me, the other cooperatives apparently got along just fine.

11. Following the method employed by Douglass Butterworth (1975), I derived these rates from a comparison of natural population increase (births less deaths) taken from municipal and district civil registries, with actual population growth as measured by 1960, 1970, and 1978 censuses.

12. A study in the Tlacolula wing of the valley of Oaxaca that compares three communities in terms of emigration and different production strategies not surprisingly demonstrates that the community that was most able to supplement agriculture with a nonagricultural occupation experienced the smallest levels of emigration (Sánchez Gómez 1995). Unfortunately, since the author uses a different method of calculating emigration rates, I cannot make a direct comparison between San Antonino and those communities.

13. For historical reasons too lengthy to delve into here, the agrarian structure of the valley of Oaxaca has never been dominated by a landed elite. (For the colonial period, see Taylor 1972; for the revolutionary period [1910–1920], see Waterbury 1975.)

14. This was demonstrated in a comparative study of three peasant communities in the Tlacolula wing of the valley of Oaxaca. Emigration was markedly lower in the one community with substantial artisanry production for the tourist market (Sánchez Gómez 1995).

15. For a general treatment of national irrigation policies as they affect peasants, see Whiteford and Bernal 1996.

16. The statement was made to Dolores Coronel Ortiz (personal communication) while she was carrying out research for her master's thesis on traders who supply Oaxaca City's large central public market. The statement, however, does not appear in the thesis itself (Coronel Ortiz 1997), and I have not had the opportunity to corroborate its accuracy.

17. *Maquiladoras* are in-bond assembly plants—in the Oaxaca case, mostly clothing—that, until NAFTA, had been confined to a strip along the U.S. border.

4

Rural Guatemala in Economic and Social Transition

Liliana R. Goldin

As rural peoples of Central America and beyond struggle to create and access new forms of market participation and means of survival under accelerating globalization processes, significant social and cultural shifts are taking place at the local level. In this chapter, I discuss some of these economic changes and their sociocultural correlates. The developments discussed here are common to most countries of Latin America. I base my analysis on research conducted for the past 15 years in the western and central highlands of Guatemala, in the departments of Sacatepéquez, Chimaltenango, Sololá, Totonicapán, and Quetzaltenango (see Maps 4.1 and 4.2), where I combined qualitative traditional anthropological fieldwork and survey research. My focus is on the analysis of overall trends, rather than an in-depth treatment of selected issues. This broad-based approach allows me to present the socioeconomic complexity of the Guatemalan highlands, where productive strategies are intertwined with cultural practices and where actors identify with diverse perspectives about the world.

Toward the end of the nineteenth century and up to the middle of the twentieth, most of the townships of the western and central highlands were well inserted into the capitalist system, but differentially so. The central areas were engaged in active commercial participation and economic development, whereas the areas that tended to contribute larger sources of labor to the coastal plantations remained peripheral and less developed (Smith 1977). From an economic perspective, the major differences in the communities and regions of today relative to those of the 1950s are those resulting from the intensification of traditional agricultural and artisan production, an increase in the use of putting-out systems of production, an increase in the number of petty industrial workshops with combinations of wage labor and unpaid family labor, further socioeconomic differentiation, and the development of new products and new markets for export, including

Map 4.1   General research area, Guatemala

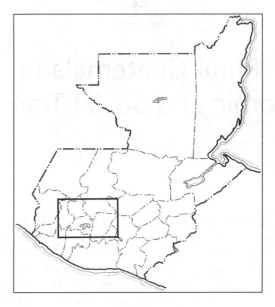

Map 4.2   Research sites

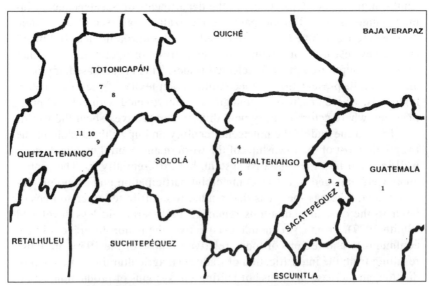

1. Guatemala City	7. San Francisco el Alto
2. Santiago Sacatepéquez	8. San Cristóbal Totonicapán
3. Santa María Cauqué	9. Zunil
4. Tecpán	10. Almolonga
5. Chimaltenango	11. Quetzaltenango
6. Patzún	

the expansion of industrial production through *maquiladora* industries as a result of economic globalization processes.

In 1950, the World Bank sent a commission to Guatemala to assess the potential of the country for economic development. The report was published in 1951 in the *Canadian Journal of Economic and Political Science* and was titled "The Economic Development of Guatemala." The report was also presented at the Association for Applied Anthropology in Montreal in June 1951 (Britnell 1958). In the report, it was noted that a major problem for Indian populations was insufficient agricultural production, due to the "cultural isolation of the indigenous population" concentrated in poor mountain lands inappropriate for the cultivation of grains. This cultural isolation contributed to the continuous use of antiquated agricultural methods that resulted in substantial erosion and deforestation of the hills. The report also attributed the minimal industrial development to the limited markets and poor conditions of the labor force.[1]

The commission suggested several solutions leading to the integration of the population into a single economy, which would then improve education, health, nutrition, and the development of new occupations for the indigenous populations of the highlands. The report also suggested the resettlement of portions of the population into regions that are "better adapted to progressive agriculture" (Britnell 1958:57). Overpopulated areas should depend less on corn production and more on cattle, milk products, and horticulture, as well as native crafts that could potentially be exported to the United States (Britnell 1958:59). In a subsequent phase, when abundant labor force and inexpensive electric energy were present, it would be possible, according to the commission, to solve the problem of unemployment through the establishment of small manufacturing plants in combination with a type of agriculture or horticulture that would employ only part of the available labor time of the people (Britnell 1958:60). In conjunction with the above recommendations, the report urged the resettlement of the population into small villages, rather than scattered hamlets, which would facilitate sanitary control and social and cultural stability.

These recommendations bear a striking resemblance to many of the recent developments in Guatemala, which include new migration patterns, resettlement efforts deriving from the establishment of *maquiladora* industries, growth of petty capitalist workshops as well as small local factories, reallocation of land in the most fertile areas for purposes of exporting vegetables, and the planned resettlements of the "development poles." The limited industrial development observed in the 1950s seems to have yielded to today's international capital, with ideal locations for assembly export production. These are areas with a large supply of potential workers willing to work for low wages who are also perceived as "docile" and "submissive." The structural adjustment policies of the 1980s in conjunction with the repressive measures of the state have, in essence, resulted in the implementation of many of the recommendations from the World Bank.

In the remainder of this chapter, I describe the effects of structural adjustment policies in Guatemala and then highlight the nature of the communities formed around current productive strategies. New identities, new religious affiliations, and changing socioeconomic positions are more consistent with the new practices and speak to the unique interactions between global trends and local ways. Our focus must shift from traditional concepts that emphasize singular unidimensional characterizations to concepts that recognize the multiple and sometimes contradictory roles that individuals participate in within the context of their everyday life.

Structural Adjustment Policies

Adjustment policies in Latin America have been precipitated by numerous events, including oil price increases in the 1970s and the rise of interest rates in the early 1980s followed by significant decreases in demands for import. The guiding ideology of neoliberal policies has been oriented toward downsizing government. Measures have included restrictions on social expenditures, such as health, education, and other social services; the privatization of public enterprises; and the denationalization of resources. Since the 1980s, the number of Latin Americans living below the poverty line has increased dramatically. At the same time, there has been an increase in the standard of living of the top 25 percent of the population. Most of the decreases are found in the rural areas of Latin America.[2]

Guatemala probably represents the most extreme situation on most economic dimensions. As is widely known, Guatemala has one of the most inequitable land distribution ratios in Latin America, as well as the highest levels of urban and rural poverty. Profound problems of malnutrition, health, environmental degradation, and rural unrest have been combined until recently with high levels of political repression. Signs of political opening after the signing of the 1996 peace accords are hopeful, but the economic situation continues to be poor. Some rural sectors, even with limited resources, have been able to take advantage of market opportunities that the new policies present. For example, some have exploited their skill base and the increased prices for nontraditional exports in foreign markets, including other Latin American markets. Examples of these exports are horticultural products and light manufactures, such as textiles and clothing. They include newly developed products for export such as vegetables and fruits (broccoli, Chinese peas, melons, and others), which are usually produced under foreign supervision. In Guatemala, the production of nontraditional agricultural goods has progressed in several ways. Some export operations are growing crops on rented or purchased land, hiring help, and then exporting the crops directly to the United States or Europe. There are also exporters who contract directly with the growers, setting high standards of quality (see, e.g., Barham et al. 1992; AVANCSO/ Pacca 1992; Calí 1992; Mendizábal and Weller 1992; Paus 1988; and Murray 1994). Those communities privileged with access to fertile land have taken Agency for International Development offers for facilitating contacts and advice for the production of fruits and vegetables. In the less-typical case that I observed—Almolonga, Quetzaltenango, a K'iche' Maya–speaking town of 11,000 located a few miles from Quetzaltenango—independent producers and local middlemen are marketing local products for the local market and also in bordering countries of Central America and Mexico. These opportunities offset the fact that prices of traditional products, including traditional vegetables and grains sold for national consumption, have dropped and that imports of cheap grain from the United States have lowered dramatically the profitability of grain production.

The production of garments for the local/national market, often restricted to urban non-Maya populations, has intensified in a few Maya townships in the country. For example, San Francisco el Alto, another K'iche' Maya–speaking town of 35,000 located in the department of Totonicapán, has seen much development due to this economic strategy. The success of the intensification of garment production by Maya townships is largely the result of the local development of styles and tastes introduced from developed countries, combined with the competitive prices generated with family labor and low wages. These producers compete primarily with the *pacas,* or resale of secondhand clothes, originating in the United States and sold at very low prices in rural Guatemala. More indirectly, they compete with the constantly expanding *maquiladora* industries. Petty industrial producers of San Francisco, for example, often rely on outputting labor from women and men who work in their houses using their own sewing machines. They receive thread and cut materials from their *patrón* (boss) that they, in turn, assemble into finished products. Some workshops are beginning to operate in the owner's shops rather than their own houses.

The people of Almolonga, of San Francisco, and of many other sites in the central and western highlands have several commonalities. They are intensifying their economic strategies, innovating, and exploring new markets. They are rapidly converting to Protestantism, and they are drawing on the cheaper labor from neighboring townships. Within the makings of such economic restructuring, we observe more profound patterns of capitalization and cultural change. These developments bring with them implicit trends of socioeconomic differentiation and uneven development (Goldin and Saenz de Tejada 1993). In the western highlands, textile (craft) producers of Totonicapán, San Cristóbal Totonicapán, Comalapa, and the towns surrounding Lake Atitlán (departments of Totonicapán, Chimaltenango, and Sololá) have also sought the market opportunities of foreign buyers. They have adapted and transformed many of the traditional products they produce to appeal to the international market (Rosenbaum and Goldin 1997). In the central highlands, the populations in the surroundings of Guatemala City and many depressed towns, in turn, have become sources of cheap labor for the *maquiladora* industries.

Sectors within the region have opted to respond differently to the limited possibilities resulting from years of repression, land scarcity, and changes in the demands of the world market. We also observe a pattern of uneven development in the country as a whole. This pattern points to increased differentiation within towns with an emphasis on semiproletarianization and a more skewed class structure combined with marked differentiation between towns as well as regions. As certain towns take advantage of opportunities (conditioned by ecological and historical factors) to explore alternative markets, they have differentially engaged in the use of internal and external sources of labor. The ongoing decline in the export of artisan products (Hernández 1997:34; Rosenbaum and Goldin 1997) and the increasing number of foreign-owned industries opening in the metropolitan area are creating important changes in the social and cultural lives of the newly proletarianized individuals and their sending communities. The experience of a few communities in the highlands of Guatemala highlight at the microlevel issues of uneven or exclusionary regional development. The mixed results lead to equivocal assessments, which depend on the focus of the analysis or the definitions of development. With serious land pressures, the new economic policies provide rural peoples with the opportunity (and the need) to rely on sources of income not always dependent on the availability of large extensions of land. Industrial opportunities, export enterprises, and intensification of petty industrial and artisan production and trade are creating new contexts that defy traditional assumptions about rural societies.

The Global in the Local:
The New Communities of Guatemala

Working for Maquiladoras

Since the 1980s, Guatemala has joined several other Latin American and Asian countries as an attractive site for *maquiladora* industries. *Maquiladoras* are factories specializing in the finishing stages of production of such diverse merchandise as garments and electronic parts. These final stages are often labor intensive and require low-level training and skills. They include the assembly of previously designed and cut parts and the packing of the finished product. The more sophisticated stages requiring higher technologies and skills take place in developed countries such as the United

States, Japan, or Korea. The finished products are returned to the originating countries without the payment of export fees. Mexico, Costa Rica, Colombia, the Philippines, and Guatemala, among others, offer investors tariff-free zones with an abundant labor force willing to work for extremely low wages and in conditions that would be unacceptable or illegal for the workers of developed countries (Ong 1987; Safa 1983; Fernandez-Kelly 1983; Nash 1983; Goldin n.d.). Studies of the *maquiladora* industry have described the conditions in the factories and documented exploitative forms of labor, sexual abuse of female workers, poor environmental conditions and hygiene practices, limited breaks, and dangerous spatial arrangements, including the lack of sufficient air and fire exits.

In Guatemala, the daily salary rarely exceeds the equivalent of U.S. $3.00. As in other places, laborers come from rural areas to work for small wages with hopes of "improving themselves." Work in the *maquiladoras* is one of the few options open to them, other than migration to the United States or other Central American countries and seasonal work in the coastal plantations. There is a direct relationship among landlessness, unemployment, and the *maquila* industry. Guatemalan peasants have been dispossessed of their lands continually since the European invasion. Work in *maquiladora* factories often involves migration to the metropolitan area of Guatemala City. Most workers are young women who are considered docile and flexible. Unionization is forbidden in most cases, and alternative associations called *"solidaridades"* replace unions. *Solidaridades* encourage employees and management to work together. In fact, it has been suggested that *solidaridades* prevent workers from joining unions, as evidenced by the fact that these associations usually stop all activities after unionizing efforts are dissolved (Petersen 1992; AVANCSO 1994).

In the 1950s, scholars predicted a new millennium where automation and a large array of robots would replace a tired working class, who would, in turn, become managers, designers, or analysts in the computer age (Sklair 1989; Holmstrom 1984). But such predictions could not foresee crucial features of the world economy—the internationalization of production and the global movement of products, labor, and capital. The need for flexibility in production, with extremely compartmentalized labor processes, would be fulfilled not by robots, but by the cheap workers of the *maquila* age. The process of production has come to be distributed around the world in small components, taking advantage of what every locale on the planet has to offer. With the formal disjointment of the labor process, production and consumption have become truly "worlds apart" (Goldin 1997b and n.d.).

Both Mayas and non-Mayas alike became the new robots of the turn of the century. In July 1997, there were 234 factories involved in the export of garments in Guatemala employing approximately 70,000 workers. Ninety of those factories are Guatemalan, and of the remainder, 122 are Korean, 17 are U.S., and five are of other origin (GEXPRONT/AGEXPRONT

1997). In 1991, President Jorge Serrano Elias chose *maquila* production and such other nontraditional exports as fruits and vegetables as the preferred development strategies for Guatemala. The growth of this industry is not only changing the lives of thousands of families, but is also changing the structure of rural communities, disrupted by the emigration of young women.[3] As the young move away from agriculture and lose the opportunities to learn the skills needed for agricultural work, many Guatemalan youth wonder about the unpredictable future. In the central highlands of Guatemala, hundreds of communities provide Maya and non-Maya workers to the international factories, some of which are located in the departments of Chimaltenango and Sacatepéquez. In those departments, local people and migrants combine production strategies by sending their sons and daughters to work in the *maquilas,* while at the same time maintaining some agricultural work with the aid of younger family members or older hired labor who do not qualify for *maquila* work.[4]

Commercial Agriculture and Petty Industrial Production: Ethnicity, Class, and the New Identities

QUESTION: People everywhere in the region say: "The people from Almolonga? Oh! They are rich, they have lots of money!" Do you think there is envy?

ANSWER FROM A TEACHER FROM ALMOLONGA: Oh, yes, I know what you are asking. . . . the problem is that they say that we are the little Israelites. Where do these people come from? From little Israel, they say. Well, they say this because the people of Almolonga are very nosy [*muy metida*]. You go to Tapachula, and you see people from Almolonga; you go to El Salvador, and there you see people from Almolonga. You go somewhere else in Guatemala, and you see people from Almolonga. We are always noticed because of the colorful outfits that our women wear, which are very well known. And they say that these people from Almolonga, just like you were saying, are very rich. Maybe it is not so much the potassium [in the soil] but the money. But I think there is some resentment, because the people here are very hard-working people. They get up at dawn, for example, not so much in times of rain but when there is no rain, in the summer. They get up at five or four in the morning, they take their shovel [to irrigate their fields], and go to work on the vegetables, and then, at seven or eight they go to plant or to harvest, or if they have to go to the coast, or just conduct their daily activities. . . . Like the expression says, *El que quiere celeste que le cueste* [the person who wants results must work hard to achieve them]. Like I said, in Almolonga we now cultivate land in Quetzaltenango, Salcajá, and San Cristóbal. Even in San Marcos, people from here have arrived to cultivate their land, to grow vegetables. Almolonga is not enough any longer, *Almolonga ya no alcanza,* there is not enough room to cultivate here. . . . Also, people here have trucks and pickups. They are not rich, they have made an effort, and they have debts with the car agencies . . . but not everyone in Almolonga is rich, no! There are some that have, but they have worked for it. When they say that everyone here is rich, no! That is a lie! Some are, some aren't, like in other places.

The populations that are succeeding in the region have had access to limited but fertile lands, coupled with knowledge of such labor-intensive techniques as the use of natural and chemical fertilizers and pesticides, and to the means of hiring a labor force that can fulfill production goals. Vegetable producers from Almolonga, for example, have hired temporary workers from surrounding townships to work in Almolonga or on their rented and newly acquired lands in the region, creating a double pattern of stratification within Almolonga and between Almolonga and neighboring townships. In the pursuit of alternative production strategies, Almolongueños have not developed into distinct classes of proprietors and workers within the village. Some people work as peons for a few days of the month, but overall, they cannot be considered exclusively as wage workers. If anything, there is exploitation of other villages through the use of their land and occasional wage labor. As between and within town economic differentiation takes place, we observe incipient indications of class formation centered on production forms and town specialization. Producers and traders of export crops (*comerciantes* or *gente de negocios*), for example, tend to see themselves as more intelligent and better equipped to succeed than others, and they are in fact wealthier, on average, than traditional (corn) agriculturalists. Traders state that they are good for the town in that, by taking vegetables for sale to El Salvador, Nicaragua, and other markets, they generate demand and are thus able to keep the price of vegetables high. The aura of progress and interest in innovation resulting in an advantaged position in the town has created a new faction around traders and middlemen and the potential for developing into a full differentiated class. This group has explored new alternatives provided by the market, has been open to change and innovation in social and economic terms, and has experienced large ideological transformations (Goldin 1996 and 1997a).

QUESTION: Who works here with you?

ANSWER FROM A GARMENT PRODUCER IN SAN FRANCISCO EL ALTO: My children—two sons and one daughter. They work here with these sewing machines. My wife, she works on the overlock machine that gives the finishing touches. I had some paid workers but it was not worth it. Not enough. It is better to work with just the family. If I had more room to put all the workers together and I could check on them . . . but it is hard when they are away in their own homes.

In San Francisco el Alto, Totonicapán, the intensive production of garments is generating a newly developed class structure that may be different from the one generated by traditional developments of the life cycle, where older people attain more established positions in the town. The new class structure is one in which those who are able to produce more for less can extract larger surplus and place themselves in privileged positions in the class spectrum. This is combined with the widespread employment of women in semiproletarianized positions (working part-time for wages), which creates a new stratum of dependent workers while providing women with the (limited) power that access to cash brings. The use of family labor complemented, when necessary, with pieceworkers who often work at home with their own equipment—machines, lighting, needles, and thread— can be profitable. Owners' statements to the effect that the availability of more rooms may allow them to gather all workers and exercise more direct control over them are reminiscent of developments described for Europe in the fifteenth century. Then, the expansion of markets generated new and expanded production needs, giving place to incipient forms of capitalist development in the form of workshops and small labor-intensive industries. Today, these small-scale enterprises provide fascinating clues about the ways in which the processes of social and economic differentiation interface with the formation of ideologies.

These communities are difficult to understand in terms of class or ethnicity alone.[5] In San Francisco, for example, we observe a class of owners of the means of production that coexists with a class of workers that has, at least temporarily, lost control of the production process but that requires low investments to start up a new business. It is not possible to conceptualize them based on classic notions of class because most actors are engaged in multiple activities, multiple identities, and truly multiple relations of production. It is difficult to identify rural sectors of the population that are clearly extracting surplus from the labor of others (Smith 1990; Goldin and Saenz de Tejada 1993; Goldin 1996). Often they do so on a temporary basis, until the worker is able to learn enough to start his or her own business. We often find individuals within households that are positioned at both ends of the economic spectrum, as exploited and as exploiters, or at multiple points in the economy. These multiple roles do not always lead an individual to choose to identify with a given class or ethnic affiliation. Rather, they use other elements of identification, such as their preferred occupation or their identification with the land, their connection with a religious group, or their main source of employment (e.g., the factory). The new communities transcend the "peasant/proletarian/bourgeois" categories. As Michael Kearney (1996:146) has pleaded, new categories placed on the borders of social and economic positions need to be defined.

The relatively fluid movement between *aprendiz operario* (apprentices) and *patróns* in the context of petty industrial production, the use of family labor, and the fine lines between owners and workers in general prevent us from generalizing traditional class dynamics. The phenomenon of regional, rather than internal, differentiation observed in the context of export agriculture is also suggestive of nontraditional differentiation patterns. In the case of *maquila* production, class statements are often made in terms of national distinctions, such as the emphasis on discussions of Guatemalans and Koreans, which appear again and again in the context of interpreting power relations in the Korean-owned factories.

Global Trends: The Production of Ideologies[6]

QUESTION: Why is it that you do not attend traditional town celebrations?

ANSWER FROM A VEGETABLE WHOLESALER FROM ALMOLONGA: When you have to travel all week, to Petén or El Salvador, there are no weekends and no time for communal fiestas. You cannot spend three or four days drinking [liquor] because, if you do, you will not be able to deliver the merchandise on time.

QUESTION: What has brought about this progress?

ANSWER FROM A SHOP OWNER FROM ALMOLONGA: I think the increase in commerce and traders, and the change in religion. Since many of them stopped drinking, now they only think about traveling and doing business, working and cultivating the land . . . because before, many people were engaged in vices, they even sold their land to pay for them; now, they take good care of it.

ANSWER FROM A PERSON FROM ALMOLONGA WORKING IN THE DEPARTMENT'S ADMINISTRATION: As I said, it is not Saint Peter [the town's patron saint] who brought progress to Almolonga, and I do not believe that it is the Evangelicals either, but the principles that people follow. But it is true that 50 percent of people are Evangelical, and they dedicate themselves more to work than to vices. Before, when they were not Evangelical, people drank and womanized more. But with the change, people work harder.

Profound cultural and ideological changes are taking place concurrent with the creation of new economic strategies or the intensification of traditional ones. This is more noticeable among the populations that have shown evidence of economic development and less so in others that have not significantly deviated from previous practices or that have remained as providers of land and/or labor for others. People are articulating justifications for moving away from customs constructed around a system of rank and prestige, rather than class, which complements an accepted discourse centered on humility and an expressed sense of community solidarity. Statements like "We are all in this together" or "Ambition is never good" are now sometimes overshadowed by a new rhetoric often associated with the needs for progress and change. There are those who are "willing to change" and those who are not, as indicated in the comments here of a university-educated cooperative worker from Almolonga:

> Everything I was doing was wrong; I realized that I had to *really* change. I was badly investing all the fruits of my work. Then I said to myself, This is the opportunity to change, and only God can help me. . . . The main idea has to be improving your life. Then you stop thinking about liquor or about fiestas and things of the like. One worries more about dressing well, improving your house, your clothes, your lifestyle. The minister at the church gives advice about how to improve your economic and social situation: avoid those fiestas, dress better, invest your money to buy, for example, a car to be able to move around, and enjoy the benefits of development . . . because money would not be good for anything if one continues living as we did before. You need to acquire more modern means of life.

In a survey conducted in Almolonga, I found that approximately 52 percent of the population there is Catholic and 48 percent Protestant. This contrasts with the finding that, during the generation of the parents of the present heads of household, only about 13 percent of the population was Protestant and the remaining 87 percent Catholic. Of the present generation's grandparents, only about 3 percent was Protestant. This recent and rapid rate of conversion is associated with a decrease in *cofradía* (the civic and religious hierarchy) participation, from approximately 42 percent during the sample's parents' generation to approximately 26 percent during the present generation, and a major decrease in the practice of traditional *costumbre* (rituals associated with the earth and other Maya deities), from approximately 82 percent during their parents' generation to approximately 42 percent for the current generation. In 1995, there were 15 Evangelical churches in the town. The largest one, located in front of the market and beside the Catholic church, was built in 1993 and has a large capacity. It is clear that Almolonga has a larger Evangelical population than most neighboring townships, where estimates suggest that conversion rates range from 10 to 30 percent. In Zunil, a neighboring town where people from Almolonga rent land, only 5 percent of the population has converted. In addition, there is more *cofradía* participation in Zunil.

Preliminary work in San Francisco suggests that conversions to Protestantism are fast and may be as prevalent as in Almolonga. Based on qualitative analysis, however, I have not observed differences in religion as a function of production strategy among men in San Francisco. Since most men in San Francisco have adopted petty industrial production, we find both Catholics and Protestants to be engaged in the activity in large numbers. However, I also have found that workshop owners tend to be Catholic and intermediaries tend to be Evangelical. It is interesting that most women engaged in the industry tend to be Protestant, suggesting that an interest in economic independence and the initiative to carry it through is more prevalent among Protestant women. I also speculate that the position of intermediary, for men, is one that entails more risk taking and departs from more traditional occupations. In Almolonga, I have observed a correlation between changes in production strategies—in particular, the practice of trade in vegetables—and the rate of conversions, and I have suggested that as people turn to commerce and find themselves traveling to new places with new ideologies, they become more open to accepting new ideas (Goldin 1992). In the department of Sacatepéquez, in a survey conducted by the Asociación de Investigación y Estudios Sociales (Asturias de Barrios 1996), it was found that approximately 40 percent of the households in the sample were involved in *maquila* production and that most of those households involved in *maquila* and other economic strategies were Evangelical.

Protestantism offers individuals a set of specific codes about proper behavior that directly address situations that have led to economic and familial stress (e.g., drinking, polygyny). These codes are linked to a broader belief system that is said to be directly rooted in religion and God's word. Formal adoption of the specific codes fosters acceptance of the broader belief system and reassures individuals with the promise of religious salvation. The codes can have favorable implications for all members of the family, thereby engendering family support.

This trend is not characteristic of only a few Guatemalan towns. For example, many Latin Americans are resorting to the new Pentecostal and other Evangelical churches for support. The new churches are constructed on ideologies that support the changes in production relations and new household strategies. They provide a framework for change, further stratification, and a sense of "brotherhood" that the Catholic Church is unable to offer (see Stoll 1990).

These cultural changes often materialize in the context of religious change: new leadership by responsive and empathetic ministers who speak the language of the people; specific guidance as to proper (different) behavior, as well as more general moral guidance; the promotion of solidarity and togetherness by the formation of clearly identifiable social networks (e.g., addressing other converts as "brother" and "sister") and working toward common (newly established) goals; the linking of everyday behavior to broader religious salvation (and achievement of earthly success); public commitment as a means of inducing behavioral conformity and belief consistency; a responsiveness to the changing needs of the community as a result of land loss and occupational changes; and a responsiveness to the problems of both men and women in the context of the family unit.

New Actors in New Fields of Practice and Analysis

The traditional migration route took highland people to the coastal lands. Presently, people from all regions are migrating to the highlands in order to work in the factories and other facilities such as chicken farms or on export agriculture. As a result, we have observed a new discourse on the subject of interethnic relations and definitions of "self" and "other" that tends to move away from agriculture. The decrease in agricultural activities by a sector of the population of the central highlands may remove one of the few economic options that offers some degree of independence, if not development. Although the production and sale of agricultural exports has been shown to offer limited development potential (Goldin 1996), it has created an opportunity for applying traditional skills to more profitable endeavors, even if at the same time these activities have generated more internal social and economic differentiation. It is clear that some Mayas have been able to achieve improved economic well-being by focusing on nontraditional agriculture (see Asturias de Barrios, Tevalán, and Romero 1996; Von Braun, Hotchkiss, and Immink 1989; and Thrupp, Bergeron, and Waters 1995). They also are obtaining steady sources of cash from assembly industrial production. In the context of export strategies, capitalism offers a few the chance for mobility at the expense of others. From the perspective of the Maya people, it is indeed preferable to have economic, political, and social resources within the communities. These may someday translate into political and social gains. However, *maquilas* and export production in general constitute a new source of dependency. The dominant element is not the landowner; it is the intermediary, the manager, and the new employers, regardless of nationality, a new *patrón*. The new communities on the fringes of the world economy are an expression of capitalist expansion. They constitute the de-skilling of rural peoples and the decampesinization of the peasantry, in the case of industrial work, and the loss of decisionmaking power, in the case of export agriculture (Goldin n.d.).

Export assembly plants and commercial agriculture are having a substantial impact on sending households and local communities located on or near *maquila* sites. They are directly affecting the extent, nature, and degree of agricultural practice. New attitudes toward work are being defined in the context of changing interpretive systems, and new perspectives on economic opportunities are emerging engendered by the new forms of labor: young men and women refer to agriculture as "our parents' jobs," and those who work in the factories are quite adamant about not wanting to participate in agriculture. This generational split is suggestive of future trends, but more research is needed to assess what these workers will be doing when they are no longer hired by the factories.

Furthermore, new gender relations have developed in the context of working side by side in the factories and, most important, as a result of allowing both women and men to provide the household independent sources of cash. In this regard, women often express regret at the loss of their teen daughters to the factories and miss their help with the younger children, but they are able to benefit from their daughters' economic contributions to the household, which go directly to their mothers. Indirectly, this gives all women an added measure of independence. Larger households that include adolescents are taking advantage of the new economic opportunities, and, on average, those engaged in multiple activities seem to be the first to convert to Evangelical religions.

Finally, communities of the central highlands are constantly receiving new migrants, are becoming more urbanized and complex, and, as a result, are experiencing many of the problems pervasive in urban settings, including delinquency and drug use (Goldin 1997b and n.d.).

From the 1930s until not too long ago, the township has been the logical unit of anthropological analysis. Township distinctions opened questions for research and yielded fundamental case studies of social-anthropological research in Guatemala. Many of the communities that we see today are essentially transformed communities in that they are global and transnational in nature. The boundaries, real or imagined, that anthropologists described in the 1940s, 1950s, and 1960s were boundaries that held the township and the nation-state as the organizing categories. The boundaries (meaningful contexts) that we find today extend to the fields, cities, and refugee camps of Mexico and the United States and the factories of Korea and Japan (see Kearney 1996:126). For example, the towns and hamlets of Sacatepéquez and Chimaltenango have seen a dramatic population increase in the last 20 years—82 percent and 59 percent, respectively (figures from Guatemalan population censuses for 1973 and 1994). With the multidirectional flows of people, produce, and requirements, new actors develop new and multiple identities associated with complex patterns of production and reproduction (Kearney 1996:159). These actors are indeed Mayas, but they are far removed from any romantic or essential notion of the Maya; these are de-essentialized Maya (see Warren 1992). They struggle with the many complex attires that they choose to wear in literal and symbolic expression of their complexity, as illustrated in the comments of a young man from Santa María Cauqué who notes that the factory allows new dress styles but sets strict (and new) work guidelines:

> Down there [in the factory] it is just a job, and if a woman wants to wear skirts or makeup, if she wants to break away [from custom], she does (*si le da la gana de safarse, se safa*). The same happens with our work up here; you do things one way here [in the town], but when you are down there in the factory, you have to do things in their particular way. And if I don't do things the way the Koreans want, then I have to go back and work in the fields. Down there, women can wear makeup or wear skirts, but up here, they have to go back to what they were before.

One interesting aspect of this characterization is that the "before" and "after" are actually simultaneous, and they refer to differing spatial and cultural categories, such as from "down there" in the factory versus from "up here" in the town, from factory to field, from Natural to Guatemalan, from field to market to the household hearth, all in one. In short, people are generating new conceptions of self. However, it is not a simple case of replacing one mode of production with another, one element of value with another, such as land over capital, or one ideology with another. Rather, it is a question of multiplicity. Changes in worldview do not replace one ideology with another. Rather, alternative and often contradictory sets of assumptions coexist (Goldin 1997b).

Conclusion

As a result of structural adjustment policies and years of political repression, we have observed several developments in the western and central highlands of Guatemala. Most notable is the apparent success of those communities that have taken advantage of niches in the export markets, such as artisan products, nontraditional crops, and industrial wage labor. This development has a mixed impact on the local communities. For one, we observe increased and new patterns of differentiation generated by the position of the various communities in the practice of the new economic strategies. Those located in areas that are deemed preferential for export agriculture are experiencing some economic improvements, but at the same time, they are dealing with the problems of a scarce labor force willing to work for them. This, in turn, encourages producers to hire labor from communities not engaged in the production of nontraditionals. A pattern of uneven development that distinguishes one community from the next is thus being generated.

As economic improvements occur due to agricultural and artisan exports, we are also documenting diminished returns. The international market for artisan products seems to be saturated, and quality and prices are going down, as they yield the lowest returns from all nontraditional exports (GEXPRONT/AGEXPRONT 1998). Returns from export of nontraditional products in general had gone up in 1996 but down by 1997 (GEXPRONT/ AGEXPRONT 1998); prices for some export vegetables, such as Chinese peas, also seem to be decreasing as the cost of labor increases; and other agricultural products are yielding higher returns, with an overall increase of 17 percent for agricultural nontraditional exports from October 1996 to October 1997 (GEXPRONT/AGEXPRONT 1998; see Asturias de Barrios et al. 1996 on recent fluctuations). Labor is orienting itself toward industrial work in the export industries. Such jobs are more attractive to young people, who no longer identify with agricultural work. Instead, they see factory work—with its biweekly checks and an atmosphere of worker solidarity—

as the wave of the future. The expansion of *maquiladora* industries, in turn, has brought significant changes at the level of both the community and the personal. Migration and urbanization of previously small towns has created new problems. New occupations create a new persona—the industrial wage worker, which still coexists with the rural agriculturalist. Petty industrial production is also presenting an opportunity, although an apparently limited one, for economic improvement. With it, we see young people willing to learn new skills in order to improve themselves. The distance, both social and temporal, between employer and employee is often short, and many in these communities are sociologically placed at several levels of the economic spectrum at the same time. In addition, workers are reevaluating their worldviews and sometimes opting to convert to new religions (Evangelicalism) so as to find better support and provide coherence to their new economic practices.

The new households of rural Guatemala are more complex today than they were in the past. Although the notion of pooling resources is old, the new households truly reflect changes in the world economy. The presence of adolescents in the household brings further sources of income, and the young and the older are now involved in multiple and different activities. Commerce, often on a larger scale than customarily seen in local marketplaces, is more widespread, and a new sector of intermediaries (mostly but not exclusively men) continues to grow.

What all these developments suggest is a need for new perspectives in the study of rural issues. The matter of multiplicity, where individuals are placed at different and formerly contradictory positions in the economy, the matter of complex households engaged in new and different activities, and the matter of economic fluidity in certain sectors and the impoverishment of those that have become subordinate to the emerging elites all require flexible research schedules and more comprehensive research instruments that will not limit the scope of any study to one productive strategy. The new identities and new ideologies generated in the context of internationalization of production can be captured through the use of a combination of qualitative and quantitative methods that allow for open areas of inquiry. The need for multimethod approaches has never been this great. In addition, the new socioeconomic dynamics, which we have until now referred to as "class dynamics," also need to be documented and reported in creative ways. The conceptual tools that we currently rely on are limited to cleaner, but consequently unrealistic, models of the economy. These models are in need of reassessment.

Notes

This chapter is based, in part, on a paper presented at a meeting of the American Anthropological Association (San Francisco, 1996) titled "Maquila Age Maya:

Assessing Our Theories, Methods, and Choices of Anthropological Socioeconomic Analysis." The research was funded, in part, by two faculty research development grants from the Office for Research, State University of New York at Albany.

1. The chief of the commission was G. E. Britnell from the University of Saskatchewan. The commission report also mentioned the poor quality of seeds, lack of use of fertilizers and insecticides, lack of agricultural markets (including transport and warehouses that were not convenient or were too expensive), lack of credit for the indigenous population with small purchasing power, inadequate agricultural production, and high cost of raw materials. In addition, Britnell cited psychological obstacles to development associated with inadequate nutrition and education of the labor force.

2. For discussions of the impact of structural adjustment policies in rural areas of Latin America, see, for example, Collins 1993; Edwards and Teitel 1986; Glewwe and de Tray 1989; Tardanico 1993; Petras and Vieux 1992a; and Goldin 1997a.

3. *Maquila*-based employment is not secure, with factories closing with short notice when conditions are found to be better in other locations. More than 60 *maquiladoras* (about 35 of which are Korean owned) had closed by the end of 1994. Many more threatened to close if their performance did not compare favorably with that of other Central American countries and Mexico. With the implementation of the North American Free Trade Agreement, many *maquila* factories have moved to the border between Guatemala and Mexico, which added to the approximate 40 percent unemployment rate of the qualified labor force in Guatemala (*El Gráfico* December 1994). The Vestuarios y Textiles (Commission of Clothing and Textiles) requested incentives for these industries (about 15,000 people were reported to have lost their jobs in the industry; *Prensa Libre* December 16, 1994).

4. In a survey conducted by the Asociación de Investígación y Estudios Sociales (Asturias de Barrios 1996), which I further analyzed, one finds that 40 percent of households sampled in Santa María Cauqué, Sacatepéquez, engaged in some form of *maquila* work, but some members of almost all of these households still maintained some footing in agricultural work. In fact, 90 percent of households involved in *maquila* work were also involved in agriculture.

5. People find themselves involved in multiple relations with multiple levels of self-identification. Scott Cook and Leigh Binford (1990:228) observed this when they discussed the nature of differentiation and the complexity of economic relations that are present in Oaxaca, which they refer to as "ambiguous" (cited in Kearney 1996:96).

6. Material in this section has been published in Goldin and Metz 1991. See Stoll 1990 for a survey and discussion of the Protestant Church in Latin America, and see Garrard Burnett 1990 for a historical analysis of Protestantism in Guatemala.

5

Ngóbe Adaptive Responses to Globalization in Panama

Philip D. Young and John R. Bort

Central American nations have been increasingly susceptible to the exploitative overtures of multinational corporations—the primary agents of globalization—since the 1980s, a decade characterized by high inflation, economic decline, and increasing national debts. In the 1990s, the nations of Central America are turning to contracts with multinationals for the exploitation of the natural resources of their rural hinterlands, particularly forests and mineral deposits, as a means to improve the health of their national economies and to service their debts. We see this as part of a process of economic and technological globalization that exacerbates the ongoing processes of cultural domination to which the indigenous peoples of the Americas have been subjected, in various forms, for 500 years.

Our purpose is not to examine the material consequences of this short-sighted strategy for the nations concerned, but rather to look at the impact on indigenous peoples and their responses. In short, as the processes of globalization impact the nation-state, the state seeks to extend and consolidate its hegemony over its indigenous (and other) ethnic minorities. We address the broad issue of the strategies of indigenous peoples to control this current intensification of the process of domination by looking at the responses of the Ngóbe of Panama.[1]

In this chapter, we describe some of the pressures that the Ngóbe have endured during the latter half of the twentieth century, and we examine Ngóbe coping strategies as they attempt to preserve—even strengthen—their sense of cultural and ethnic identity and adjust to changing circumstances that seem largely beyond their control.[2] We will focus in particular on the impact of demographic, economic, and ecological changes and Ngóbe responses within a context of limited alternatives.

These changes are ongoing and represent interrelated aspects of the general process of globalization that is affecting the Republic of Panama

111

and, in turn, the Ngóbe, as well as Panama's other indigenous groups and its large campesino (subsistence farmer) population. Contemporary Ngóbe responses are thus to be understood within this context, although, as will be evident in what follows, the impact of globalization has not always been direct. Ngóbe responses are themselves continuations of dynamic interactions with shifting forms of domination that greatly antedate the time when the term "globalization" became dimly visible on the lexical horizon.

Anthropologist Guillermo Bonfil Batalla suggests that indigenous responses to domination consist of three interrelated processes: resistance, innovation, and appropriation (1990:206–209). Resistance may periodically take the form of open rebellion, but ordinary, everyday resistance is, by far, the more pervasive variety.[3] In this process, aspects of the dominant culture are reinterpreted as they are incorporated within the existing indigenous worldview. Much that has been called "syncretism" in the ethnographic literature is better understood, Bonfil Batalla says, as reinterpretation that facilitates the continued viability of indigenous belief systems. Innovations, in his sense, are seldom the great events that significantly alter historical trajectories. Rather, they are the small daily changes by which indigenous cultures adapt while maintaining continuity of perceived cultural identity. Appropriation is the process by which indigenous peoples seek to control and make use of foreign cultural elements, material and nonmaterial (e.g., ideas), even though they lack the capacity to produce or reproduce them.

Ngóbe responses to globalizing forces during the latter half of the twentieth century display elements of all three processes. Each serves as a way to exercise (at least potentially) some control over the general process of domination. In our view, there is a significant difference between Bonfil Batalla's views and the acculturation theory of an earlier era. Acculturation theory, in its various permutations, implicitly or explicitly viewed the "natives" as passive recipients of a largely one-way process of cultural transfer—from the dominant to the dominated (with some lip service to influences flowing in the other direction). Bonfil Batalla's perspective—and ours—on the other hand, places heavy emphasis on the active manipulation of the domination process by the members of the subordinate or dominated culture.

The Recent Historical Context

Livelihood

> There does not exist in Panama a policy for indigenous peoples that responds adequately to indigenous problems. Generally the central conflict, that of land [rights], is brushed aside. (Aparicio 1995:16)

The Ngóbe, although less well known than the Kuna, are the largest group of indigenous people in the Republic of Panama and indeed, except for the Maya, the largest indigenous group in Central America (see Table 5.1). They occupy an area of approximately 6,500 square kilometers (about 2,500 square miles) in the three westernmost provinces of Panama: Bocas del Toro, Chiriquí, and Veraguas (see Map 5.1).[4]

Elsewhere, we have documented many features of Ngóbe traditional culture that survived beyond the mid-twentieth century (Young 1970, 1971, 1976, 1978a, 1985; Young and Bort 1976). We have examined many of the problems and pressures the Ngóbe have faced in recent decades and the changes that have occurred in their culture and society as they have sought to cope effectively with the various forces of modernization and exploitation impinging upon them from the outside world (Bort and Young 1982, 1985; Young 1971; Young and Bort 1979). The account provided here is deliberately brief.

During the late nineteenth and early twentieth centuries, the Ngóbe relied upon a subsistence economy heavily dependent upon slash-and-burn agriculture, supplemented by cattle keeping (along with other domestic animals, mainly chickens and pigs), a few tree crops (most notably the peach palm), hunting, gathering, and, when possible, fishing. By 1960, Ngóbe population density was about six people per square kilometer, an average believed to be a sustainable density for swidden agriculturalists in the tropics (Young 1971). The major crops upon which the Ngóbe rely are maize,

Table 5.1   Indigenous Population of Bocas del Toro, Chiriquí, and Veraguas Provinces, 1970 and 1990

Province	Males		Females		Total		
	1970	1990	1970	1990	1970	1990	% Change
Bocas del Toro	7,087	29,067	7,309	26,338	14,396	55,405	285
Chiriquí	12,891	32,830	13,034	30,547	25,925	63,377	145
Veraguas	2,269	4,471	2,204	4,084	4,473	8,555	91
Totals	22,247	66,368	22,547	60,969	44,794	127,337[a]	184

Sources: Censos Nacionales de 1970, vol. 3, p. 27; República de Panamá 1975, vol. 3:27; 1993:24.

Notes: a. This total includes the small populations of Naso (Teribe) in Bocas del Toro and Buglé in Veraguas and Bocas del Toro. The total Ngóbe population of these three provinces is estimated to be 121,769 (*Drü* 30[1992]:14). Of these, we estimate that somewhat less than 109,000 are living within the territory claimed by the Ngóbe. This estimate has been arrived at by subtracting the Ngóbe population totals for those districts in Chiriquí and Veraguas that lie totally outside the territory claimed by the Ngóbe. It was not possible to do the same for the province of Bocas del Toro because that province is divided into only three very large districts, each of which lies partially within Ngóbe territory.

Map 5.1 Western Panama, showing approximate boundary of Ngóbe *comarca*

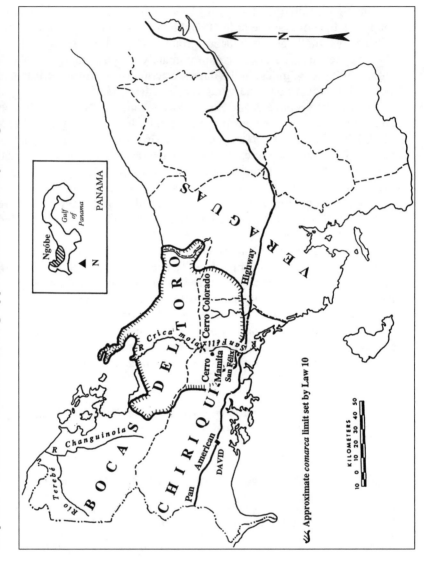

beans, bananas, sweet manioc, and the New World species of taro. Dry upland rice has also become important in recent years. Due to climatic differences—a true dry season of approximately three months' duration on the Pacific side of the isthmus, and no marked dry season on the Caribbean side—the Ngóbe of the Pacific slopes are more dependent upon seed crops, while those of the Caribbean slopes rely more heavily on root crops.

Wage labor during the first half of the twentieth century was a minor factor in their overall economy. Contact with the world outside Ngóbe territory was usually sporadic and of brief duration and was limited in the main to brief stints of wage labor, occasional trips to small Panamanian towns, and itinerant *Latino*[5] cattle buyers who periodically traveled through parts of Ngóbe country.

During the latter half of the twentieth century, the Ngóbe have shifted at an accelerating rate from this largely swidden-agriculture-based subsistence economy to greater dependence on the market economy of Panama. Market participation has taken the form of temporary day labor, some more permanent unskilled labor, and commodity purchases and sales. And, it should be noted, neither Panamanians nor foreign nationals have hesitated to take advantage of the Ngóbe. Although some participation in the cash economy has long been a part of their livelihood, recent events have forced the Ngóbe to seek greater involvement in outside markets. At the same time, Ngóbe labor has become indispensable to the agrarian industries of western Panama. Vegetable and coffee growers in Chiriquí Province and the banana plantations in Chiriquí and Bocas del Toro Provinces could not be maintained without it. Even the coffee growers of the eastern highlands of Costa Rica have come to rely on Ngóbe labor to harvest their crops in recent years.

Today, the Ngóbe serve as a cheap labor pool for these agroindustries. This has occurred at a time when inflation is high in Panama, wages for unskilled labor are stagnant, and jobs are scarce. Under these circumstances, labor can be sought and dismissed as needed, making the Ngóbe more vulnerable than ever to fluctuations in the prices of international commodities. Due to population increase, coupled with climatic irregularities that exacerbate the situation, the viability of their internal subsistence economy has become increasingly precarious.

Normative features of traditional socioeconomic organization in the past provided security against irregular agricultural yields from year to year. These consisted of generalized and balanced reciprocity among kinsmen, sharing, barter, and cooperative labor parties based on payment in kind (Bort and Young 1985). These forms of distribution and exchange have become difficult to sustain in the face of rampant population growth, decrease in per capita yields, and the continuing shift from a nonmonetary subsistence economy to one based on cash and subject to market fluctuations.

Wage labor was, and remains, the main source of cash income for the Ngóbe, and it has many drawbacks in addition to salaries so low that they do not constitute a living wage. Philippe Bourgois (1985, 1989) documents the near-inhuman conditions under which the Ngóbe labor and live on the banana plantations. Conditions are not much better for Ngóbe laborers on the coffee *fincas* (farms), cattle ranches, and sugar *ingenios* (plantation factories) in the region.

Revitalization

Unsatisfying interaction with the non-Ngóbe world led, in the 1960s, to a revitalistic religious movement, briefly described below. The movement stimulated the development of ethnic pride and a process of politicization (Young 1971, 1975, 1978b), as well as the formation of the Ngóbe Voluntary Teachers Association (Ottey 1977) that resulted (largely indirectly) in greater literacy and a small number of experiments in individual and collective entrepreneurship (Bort 1976).

In late 1961, a young Ngóbe woman who came to be known as Mama Chi (Little Mother), the wife of a man who had worked on the banana plantations, saw a heavenly vision that provided her with a message from the Christian God and formed the basis for a religious movement called the Mama Chi religion.[6] Whereas the roots of Ngóbe economic, social, political, and religious domination lie far back in time, and the pressures of domination and dependency accelerated beginning in the 1930s, the precipitative or immediate cause of the movement appears to have been the crisis produced by mechanization and unionization on the banana plantations in 1961. The number of Ngóbe annually employed on the Chiriquí plantations was suddenly reduced from about 2,000 to approximately 300.

The teachings of Mama Chi spread rapidly throughout the Ngóbe population. At its height, this religious movement affected all Ngóbe (though not all in the same way), both inside and outside the traditional territory. Following A. F. C. Wallace (1956), we refer to the Mama Chi religion as a "revitalization" movement.[7] As a revitalization movement, the Mama Chi religion did not achieve Wallace's fifth and final stage of routinization to reach a new steady state. However, whereas classificatory labels may be important for cross-cultural comparison, what is of central importance for our purposes is an understanding of the transformation of social consciousness that was accomplished by the movement during its active life.[8] By initially seeking as much withdrawal from contact with the Panamanian world as could be achieved, the teachings of Mama Chi addressed the fundamental nature of the relationships of subordination and dependency that existed between the Ngóbe and the outside world. By prohibiting the performance of certain traditional rituals and banning the consumption of

alcohol (which was an integral part of the rituals), and by vigorously promoting, through prayers and new rituals, the idea of Pan-Ngóbe sister- and
brotherhood, the movement served to restructure the very foundations of
Ngóbe culture as the Ngóbe themselves understood it.

The Mama Chi religion went through many changes and offshoot in-
terpretations before it eventually lost its force as a significant social movement sometime between 1970 and 1972. But its accomplishments in terms
of a restructuring of Ngóbe internal and external relationships were far-
reaching.

In 1964–1965, a group of younger leaders who became prominent in
the movement shifted the focus of concerns from the religious to the political. This shift in orientation marks the beginning of a process of politicization among the Ngóbe that continues and has gained strength. By the
late 1960s, the political activists had largely disassociated themselves and
their activities from the followers of Mama Chi. By the early 1970s, the
Mama Chi religion was no longer exerting a discernible impact on the
course of events in Ngóbe society. But this is not to say that the movement
left no legacy.

In brief, the movement had clearly engendered conscious reflection
upon and rejection of the derogatory Panamanian stereotypes of Ngóbe
that even the Ngóbe themselves had tended to accept prior to the movement. In seeking ways to restructure their relationship with the dominant
society, the Ngóbe responded in a way that treated their subordination as,
in part, a state of mind rather than an unalterable condition of life; and
they developed a new sense of solidarity.

Second, despite Mama Chi's order to remove all Ngóbe children from
outside schools (or perhaps because of it), the Ngóbe developed a heightened sense of awareness of the value of formal education, especially literacy in Spanish, as a powerful tool in dealing with merchants and bureau-
crats and, indeed, with a whole range of opportunistic outsiders. By 1968,
the few Ngóbe who had received some schooling had formed a voluntary
teachers organization and were beginning to offer instruction that the government had failed to provide within the territory.

Third, the restriction of contact with, and the use of goods from, the
outside world fostered a much-heightened awareness of the extent to
which they had become dependent on the market economy and were no
longer in control of their own economic destiny. This stimulated a consideration of alternative means of adaptation to a cash economy. One result
was an increase in small-scale entrepreneurship and some experimentation
with cooperative ventures.[9] In an absolute sense, the Ngóbe are worse off
now, economically, than they were before the movement began, but the
recognition generated by the movement—that there are alternatives to dependency—has arguably strengthened their resolve in dealing with the

government and, since 1970, a parade of multinational corporations and development agencies.

Fourth, an emphasis on political autonomy during one phase of the movement, although even at the time viewed as impractical and unattainable by many, stimulated a greater awareness of the possibilities of using political means to achieve socioeconomic ends. The Mama Chi religion, perhaps unintentionally, initiated the process of politicization.

The Transformation of the Body Politic

By 1970, the advocates of political means to achieve societal ends had selected a *cacique* (chief) for each of the three provinces. These chiefs had designated *jefes inmediatos* (local-level representatives). Of those Ngóbe interviewed in 1970 (certainly not a representative sample), most had no idea how they had come to have provincial chiefs. A few thought that the selection had been made at a *congreso* (regional meeting) held in Veraguas sometime in 1968. (This was partially true.) At this point in time, the debate was rather heated about the legitimacy of the chiefs and the new political structure that had been superimposed upon the authority of kin groups. Many Ngóbe openly refused to honor the decisions or otherwise to cooperate with the chiefs or with their appointed local representatives. In part, this unwillingness stemmed from the fact that, by 1970, General Omar Torrijos had publicly and officially acknowledged the provincial chiefs as the legitimate leaders of the Ngóbe. Many suspected that the government may have had more to do with choosing the chiefs than met the eye, although, so far as we know, this was not the case.

As late as 1978, the Ngóbe were internally divided on the question of the legitimacy of the provincial chiefs to represent them. More serious in terms of their chances of successfully negotiating with the government, they were still unable to present a united front to outside agencies. At the same time, several events, activities, and outside forces, beginning about 1970, were making their situation more desperate and unity more urgent.

The late 1970s saw the beginnings of penetration of a few access roads in Chiriquí and Veraguas where none had existed before. In many respects, it may be argued that road penetration has served outside interests better than it has served the Ngóbe. External entrepreneurs are able more easily to buy and transport maize, rice, and beans at seasonally low prices during the harvest periods when cash-strapped Ngóbe are willing to sell. The roads also facilitate the transportation into the area of commodities that can be sold at high prices during periods of scarcity.[10]

The 1970s was also a period in which, under the Torrijos government, the Ngóbe became the intended beneficiaries of a continuing series of national and international development efforts, beginning with the nonformal education project for the Ngóbe popularly called (at the time) "Plan Guaymí." Most of these projects have been designed for the Ngóbe with little or no input from them. Plan Guaymí served to hasten a process of politicization among the Ngóbe that was already well under way, but the project seems to have had no other lasting impact.[11] Other projects also seem to have had no significant positive impact, at least with regard to the alleviation of poverty, hunger, poor health conditions, and oppression. Recent projects designed to generate environmental improvements—for example, the Ngóbe Agroforestry Project—have so far had only very modest discernible impact. Problems of Ngóbe agricultural technology have not been addressed in any sensible and significant way. Until recently, demands for legal title to their land in the form of a *comarca* (reservation) were continuously brushed aside by the Panamanian government. However, in 1997, the government granted the Ngóbe their *comarca* (see below).

Perhaps the most notable event of the 1970s, in terms of impact on the Ngóbe, was the beginning of intensive mining exploration in the Ngóbe area—particularly around Cerro Colorado. Chris Gjording (1991) documents for the 1970s and 1980s the frustrating interactions of the Ngóbe with the Panamanian government, the government-run mining corporation (a parastatal), and the various foreign corporations that paraded through the area over the years, with exploration rights granted by the government without consultation with the Ngóbe. The title of Gjording's book, *Conditions Not of Their Choosing,* is aptly descriptive of Ngóbe circumstances then and now.

In the midst of this, the Ngóbe were attempting to consolidate and strengthen a centralized political structure to aid them in their attempts to achieve a modicum of control over events that would fundamentally alter their economy and society—indeed, their very existence and identity as Ngóbe. Despite the parallels with the Kuna political structure that gives the evolving Ngóbe system the appearance of appropriation, the Ngóbe themselves view their new political structure in terms of what Bonfil Batalla calls an "innovation."[12]

By 1980, at a general congress held in Ngóbe country at which the minister of government and justice of the Republic of Panama presented the government's proposals to mine the copper deposit at Cerro Colorado and to construct a large hydroelectric dam in the Terebé-Changuinola drainage system, 4,000 Ngóbe delegates to the congress from all parts of the territory, who had been discussing these projects for two days before the minister arrived, unanimously rejected the government's plans. We present here a summary of some of the more important factors that brought about this remarkable transformation.[13]

Cerro Colorado and Solidarity

In 1972, under the Torrijos government, elections were held for representatives to the national legislature. There was to be one representative for each of the political districts (equivalent to a county in the United States). And, due to constitutional changes, for the first time in Panama's history, those standing for election had to be residents of the districts in which they were running. This meant that several Ngóbe were elected, and a new kind of political education began for them. Although they lacked any power in the legislative assembly, their experience of politics at this national level surely fed back into the local process of politicization.

Cerro Colorado is a mountain of low-grade copper ore in the center of Ngóbe territory. Between 1970 and 1981, a series of three mining companies contracted with the government of Panama for mining exploration rights at and around Cerro Colorado. In chronological order, these companies were Canadian Javelin, Texasgulf, and Rio Tinto Zinc. Extensive explorations were conducted by each company in turn, and an access road was constructed from the town of San Félix on the edge of Ngóbe territory in Chiriquí to Cerro Colorado, as was a penetration road from the Pan American Highway through Tole District to the mine site. A few Ngóbe were employed as unskilled laborers but never more than about 100 at any given time. The road construction and exploration activities damaged Ngóbe lands, crops, and water supplies, but both the damage and the complaints were confined to a small part of the Ngóbe territory. The Corporación de Desarrollo Minero (CODEMIN), the Panamanian government mining corporation, counterpart to the multinationals, agreed to reimburse Ngóbe only for damage to existing crops. This was, of course, tokenism in the extreme, as most of the damage to the land was of a much more permanent nature.

Cerro Colorado was to be a massive open-pit mine that would require for its operation substantial quantities of water and electricity; thus the need for the proposed hydroelectric dam in the Terebé-Changuinola river basin.

During this same period, the Ngóbe were subjected to several development projects by both the Panamanian government and international agencies (see above). For most of their history, the Ngóbe had simply been ignored by the government; now they had become the object of an assimilation policy disguised as concern for their welfare and implemented with "development projects." Always suspicious of the government, though for some reason more trusting of General Torrijos himself, their distrust heightened as the Cerro Colorado explorations intensified.

Ngóbe living in Panama City, some attending the university, formed an indigenous organization and eventually also joined with the Kuna and the Choco in a Panamanian pan-indigenous organization. In the late 1970s, leaders in the Ngóbe organization began to receive technical guidance from a Panama City–based nongovernmental organization, Centro de Estudios y Acción Social-Panama (CEASPA), regarding the potential impact of the Cerro Colorado mine on the Ngóbe. CEASPA had been founded by a Jesuit priest. Some guidance was also provided to Ngóbe communities and representatives by Jesuits and concerned non-Ngóbe laypersons. It should be noted that the Jesuits did their best to act as a disinterested third party in this process of helping the Ngóbe to understand the impact that the mine would have on their lives and their environment. It should also be noted that several members of the Ngóbe leadership requested their help.[14]

It was within this ominous context of multinationals and megaprojects that the Ngóbe struggled to restructure their political organization and make the new system function effectively. At first, there was disagreement and uncertainty among them about who should represent them and what should be the extent and limits of their authority. It was far from clear, for example, whether this new structure of provincial *caciques* and local *jefes inmediatos* should concern itself with internal affairs or only with external affairs, and whether it was intended to supplant existing forms of authority or only to supplement these. Initially, the fledgling structure of provincial chiefs, their appointed deputies, and local chiefs held local and sometimes regional (or provincial) congresses that were attended mainly by the residents of nearby hamlets.

Most of the discussion at these early congress meetings was taken up with one issue: the *comarca*. From the beginning, the Ngóbe were nearly unanimous in wanting to obtain legal title from the Panamanian government to the lands they occupied, not as individuals, but as a group. Such title, in the Ngóbe view, should be accompanied by a *carta orgánica*, a legal document that specifies the details of semiautonomous self-governance. (The Kuna have had a *comarca* since 1930 and a *carta orgánica* since 1945.) Only in those areas being directly affected by mining exploration was the issue of the mine being raised and discussed at local meetings.

Gradually, as explorations expanded and large earth-moving machines worked their destructive magic on the landscape, the issue of the mine became a widespread concern. At the same time, there developed more widespread acceptance of the chiefs and their representatives, and, although it appears to have been the result of an unspoken process rather than a deliberated decision, the new political structure came to focus on external affairs. In meetings leading up to the first Ngóbe General Congress, held in 1979, the Ngóbe became painfully aware that they could not, by themselves, control the political dynamics involved in dealing with transnational corporations and the Panamanian government. At this point, the leadership began actively to seek outside help and support and to make use of research, documentation, and, when possible, the public media to actively promote their cause and to expose government and corporate duplicity.

Even so, at the first general congress in 1979, the Ngóbe were not of one mind on the issue of the mine. Some believed the government's vague promises of economic and social benefits; others felt they did not yet have sufficient information upon which to base a decision. Still others, particularly those who lived in the near vicinity of the roads, the exploratory operations, and the camps, had personal adverse experiences with CODEMIN and the mining multinationals, which convinced them that no good was going to come to them from this mine, so they openly opposed the government's plans. Many simply could not yet comprehend the potential impact of the proposed mine.

In the period between the first general congress in September 1979 and an extraordinary general congress held in April 1980, solidarity in opposition to the mine was achieved. More remarkable still, the Ngóbe leadership skillfully tied the issue of the mine to that of the *comarca* and put the government on notice that the Ngóbe would continue to oppose the mine until the government fulfilled the promise made by Torrijos several years previously to grant the Ngóbe their *comarca*. By this time, the environmental and human rights issues surrounding the proposed Cerro Colorado mine were receiving some international attention, and this strengthened the Ngóbe position. It is doubtful, however, that issues of human rights and environmental damage would have stopped the multinationals had potential profits been great enough. What did stop them was high inflation coupled with copper prices on the world market that were both too low and too unstable, as well as several lesser problems having to do with their negotiations with the Panamanian government. By late 1981, Rio Tinto Zinc, the third in the succession of Panama's mining partners, suspended plans to open the mine.[15]

The Ngóbe have become increasingly and justifiably adamant in their demands that they be involved in decisions about the exploitation of resources in their territory and about any projects that will affect them. The government, on the other hand, has remained staunchly intransigent in its position that the natural resources of the Ngóbe area belong to the nation and that the government will make decisions regarding the exploration and exploitation of these resources for the good of the nation. This position is incorporated in Law 10, Article 48, of March 7, 1997, establishing the Ngóbe-Buglé *comarca*. We resume our discussion of Cerro Colorado below.

The 1990s: Problems and Responses

The Demographic Problem

Today, if 1990 census figures can be believed, there are about 109,000 Ngóbe living within an area of approximately 6,500 square kilometers in the western Panamanian provinces of Bocas del Toro, Chiriquí, and Veraguas (see Table 5.1). The average population density is thus 16.8 per square kilometer.[16] Assuming that about half of their land is useable for agriculture and pasture—a generous estimate given the ruggedness of the terrain and the amount of environmental degradation that has occurred since the early 1960s—population density in relation to agricultural land is now apparently greater than 33 people per square kilometer. At even half this density, an ecological crisis is inevitable if agricultural technology remains that of the slash-and-burn type. And, for the vast majority of Ngóbe, it has.

Agroecological Crisis

It is common knowledge that swidden agriculture in the tropics is a sustainable long-term agricultural system only under conditions of low population density. Ngóbe population increase since 1950, even taking account of the possibility that the census figures (especially for 1990) are substantially inflated, has pushed their swidden system beyond the limits of sustainability.[17]

An early response to the basic food problem created by a rapidly increasing population on a stable (or in some areas shrinking) land base was to decrease the length of the fallow period. This was already ongoing in the 1960s and had the predictable consequences of environmental degradation, particularly deforestation, soil nutrient depletion and erosion, and declining yields. Although we have no exact figures, forest cover in Chiriquí Province has declined noticeably, and eroded hillsides have become more evident since Philip Young initiated his research in the area in 1964.

Two subsequent changes noted by John Bort in the 1990s in Chiriquí Province have been a decrease in the amount of pastureland and the number of cattle, and an increase in land area devoted to expansion of the cultivation of bananas, a dietary staple. We do not know how widespread these practices may be. Increased banana production seems to place greater emphasis on an increase in the production of calories derived from carbohydrates.[18] In some areas, significant undernutrition among children has been noted by Jesuit priests (Vasques 1995). The decrease in numbers of cattle appears not to be due to disease, as in the 1950s (Young 1971), but rather to a deliberate attempt to increase the amount of cropland. It is important to note that these are adjustments within the framework of an existing agricultural system. That is, the changes reflect amounts of land devoted to particular crops versus pasture. We think many Ngóbe are probably "experimenting" with ways to improve food production within a context of scarce economic resources.[19] An example observed in 1997 is the planting of garden crops in the patio areas surrounding houses, a practice not previously observed. Such changes may mitigate the food crisis to some extent at the local level, and those noted would appear to be ecologically sound measures, but they do not address the population problem. And they do not represent innovative changes in agricultural technology itself. Indeed, it is hard to imagine what types of changes in agricultural technology might be ecologically sustainable in the long term and, at the same time, entail transaction costs that would put them within reach of the ordinary Ngóbe farmer in the field.

Erratic Weather and Climate

Whether the shifts in climatic patterns in many parts of the world are due to global warming or long-term climatic fluctuations is an unresolved scientific question. For the Ngóbe, however, the problem of irregularities in yearly weather patterns is immediate and consequential. The Ngóbe observe that the weather in the late 1980s and 1990s has not conformed to long-predictable patterns upon which their swidden agricultural system is based. Rain has continued well into what they normally consider the dry season, and there have been extended dry periods when they expected rain. There is no doubt that their observations are accurate. Much, if not all, of the irregularity in weather patterns may be attributable to the El Niño effect.[20] The Ngóbe may not know the cause(s), but they are suffering the consequences. The result for their system of swidden agriculture has been a substantial decline in yields of dietary staples such as maize, beans, and rice.

These irregularities of weather make the burning of slash problematic, cause planting to be off the normal schedule, and result in uncertain, irregular harvests that are in general much below anticipated average yields. The result is hunger. This is the dire situation described by a Ngóbe friend:

> My brother, this year just past [1995] has been the worst of all the years for the Ngóbe. Almost no one was able to burn [the slash] because the rains fell early. There was much hunger and it continues still. Many have nothing. In general this is how it is among the Ngóbe. I too had a bad time and it continues. The only thing that saved me were the beans [I planted], which turned out well. . . . The situation is very difficult. Everything is going up in price and we Ngóbe are in a food crisis. There is little maize because of disease. The bean fields were damaged from too much rain. The rain is still falling in this month of February.[21]

In 1997, the Ngóbe in San Félix District had the opposite problem. By the end of August, the rains had not yet begun, although other parts of Panama were experiencing unusually heavy rains and flooding.

It is quite likely that such fluctuations in weather patterns occurred in the past, possibly on a regular basis if there is anything to the theory of climatic cyclicity. Under past conditions of low population density, sharing and other cultural practices (e.g., deliberate overproduction for ritual expenditures necessary for advancement in the prestige system) institutionalized within Ngóbe socioeconomic organization served to buffer— probably with success in most instances—the impact of local and regional shortages. Under current circumstances, these buffering mechanisms are no longer adequate to relieve the scarcity of resources. In a word, there is no surplus anywhere; there is only scarcity. The weather is thus another factor in the 1990s that is pushing more Ngóbe into the labor market of Panama and, already to a limited extent, into that of Costa Rica.

Market Participation

Wage labor has always been, and remains today, the main source of cash income for the Ngóbe. As the population has increased, so too has the need for cash to meet family dietary needs that are no longer being met through traditional subsistence agriculture and institutionalized food distribution mechanisms.

Thus, a third response to the combination of population increase and declining per capita crop yields has been an increasing exodus of Ngóbe, particularly males, in search of wage labor to supplement, and in some cases wholly to supplant, subsistence agriculture. Today, most Ngóbe males seek wage labor at some time during any given year. The months of June and July are considered to be particularly lean because the harvest in Ngóbe country does not begin until August and September, and this is also a time of the year when few wage labor opportunities are available.

Younger males sometimes leave the area permanently for employment. We estimate that nearly 12,000 Ngóbe are currently living permanently outside of Ngóbe territory in the province of Chiriquí alone.[22] Many, we are sure, are unemployed or underemployed, for the exodus is taking place in the context of a shrinking labor market. In absolute, not just relative, numbers, there appear to be fewer jobs available for day laborers and other unskilled labor, the only kinds of jobs for which most Ngóbe are qualified. For example, in three corporations that employ significant numbers of unskilled laborers in the provinces where the Ngóbe live—Cítricos de Chiriquí, Corporación Azucarera La Victoria, and Corporación Bananera del Atlántico—the total number of employees decreased from 3,137 in 1986 to 1,928 in 1990. Ngóbe compete for these jobs with other Panamanians, and this clearly means fewer jobs for Ngóbe, who often encounter discrimination in the workplace (Bourgois 1989; República de Panamá 1993).

Recently, wage labor availability has also been incorporated into the equation, further restricting opportunities for some. Seasonal wage labor is now organized to the point where employers send word to Ngóbe who have worked for them in the past that work will be available for a specific number of men on a specific date. As an enticement, employers offer bus fare in advance and enlist Ngóbe to recruit workers for them. Because of this, many Ngóbe now fear going to search for work without prior contact with employers. In 1994 and 1995, Bort encountered men who had sought work without established contacts and who were forced to return home after unsuccessful efforts to secure employment. In short, employers can specify how many men they want to hire and when they want them to appear, with the expectation that their precise labor needs will be met. Ngóbe laborers are very much at the mercy of employers.

Increasing numbers of Ngóbe are now crossing the border into Costa Rica in search of work. The international coffee market directly influences job availability and wages. When the price of coffee went up a few years ago, coffee tree plantings were substantially expanded in Costa Rica, increasing the need for labor to tend and harvest the coffee. Interestingly, the Ngóbe are not going to Costa Rica for better wages. Wages are comparable to those in Panama and sometimes slightly lower. They go because there are simply not enough jobs in Panama for the vast number of Ngóbe who now depend on wage labor.

Other sources of cash income for the Ngóbe make only a minimal contribution to Ngóbe livelihood. Cattle, once a significant source of cash for many families, are declining in numbers, as noted. Net bags made by women, and beaded collars made by both men and women, mostly in eastern Chiriquí and Veraguas, are nowhere near as popular on the tourist market as Kuna *molas* (colorful cloth appliqué panels). They bring in only small amounts of cash and require a great deal of labor.

The Impact of Inflation

During the period from 1965 to 1975, the average cost of the 15 products most frequently purchased by the Ngóbe rose by 155 percent, while their average cash income increased by only 73 percent (Young and Bort 1979:86). Between 1970 and 1987, inflation pushed the cost of consumer goods up by 173 percent, an annual rate of inflation of slightly more than 10 percent. Between 1987 and 1990, the annual inflation rate averaged over 17 percent (República de Panamá 1993:156). As the Ngóbe attempt to compensate in the wage sector for deficiencies in returns from subsistence agriculture, they are clearly losing ground (as are most Panamanians). Average monthly wages (of all jobs) for three companies likely to hire Ngóbe showed only a slight increase between 1986 and 1990—from U.S.$243 to $253—an increase of about 1 percent per year, far behind the rate of inflation (República de Panamá 1993). If there were any way of disaggregating the wages paid to unskilled laborers from those of supervisors, administrators, and the like, it is certain that the picture would be even more gloomy.

Against this bleak economic backdrop, potential large-scale mining development has emerged once again.

Mining, Multinationals, and Development Projects

> The government has granted mining concessions for 80 percent of the area occupied by the Ngóbe and this has been done without any consultation whatsoever with the Ngóbe. (Sarsanedas 1995:2)

The saga of Cerro Colorado, so eloquently documented by Gjording (1991), came to an end, or so the Ngóbe thought, in 1981 when Rio Tinto Zinc, the multinational corporation that was to open the mine and control its operations, decided that the venture would be unprofitable. Although the Ngóbe organized in strong opposition to the project, and received more than moral support from outside agencies including the Catholic Church, it was ultimately the price of copper on the world market that doomed the Cerro Colorado mine.

But times have changed. The Panamanian government is again seriously considering the possibility of exploiting the Cerro Colorado copper deposit, and the Ngóbe are again organizing in opposition to the mine. What was thought to be a closed book was only a closed chapter, and the 1990s have opened a new, but familiar and repetitious, chapter in the story of relations between the Panamanian government and the Ngóbe. In the 1970s, the Ngóbe saw clearly that, government promises aside, they would receive little benefit and probably much harm from the Cerro Colorado mine. They insisted then, as they insist now, that they would not reconsider their opposition to the mine until the government granted them title to their land in the form of legal status as a *comarca*. Ignoring their concerns, the government has now granted mining concessions, at least for exploratory purposes, for more than 80 percent of the territory claimed by the Ngóbe (Sarsanedas 1995:2).

In 1996, the Panamanian government signed a contract with Empresa Panacobre, a subsidiary of Tiomin Resources, Inc. (registered in Canada), to exploit the copper deposit. When or if this will happen is not known, but as the Ngóbe themselves see it, "This mining project will affect the future of our community and will have negative consequences for the natural environment, the life and the social and political institutions of our community."[23] This new development makes issues of land rights and local control of resources extremely problematic.

In January 1997, after a struggle that had lasted for decades, the Panamanian National Assembly did finally grant the Ngóbe *comarca* status for their territory, and the president of the Republic, Ernesto Pérez Balladares, signed the measure into law in March. But the Ngóbe leadership is justifiably unsatisfied with several of the provisions of this law. Aside from the fact that the Ngóbe received only half the territory they were demanding, the government did not declare null and void the contract with Panacobre. In addition, provisions of the law include (among other problematic articles) retention by the government of ownership and ultimate rights of disposition of the natural resources of the territory. Ngóbe authorities will be permitted to offer only opinions on planned development projects and to make observations on environmental and social impact assessments. This does not honor even the spirit of Ngóbe demands for self-governance and local control. These and other provisions of the new law are likely to remain points of contention for some time to come.

We speculate that a factor that probably contributed to the government's decision to grant the *comarca* was pressure from the Canadian mining company. Tiomin is a relatively small firm that seems to specialize in getting promising ventures up and running and then selling them at handsome profits to much larger corporations. For the company successfully to do this, it does not want political and social unrest in the area. Even large multinationals are not likely to purchase trouble deliberately.

The Ngóbe continue to oppose all government projects within their territory. However, they claim that they are not against the idea of projects and development. They simply insist that they should have a say—indeed, a definitive voice—in matters that will have a profound impact on their lives and their future. As one Ngóbe spokesperson put it, the Ngóbe community, "in rejecting these [several] government and transnational projects, is not rejecting either national development or development per se. It is rejecting the imposition, the injustice and the usurpation of its lands and the exploitation of its natural resources" without allowing the Ngóbe to have a voice in these matters that vitally affect their livelihood and their very survival (Jaén 1991:13).

One project of the 1980s that the Ngóbe opposed and that the Panamanian government did complete, with financing from multinationals, was the petroleum pipeline from near Puerto Armuelles in Chiriquí to Laguna de Chiriquí in Bocas del Toro. This was done in 1981–1982. In order to complete this project, it was necessary to construct a trans-Isthmian road paralleling the pipeline. The Ngóbe feared that this road would open up their territory in Bocas del Toro to further encroachment by Panamanian cattle ranchers from Chiriquí. For this reason, as well as environmental concerns, they opposed the pipeline. Data on numbers of cattle in Bocas del Toro indicate an increase from 11,800 in 1969 to 33,800 in 1987 (República de Panamá 1993), thus confirming Ngóbe fears.

Operation of the pipeline, suspended in July 1995, faces an uncertain future with the decline of the Alaskan North Slope oil fields. The road, however, opened up Bocas del Toro to massive global influence and has transformed Chiriquí Grande into the primary commercial center in the province. Ferry service from Chiriquí Grande, capable of accommodating 18-wheel tractor-trailer rigs, connects the banana plantations in the Changuinola valley to the rest of Panama. Chiriquí Grande has supplanted Almirante as the commercial center serving the rest of the province. The Ngóbe in Bocas del Toro now do most of their trading there and are by far the largest segment of the labor force on the banana plantations.

Chiriquí Grande is being turned into a major shipment point for containerized bananas. Bananas from Chiriquí Province are going to be trucked over the mountains and loaded at Chiriquí Grande. Bananas from Costa Rica are also going to be trucked in. Almirante is going to be closed as a banana port, the bananas now to be sent to Chiriquí Grande by ferry. The very large holding areas were nearly complete in the summer of 1996. The facilities will also be used to ship other fruits and vegetables. Melons and papayas have become increasingly important commercial crops in recent years.

In addition to projects designed to benefit the government and multinationals, the Ngóbe have also been the intended beneficiaries of several development projects ostensibly designed to improve their lives and their livelihood, ranging from the failed fishponds of Veraguas (a United States Agency for International Development–sponsored project) to the impractical attempt in Chiriquí to teach the Ngóbe how to grow eggplant (a Panamanian National Guard project). With one possible exception, the only projects of this nature that appear to have achieved a modicum of success are those that provide technical training to individual Ngóbe.

The exception may be the Ngóbe Agroforestry Project (the original name during the planning stage was Desarrollo de Sistemas Forestales y Agroforestales para el Area Ngóbe de Chiriquí). This project is managed jointly by the National Institute of Natural and Renewable Resources and the German Development Corporation (GTZ) and funded by GTZ as part of Panama's Food and Agriculture Organization–sponsored Tropical Forestry Action Plan. By December 1994, the project had been operating for two years. It has its base of operations in San Félix in the province of Chiriquí and activities in the districts of San Félix, Remedios, and San Lorenzo (Jaén 1994). Bort's observational data from two of the four project sites shows that, in 1994, despite its name and avowed mission, the activities of this project were focused almost exclusively on reforestation, with no emphasis on improvement of food resources, short-term or long-term.[24] Beyond the establishment of modest nurseries for the production of seedlings, the project appeared to have accomplished little. In its favor, this project did apparently have input from some Ngóbe in the design stage, and it does employ Ngóbe technicians and a Ngóbe coordinator trained at the agricultural institute in David, Chiriquí. Although seemingly well intentioned, the agenda apparently is set in Europe in terms of some notion of reforestation as a means of improving the environment and vaguely helping people. Overall, as with many development projects, it appears that a great deal of money was spent for very few trees that may or may not end up being eaten by horses and cows before the seedlings can grow large enough to survive. Funding has been extended, and the project continues as of this writing.

In 1997, the focus of phase two of the project was on the improvement of agricultural technology and on crop diversification. Ngóbe men and women with whom we spoke and those who we observed while they were engaged in project activities seem genuinely enthusiastic and interested in this phase of the project. The directions of the Agroforestry Project are apparently being reassessed with an eye toward enhanced local benefits. As of August 1997, it appeared that interests might be moving in the direction of working more with crops such as coffee that have more immediate potential value to the Ngóbe. Most development projects for the Ngóbe have been designed and implemented with little or no input from the Ngóbe themselves, nor have their needs, aspirations, and desires even been taken into consideration by the sponsoring development agencies. The GTZ project, however, especially its second phase, appears to be exceptional in soliciting the input and active participation of the Ngóbe.

Education

Out of Ngóbe struggles to control their land and their destiny has arisen an increasing recognition of the need for more formal education—for both females and males. The recognition of the importance of education became prominent during the latter days of the Mama Chi revitalization movement and was acknowledged by the formation of the Ngóbe Voluntary Teachers Association in the late 1960s. At that time, to the best of our knowledge, only a handful of Ngóbe males had completed secondary education, and, of these, few had returned to their Ngóbe communities. By the 1990s, a substantial number had completed their secondary education, and several had some university education or technical training. Many of these are using their knowledge and abilities to the potential benefit of the Ngóbe community. Examples include the Ngóbe working for the Agroforestry Project in Chiriquí, as well as several Ngóbe teachers now working in the indigenous area.

Trends in recent years suggest that a pattern of accelerating change in the home areas may be a direct consequence of education. A whole generation of Ngóbe is now at least minimally literate, including a large proportion of the females. Overall, women still appear to be more conservative and traditional, and less affected directly by external forces, but the situation is far more ambiguous than it was 20 or even 10 years ago. The first group of females from San Félix District in Chiriquí to further their education is currently in residence at the Jesuit secondary school in San Félix, with church support, and it appears that most will probably complete their schooling. The Jesuit in charge of promoting educational efforts says he wishes to provide an example of potential alternatives for women. He seems to be receiving good support. The mothers of these young women are taking turns spending a week in San Félix to attend to cooking, washing, and the like, for them. The outcome is still uncertain. These young women could easily move out into the *Latino* world and have no impact on the home areas. On the other hand, if they do return to their communities, their influence might be substantial.

The following is another indication of the far-reaching impact of education that could be indicative of things to come: a Ngóbe woman we know is now pregnant with her sixth child. Both she and her husband think six children are enough, and the woman openly has said that she is planning to try birth control (oral contraceptives). This appears to be entirely her own idea. This is the first time we have heard a Ngóbe woman actively consider the idea, let alone plan how to do it.

Politics, Protest, Solidarity, and Identity

From shaky beginnings in the 1960s (as documented in Bort and Young 1985; Young 1971; and Young and Bort 1979), the Ngóbe have achieved a significant degree of political centralization characterized by three provincial *caciques* who attempt to work together in the interests of the entire Ngóbe-Buglé community through annual as well as special congresses.[25] These congresses are well attended, and the chiefs appear to have more popular support in the 1990s than was the case in the 1970s. The congresses deal predominantly, if not exclusively, with external affairs. At one of these congresses (in 1993), those present agreed on "Ngóbe-Buglé" as the official designation for their community, and this name has been used since that time. But this is much more than just a name. This is the culmination in a political act of a long and often difficult political process, that of achieving solidarity as a community and collectively agreeing upon an ethnic identity. For whatever else ethnic identity may entail, it is inherently political.

The 1990s have witnessed mass public protests by the Ngóbe against government policies and acts. For example, in July 1993, the Pan American Highway was blocked to transit in Chiriquí on two separate days as a means of bringing the issue of the *comarca* to the attention of the Panamanian public. The effort was well organized and involved barricading the highway in two locations, using logs as well as a human barrier to block passage. In October 1996, about 100 Ngóbe-Buglé walked more than 400 kilometers to Panama City to demand an audience with the president of Panama. On this occasion, the Ngóbe leadership displayed considerable skill in capturing the sympathetic attention of the media for several weeks. Such protests were both unheard of and unthought of in the 1960s. Public protest and other displays of solidarity have brought upon the Ngóbe more active repression from the government and the *Latino* community, and more human rights violations than in the past (Anonymous 1993), yet the evidence indicates that these actions have also strengthened the Ngóbe will to take charge of their destiny and to survive as a culture and as a people.

Summary and Conclusion: Ngóbe Cultural Survival in the Twenty-first Century

Much of what we have described is, in general terms, the story of countless indigenous groups throughout Latin America. Economic stagnation and decline in Latin America since the 1980s have had a heavy impact on indigenous communities and cultures. The global system has in many ways adversely impacted national systems in Latin America, and these, in turn, in a desperate attempt to find solutions to their own growing economic (and social) problems, have looked to the lands still occupied, even after 500 years of cultural domination, by indigenous peoples. National governments covet the mineral and natural resources of these indigenous lands, as well as the land itself. The responses of indigenous peoples to this renewed domination and exploitation have been varied. Almost without exception, responses have involved a rapid process of politicization culminating in the formation of politically active indigenous organizations as a major coping strategy to confront the renewed encroachment of national systems. Enduring internal institutions able to cope with external pressures have been slow to develop among the Ngóbe. Nonetheless, progress since the early 1970s in this regard has been quite significant. Ngóbe responses to recent waves of external domination, as discussed above, may appear reactive rather than proactive. To some extent, this is true. However, as Bonfil Batalla has argued, the indigenous response has never been merely reactive. It is a historic strategy manifest in different tactics depending on the circumstances of the moment (1990:209).

Since the 1950s, rapid population growth has placed increasing strains on the Ngóbe socioeconomic system. This has resulted, among other things, in overuse of the land, declining yields, and general environmental deterioration. The irregular weather patterns of recent years have exacerbated the situation. Forced to supplement their internal economy through greater participation in the market economy of Panama, the Ngóbe have confronted a declining job market, increasing control of that market by employers, wage stagnation, and high inflation. In the space of 40 years, they have gone from a condition of marginality to one of dependency. Multinationals in league with the government have contributed to their crisis by attempting to exploit the mineral wealth within their territory, while Panamanians have renewed their encroachment upon Ngóbe lands, turning forests into pasture.

Remarkably, through all of this, the Ngóbe have undergone a process of cultural revitalization, consolidated their sense of ethnic identity, and developed a political structure capable of presenting a unified front to the government and multinationals. The process has not been smooth, and problems remain. Many changes have occurred in Ngóbe institutions in the past few years as traditional coping strategies proved inadequate to meet new challenges. Even though the Panamanian government has now granted them legal title to their lands, many Ngóbe are not satisfied with the terms of this law. In particular, they object to the fact that the government reserves for itself all rights to the natural resources of the area, has refused to declare null and void the mining concessions previously granted in what is now legally the Ngóbe-Buglé *comarca,* and has granted the Ngóbe only the right to offer advice with regard to any planned development in their territory. Although the law, if enforced, protects the Ngóbe from further encroachment on their lands by local non-Ngóbe, it is clear that the provisions of this law provide no protection from the greater threat of exploitation by the government itself and by large national and multinational corporations that establish contracts with the government.[26] Recent public criticism by Ngóbe activists makes it clear that they intend to contest objectionable provisions of the law and that they view the law as a basis for a new round in an ongoing process of negotiation with the government, rather than as an end to the process.

Considering what the Ngóbe have been through during the past 40 years, and how well they have been able to adapt their coping strategies to confront and control the process of domination, we believe that they will remain cultural survivors into the twenty-first century. Despite the impact of globalization, that elusive abstraction known as "Ngóbe culture," embodying all that the Ngóbe think and believe and practice as a people and all that makes them distinct from others around them, is likely to endure. Perhaps it will even prosper as they become more skillful at renegotiating their articulation with an ever-changing world.

Notes

This chapter is a substantially revised version of a paper titled "Ngóbe Agroecological Crisis and Response: Cultural Survival in a Changing World," presented at the annual meeting of the Society for Applied Anthropology in Baltimore, MD, in

March 1996. We wish to thank Gloria Rudolf and Harry Wolcott for their careful reading and comments on the earlier version of the paper.

1. Just a word about wording. As will be evident, there are many places in this chapter where we report Ngóbe views. Over the course of the years since the early 1970s, we have gathered expressions of opinion on a variety of topics from a number of Ngóbe, some of them close friends, others more casual acquaintances, relatives of friends, and so forth. Most of those whose opinions are summarized here are males, and most live in Chiriquí Province. Admittedly, our sample is not random, and we make no pretense at statistical validity. However, we do believe that we have achieved a solid understanding of the *range* of views represented among the Ngóbe on a number of issues. (We are less certain of the reasons some people hold the views that they do.) We also wish to state explicitly that we are speaking *about* the Ngóbe and not *for* them. Some would agree with what we have to say, and others would not.

2. The spelling "Ngóbe" is apparently agreed upon by the Ngóbe themselves and is used in their newsletter. We follow their convention here. In earlier writings, we have used the spelling "Ngawbe." In terms of pronunciation, [ng] is the equivalent of the /ng/ in the English word "sing"; [ó] is the equivalent of /au/ in the English "cause"; [b] is pronounced like /b/ in the English "boy"; and [e] is the equivalent of /ay/ in the English "bay." In the pre-1990s literature, the Ngóbe are commonly referred to as Guaymí.

3. We would like to make clear that all three of these processes—resistance, innovation, and appropriation—do not occur exclusively as responses to attempts at domination by outside forces. This is simply the context in which we are examining certain behaviors, activities, and actions of the Ngóbe in this chapter. By "resistance," we mean any act on the part of an individual or group that is in whole or in part designed or intended to oppose, withstand, thwart, subvert, reshape, redirect, or co-opt for one's own purposes an action on the part of any other individual or group (such as the state or any of its agencies). We believe there are differences in both types and frequencies of the acts of resistance of peasants who are part and parcel of a larger system, as described by James Scott (1985) for Malaysia, and those of indigenous peoples like the Ngóbe who are still largely outside the social, cultural, and political systems of the nation-state or, perhaps more important, believe themselves to be so and who are attempting to structure on their own terms the nature of their linkages to those systems. However, this is not the place to expand on this point. Further, were it not for a recent article by Michael Brown (1996) expounding on the dangers of overusing and overtheorizing the term "resistance" in contemporary ethnography, we would have thought it obvious that even explicit acts of resistance are, more often than not, complexly motivated. We acknowledge Brown's point, and we hope it will be evident in this essay and others we have written that we do not believe that everything the Ngóbe do within the context of interaction with the outside world can be theorized as resistance.

4. Our research has focused on the Ngóbe of Chiriquí and, to a lesser extent, on those of Bocas del Toro. We have visited some Ngóbe areas in Veraguas. We feel confident in generalizing to the entire Ngóbe population in terms of the general conditions, processes of change, and responses to change that we describe in this chapter.

5. "*Latino*" is the term used by the Ngóbe to refer to Panamanians. It is equivalent to "*Ladino*" in Guatemala and "*Mestizo*" in most other parts of Spanish-speaking Latin America.

6. The Ngóbe have been subjected to Christian influence, off and on, since the time of the Spanish invasion, but it would not be accurate to say that very many of them are "christianized," even today.

7. Scholars have used other terms for social movements that have many or all of the features of the Mama Chi religion. For example, D. F. Aberle (1966) uses the term "transformative" movement; for F. W. Voget (1956), it would be an example of "reformative nativism"; and for B. R. Wilson (1973), it would be a form of "non-military revolutionist nativism" or "millenarian nativism."

8. The Mama Chi religion has not totally disappeared but reportedly has only a very small number of followers at present and thus has taken on the status of a cult.

9. See Bort 1976 for a detailed account.

10. Along the road to the Cerro Colorado mine site, vegetable production for outside markets and even semipermanent settlement by *Latinos* have also been facilitated by the presence of the road.

11. Philip Young was director of this project for the Interamerican Development Institute from October 1976 to July 1978.

12. For those who are familiar with the Kuna political structure as described by Jim Howe (1986), the Ngóbe model of regional chiefs, local chiefs, and congresses at various levels will appear to have been borrowed. Although it is clear that some Ngóbe had knowledge of the Kuna model, they insist that they did not borrow their new political structure from the Kuna (and, as Gjording [1991] notes, many are insulted by the suggestion).

13. Gjording (1991) provides an eloquent and detailed account of Ngóbe dealings with the Panamanian government and multinational corporations between 1970 and 1981.

14. Catholic Church involvement with the Ngóbe on the issue of the copper mine is documented in detail in Gjording 1991.

15. See Gjording 1991 for details of the involvement of the mining multinationals and their negotiations with the government of Panama.

16. The average nonmetropolitan density in Panama is 18 people per square kilometer (República de Panamá 1993:2).

17. We believe that the 1990 Panamanian census figures for the Ngóbe population, especially for the province of Bocas del Toro, but also in somewhat lesser degree for Chiriquí, are much too high. However, we wish to note that the Ngóbe themselves believe the Bocas del Toro and Chiriquí figures are accurate (or at least not too high) and that the total for Veraguas Province is too low.

18. The Ngóbe consume almost all their bananas green, cooking them by boiling or roasting.

19. Increased rainfall and a less predictable dry season could logically result in people on the Pacific side experimenting with increasing their dependence on root crops. However, we have no evidence that this is being done.

20. An El Niño is a disruption of the ocean-atmosphere system in the tropical Pacific Ocean. The net effect is a disruption of weather patterns globally.

21. This quotation is taken from two letters to Young, dated December 14, 1995, and February 9, 1996. Translations from the Spanish, made by Young, are intended to convey as nearly as possible the meaning in English and thus are not literal translations. Regarding the comments, note that the dry season normally begins on the Pacific side of Panama by mid-December, and the rains begin by May.

22. This estimate was arrived at by adding up the number of Ngóbe living in districts of Chiriquí Province that are wholly outside the territory claimed by the Ngóbe. Because there are also Ngóbe living outside their territory in districts in Chiriquí that extend into their territory, it is likely that 12,000 is a conservative estimate. The data we used are derived from the Panamanian census of 1990 and are to be found in the Ngóbe newsletter *Drü* 5 (29):13, of 1992.

23. This quotation was translated from the cover letter accompanying the June–July 1996 issue of *Drü,* mailed to the authors.

24. "The project has been focused on improving existing traditional agroforestry systems; incorporating innovative agroforestry systems; promoting family and community level reforestation; training Ngóbe producers in the adequate use of their renewable natural resources; providing technical assistance to improve agricultural production and conserve soils; helping producers in alternative productive activities such as arts and crafts, etc." (Jaén 1994:14).

25. Several articles in Law 10 of 1997, establishing the *comarca,* outline a more elaborate, and in some ways redundant, set of political offices. In Article 24, for example, the state recognizes as traditional Ngóbe-Buglé authorities a general chief of the entire *comarca,* three regional chiefs, local district chiefs, *jefes inmediatos* at the *corregimiento* level, and community representatives. Article 33 establishes the office of governor of the *comarca,* whose duties as specified cannot be disambiguated from those of the general chief. Article 36 establishes district mayors parallel to the local chiefs. Several other offices, as well as commissions and committees, are specified elsewhere in the document. At this writing, this new political structure is not operational, and, given both its complexity and its vagueness, the Ngóbe may seek modifications. The full text of Law 10 (except for Article 2, which defines the cadastral boundaries of the *comarca*) is reprinted in the January–February 1997 issue of *Drü,* the newsletter of the Ngóbe-Buglé nation.

26. There exists the possibility of overwhelming local change if a copper mine at Cerro Colorado becomes a reality. A highly Latinoized corridor along the road to the mine could easily develop. Under the provisions of the current version of Law 10, the law that established the Ngóbe-Buglé *comarca* in 1997, the government could easily allow this to happen under the guise of natural resource exploitation in the national interest.

6

Water Demand Management and Farmer-Managed Irrigation Systems in the Colca Valley, Peru

David Guillet

In recent years, a shift in national and international water management policy raises significant questions for the sustainable development of farmer-managed irrigation systems (FMIS). This shift has occurred because of criticism surrounding the increasing financial, economic, and environmental costs of dams and other large-scale waterworks considered necessary to increase supply. In rejecting the increase of the supply of water, policymakers advocate the management of demand. Demand management entails recognizing the value of water in relation to its provision costs and introducing policies to require consumers to adjust their usage more closely to those costs. Demand management measures include water markets, transferable water rights, charges and tariffs calculated on the basis of the amount consumed, and punitive costs for wastage. Policymakers recognize demand management as one of a set of reforms to bring economic sectors of targeted countries into a closer relationship with global market forces.

In many Latin American rural contexts, irrigation systems built and operated by farmers constitute more than half of the total irrigated area and are some of the world's oldest. These systems range from large river diversion systems of thousands of hectares to small mountain systems with less than 100 hectares. Many of these FMIS make water available on demand at no or minimal costs and do not measure water use.

The stimulus for applying demand management in Latin America can be traced to Chile's neoliberal reforms in the 1980s, in particular, the enactment in 1981 of the National Water Code establishing a system of transferable water use rights (Brehm and Quíroz Castro 1995; Easter and Hearne 1994). The Chilean reforms have been especially influential in agrarian policymaking circles, and their successes and failures are closely

137

watched. Although water remains a national resource for public use, concessions can be granted to private parties. Concessions become, in effect,
private property, allowing permanent and transferable rights to the use of
the water. Water rights are completely separate from land rights.

The law recognizes both consumptive and nonconsumptive use rights
allocated on the basis of flow volume per unit of time. Nonconsumptive
rights require users to return water in a form specified by the right while
avoiding damage to the rights of other users. Consumptive use right holders enjoy the full use of the water specified in the right and are under no
obligation to return it. Downstream users have no rights to the return flows
generated by consumptive rights holders upstream. Water users in a downstream section of a river do have rights to the water entering the river from
springs, rainfall, and discharges of excess water, but these rights are not
absolute. The law places no obstacles to interbasin transfers of water. Private parties are required to obtain rights to groundwater by application to
a government agency. An application must state the yield of the well at a
given depth and guarantee that the location falls outside that established
for existing wells.

The recognition of existing rights to water restricted the expansion of
new concessions since, by 1981, most of the rivers in the north and central
valleys had already been allocated. Exchanges of water use rights are also
most frequent in these water-scarce valleys; elsewhere, transactions are
limited. Technological changes have been necessary to facilitate water
transfers, primarily replacing fixed flow dividers with movable sluice
gates to allow water to be diverted. All rights and transfers are supposed to
be recorded in the local real estate registry. This is rarely the case, however. Most transfers occur informally within FMIS that minimize transaction costs; outside of these institutions, water rights are not formally
recorded. The government has begun the process of extending formal titles
to long-term use of water by FMIS (Brehm and Quíroz Castro 1995).

The Chilean, and the more recent (1994) Mexican, water laws represent strong forms of demand management in separating water rights from
land and allowing them to be transferred.[1] The experiences are increasing
the pressure throughout Latin America to privatize water used for irrigation. At first glance, Latin American FMIS would appear apt targets for the
initiatives. Many Latin American FMIS have poorly specified, flexible,
and, at best, approximately measured water rights. Constantly flowing
canals, unmeasured water use, and on-demand access at low or no cost
would appear to yield to water savings. Surplus water could be recouped
to irrigate new land and meet the demands of new urban, industrial, and
domestic users. Recovered provision costs could be used to maintain existing and build new infrastructure.

Yet the rush to apply demand management to Latin American FMIS
is ill-considered, putting the long-term, sustainable development of rural

communities at risk. It raises several issues adroitly sidestepped in an almost hagiographic literature on the benefits of demand management. This chapter will address the effects of the policy change on the efficiency, equity, and economic orientation of Latin American smallholders—farmers who practice intensive, permanent, diversified agriculture on relatively small farms in areas of dense population (Netting 1993).

These issues will be discussed in the context of Peru. Farmer-managed irrigation systems are widespread in the Peruvian highlands, and many antedate the Inca expansion. Irrigation, together with terracing of the slopes and the cultivation of maize, enabled indigenous Andean peoples to achieve population densities yet to be reached in the contemporary period. Whereas irrigation systems are found throughout the highlands, they are most prominent on the semiarid western slopes of the Peruvian Andes where moist green patches stand out against a brown dry background. In a survey of 99 percent of the officially recognized peasant communities in Peru, 59 percent (or 1,589 communities) reported employing irrigation, and, of these, 61 percent (970) distributed the water communally. The bulk of these systems were in the departments of Cuzco (321), Lima (226), and Ayacucho (214) (Guillet and Mitchell 1994:2).

Peru has embarked on a program of widespread market-based reforms that include removing restrictions on the transfer of agricultural land, liberalizing rules for private-sector investment in irrigation, transferring the responsibility for operation and maintenance of the irrigation systems to water users' organizations, and strengthening these organizations. At the core of the reforms is a proposed new water law in which water rights will be freely tradable in a market-based system of distribution, similar to those found in Chile and Mexico. Whatever form the new law takes, the effects on water management and farmer-managed irrigation systems are expected to be profound (ECLAC 1997).

Andean Farmer-Managed Irrigation Systems

Andean FMIS consist of numerous decentralized village and intervillage irrigation structures in two distinct ecological zones: valley bottoms and highland slopes. Highland slope systems draw water from rivers, springs, and runoff from high-altitude seeps and snowmelts into open canals for transport directly, and indirectly following storage in reservoirs, to fields. Valley bottom systems normally rely on the diversion of water from rivers into transport systems of open canals. Most farmers in these warm valleys are able to grow two crops a year, one in the rainy season and another in the dry season.

Farmers hold numerous parcels, scattered across the landscape. In irrigated regimes, these parcels are subject to communal controls. Following the harvest, one's fields are opened to communal pasturing. The village organizes the transition from cropping to grazing on the stubble by scheduling the opening and closing of clusters of land that correspond to irrigation divisions. While grazing on the stubble, villagers are not allowed to collect firewood, herbs, or other resources from the field. The entire system is coordinated by a village assembly. Communal management of cropping practices thus exerts itself indirectly through controls over water, rather than directly through the regulation of cropping practices as in sectoral fallowing (Fonseca Martel 1983; Guillet 1992). Canal and reservoir construction and maintenance, water allocation and distribution, and conflict resolution are often managed collectively, through consensual decisionmaking at the village or interhamlet level.

Although water rights are attached to land, they are not absolute and cannot be alienated. The right to water includes the duty to contribute labor to the maintenance of the hydraulic structure of main and secondary canals. Rights and duties are tacit rather than explicit and are not the subject of ordinary discourse. They are most comfortably expressed using the language of reciprocity. When cultural norms were insufficient in themselves to motivate compliance, fines began to emerge.

Good examples of FMIS can be found in the Colca valley of southwestern Peru (see Map 6.1). The valley lies among the semiarid western slopes of the western branch of the Andean Cordillera, in the department of Arequipa. The middle Colca valley is a catchment basin for precipitation that falls on the peaks surrounding it. Five Colca valley irrigation systems have been studied extensively, from east to west and by declining altitude: Yanque (Valderrama and Escalante Gutiérrez 1988), Coporaque (Treacy 1989, 1992), Lari (Guillet 1992), Cabanaconde (Gelles 1988, 1994), and Topay (Paerregaard 1989, 1994). Villages capture the runoff and divert it into canals that transport it downslope to irrigate fields. Irrigation extends the cropping season for maize and increases the predictability and availability of water for crops. Water is abundant in the higher elevations, and moving it downslope to areas with favorable thermal conditions augments the quantity and duration and eases the irregularities of limited rainfall (Winterhalder 1994:59–60). On the lower slopes, springs are tapped. The Colca River itself is too far below the villages to offer a cost-effective source of water for irrigation. The relatively self-contained nature of Colca valley irrigation systems, with their own source of water for irrigation, is quite common throughout the Central Andes (Guillet and Mitchell 1994).

Irrigation organization in the five Colca valley villages is summarized in Table 6.1. The division of society into overlapping social and territorial halves, known as moieties, has been an important traditional principle of spatial and social organization, as well as water distribution. In the Colca valley, these divisions are known as *saya*. In Yanque, each *saya* has its

Map 6.1   The Colca Valley Region of Southwestern Peru

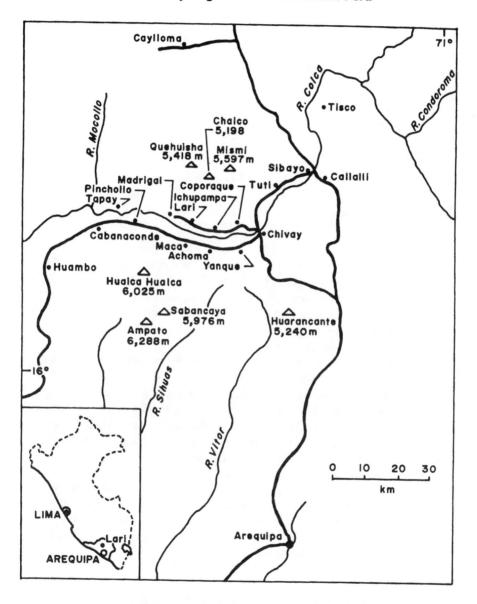

Table 6.1   Irrigation Organizations in Five Colca Valley Villages

	Yanque	Coporaque	Lari	Cabana	Tapay
Moiety principles in:					
Water distribution	+	+		+	
Contiguous spatial divisions	+		+		+
Noncontiguous field divisions				+	
Social organization	+		+	+	
Dominant water source:					
Surface water	+	+	+	+	
Groundwater					+
Irrigation organization:					
Water judges	+	+	+	+	+
Irrigation commission	+	+	+	+	

Source: Guillet 1994:176, table 7.2.
Note: In Cabanaconde, water judges are the only individuals identified as belonging to Hanansaya or Hurinsaya and then only during their service as water judges.

own irrigation system with a set of irrigation clusters and water judges. The state has respected this system by according each division its own irrigation commission. The nucleated settlement of Yanque also has a quadripartite division of barrios. In Coporaque, although there are no *saya* land divisions, *saya* affiliation governs water distribution and labor recruitment. In Lari, nothing imposes itself between irrigation clusters and a village-level irrigation association in terms of water allocation and distribution. Moiety affiliation is used only for the recruitment of labor for the maintenance of irrigation infrastructure and water ritual. In Cabanaconde, large contiguous blocks of land are divided along *saya* lines, but some of the opposite *saya's* fields are interspersed among them. Water sources are not divided by moiety. Despite the weakness of dual divisions, each *saya* names its own set of *regidores*. In the decentralized system of Tapay, there are no levels of organization above the irrigation cluster other than in ritual.

Colca valley systems are similar in most respects to other Peruvian highland irrigation systems. How would a program of demand management affect the integrity of these systems? To address this question, we now turn to a consideration of the issues of equity, efficiency, and smallholder production orientation.

Issues in Water Demand Management

Water Use Efficiency

Proponents of demand management argue that instituting measures to compel farmers to take into account the full costs of water will wring out inefficiency in water use. Efficiency here refers to the relationship between the amount of water required for a particular purpose and the quantity of water delivered (Xie, Küffner, and Le Moigne 1993). Constantly flowing canals, unmeasured water use, and on-demand access at low or no cost introduce inefficiency into the relationship. Such principles mock the notion of water as an economic resource. Tariffs levied on the basis of irrigated area, rather than the volume consumed, further promote inefficiency by their lack of incentives to save water. Irrigators attempting to use water efficiently are punished.

In the 1960s, an analogous debate was waged over the presumed inefficiencies of land and labor use in traditional agriculture. Theodore Schultz's *Transforming Traditional Agriculture* (1964) argued, in contrast, that traditional farmers were "poor but efficient" managers of land and labor, given the knowledge and stock of production factors with which they had to work. This argument proved persuasive, and the book became widely accepted during the late 1960s and 1970s as "*the* authoritative reference for agricultural development programs and policy emanating from U.S. and many western international agencies" (Michie 1994:396).

Although the 1960s debate over "poor but efficient" farmers would seem appropriate to the assumptions behind water use underlying demand management, it is curiously missing from these discussions. One reason is that the physical characteristics of water lead to common pool management and Pareto optimality criteria. When examined from this perspective, unquestionably, one can find examples of poorly managed common water management regimes. Inefficient common pool resource institutions can develop as the outcome of repeated plays of n-sum games, as game theorists have shown; power holders may also find them in their own interest (Binger and Hoffman 1989; North 1990). On the other hand, theoretical and empirical research increasingly documents cases of successful common pool resources. They include sophisticated and cost-effective arrangements for operating, maintaining, and sharing the benefits of common water systems (White and Runge 1993; Ostrom 1990). In these FMIS, the costs of incorporating sophisticated, absolute, volumetric measuring devices may outweigh the return in lowered consumption when compared with existing, low-cost methods such as allocation by proportionate shares or time. For example, sluice (or Roman) gates facilitate volumetric measuring of water and are one of the first "improvements" suggested by irrigation engineers. Yet they require constant monitoring and adjustment and can be easily sabotaged. Traditional proportional allocation remains cost free, is easily verified, and adjusts to variable water flow. At the very least, policy planners should verify empirically the assumption of inefficient water use in FMIS.[2]

Further, discussions of inefficiency in water use often fail to distinguish which of three levels of an irrigation system is at issue: conveyance, distribution, or field (on-farm distribution) application.[3] In FMIS organized as common water management regimes, conveyance and distribution are under communal control, whereas field application is a household function. Household heads allocate water, along with land, labor, and capital, in meeting subsistence and market goals. It is quite possible for household water use to be efficient while the conveyance and distribution of water to households, managed communally, is inefficient, and vice versa. For example, irrigating crops at certain crucial stages of plant growth is of obvious importance whether one's goals are subsistence or market production. A farmer would want a high degree of control over where to water and how much to water. In planning one's production and cropping mix, one would like to be certain that water would be available at the times and the quantities needed at different stages of the crop growth. Conflating water use and management at the household and communal levels, and judging them inefficient, bypasses this crucial distinction.

Last, gravity flow, dirt canals, field inundation, and furrow irrigation are clearly obsolete in a world replete with laser-leveled fields, global positioning systems–equipped tractors, and computer-managed drip irrigation. Yet replacement of these traditional practices with new and more efficient irrigation technologies, such as drip, pulse, and sprinkler irrigation, is lagging. Explaining this lag raises questions similar to those that drove the earlier debate over farmers' reluctance to adopt agricultural innovations. Innovation of these more efficient water use technologies lies at the household level. Schultz's analysis uses high risk and the small scale of production to show the rationality of such behavior. It is apposite to the debate over demand management and the adoption of new irrigation technology, lest it devolve to old clichés of tradition-bound, conservative, and irrational farmers.

Water use efficiency in the Colca valley. The irrigated agricultural terraces of the Colca valley, though impressive engineering feats, rely on gravity flow, dirt canals, field inundation, and furrow irrigation for water delivery—all highly inefficient processes in light of modern technologies. State agencies and nongovernmental organizations in recent years have made efforts to line main canals throughout the valley with cement to reduce water loss. Aside from these highly subsidized improvements, Colca farmers are reluctant to invest in new delivery technologies. They are only marginally integrated into regional markets, and the capital necessary to acquire new delivery systems is severely circumscribed. Risk and scale of production, therefore, go a long way toward explaining the "traditional" nature of these farmers' conveyance and distribution technologies.

Beyond the obvious, how efficient are Colca farmers in their use of water with their existing technology and accumulated knowledge? Unfortunately, detailed studies of water use efficiency do not exist. However, indirect indicators point to a remarkably productive and sustainable record of agricultural productivity. Most Colca valley topsoils are relatively thick, organic matter–rich Mollisols. Soil structure and bulk density indicate good soil tilth, favorable permeability and aeration, high available water capacity, and a good porosity. Soils appear generally fertile in terms of nitrogen and phosphorous, with levels of organic matter comparable to Mollisols of the U.S. Midwest. The pH range is optimal for nutrient availability for the crops. No evidence can be found to indicate land degradation in the form of the soil salinity that often attends long-term irrigation.

Productive soils are also indicated by crop yields. In Lari, yields of 3.5 metric tons per hectare were obtained for maize and 2.9 metric tons per hectare for barley. These yields are substantially higher than those reported by the Ministry of Agriculture and Coporaque farmers (1.2 metric tons per hectare) or the average U.S. yields for 1974 (for barley, 1.7 metric tons) (Janick et al. 1974; Sandor 1987, 1989). Yields in the United States have almost doubled in the period since 1974 (Jon Sandor, personal communication), and farmers' estimates of yields are subject to exaggeration on some occasions and underestimation on others. Nonetheless, they do indicate rather high yields by regional and U.S. standards.

Communal resource management of land and water contributes much to this record of high and sustainable agricultural productivity. All Colca valley FMIS exert direct communal controls, in one form or another, over conveyance and distribution. Arrangements for operating, maintaining, and sharing the benefits of common water systems are sophisticated and cost-effective. For example, simple diversion structures, easily monitored and adjusted, allow the proportionate distribution of water from main canals.

Communal controls also extend, albeit indirectly, to household production through principles of irrigation by crop and emergency water regimes during droughts. Water is allocated to irrigation clusters on the understanding that it will be distributed by crop in a general sequence of maize, broad beans, barley, and potatoes. Under normal conditions, farmers are given water sufficient to cover the requirements of their fields, a proportional allocation principle with Inca antecedents (Garcilaso de la Vega [1609] 1966: vol. 1, 248). In many villages, when water scarcity threatens, this principle is modified, and actions are taken to ensure that each household has access to a subsistence minimum. The Ministry of Agriculture has attempted to get Colca valley villages to change from distribution by *sayas* to a system of irrigating one adjacent field after another. The introduced system is known by various names: *mita, mita global,* and *riego canto a canto* in Coporaque; *mita* in Lari; and *de canto* in Cabanaconde. The Ministry of Agriculture initially attempts to introduce continuous irrigation as an emergency water regime; if successful, it moves to institute it as the sole system of irrigation. It has been unable, however, to expand it as the dominant system in those villages where water is distributed along moiety lines. In some villages, one *saya* benefits disproportionately, and its members are able to resist dismantling the system. In Cabanaconde, on the other hand, villagers resist because they feel moiety competition motivates irrigation judges to advance quickly through the irrigation cycle (Gelles 1994). In Lari, continuous irrigation uninfluenced by moiety principles was already in effect prior to the formation of a village irrigation association and contact with the Ministry of Agriculture.

A second thrust of emergency water regimes is to reduce water demand by limiting the amount of land a household can cultivate, restricting the water available to households for irrigation, or eliminating the irrigation of alfalfa in favor of subsistence crops. During a drought in Lari in 1983–1984, the maximum was set initially at an amount sufficient to irrigate two *yuntadas* of land; later it was reduced to one *yuntada* with further shortfalls.[4] The effect of limits is to force large landholders to fallow land in irrigation clusters where their fields are concentrated because the amount of land one can cultivate is constrained by the maximum that can be watered. If land is left uncultivated for a long period of time, it risks being categorized as "abandoned" land, making it extremely difficult to obtain water. Limits on water during droughts contribute to the tendency toward diversification of landholdings across irrigation clusters, weakening tendencies to land concentration and stratification.

The acceptance by farmers of these indirect controls is predicated on a shrewd, if perhaps unconscious, evaluation of their costs and benefits. On the cost side, water management principles make it difficult, though not impossible, to experiment with new crops, specialize in one crop, farm all of one's land, or reclaim abandoned land. But the long-term returns are substantial. Indeed, the logic and track record of a water management system that has stood the farmers in good stead through years of adequate rainfall and years of drought are hard to assail. Such acceptance also illustrates their willingness to trade off immediate gains for longer-term economic security and environmental sustainability.

Instituting demand management in Colca communities would have several effects. First, it would do nothing to solve the basic cause of inefficient water use. Even accepting the claims of management efficiencies brought about by reform policies, conveyance technologies would remain the same. More important, instituting transferable and permanent rights to water would represent a frontal attack on communal controls over water and land that have contributed to the excellent soil structure, good soil fertility, and high and sustained crop yields for over 450 years of land use since the Spanish Conquest (Sandor and Furbee 1996). Farmers would be able to claim water to irrigate crops outside of the irrigation-by-crop sequence, which would jeopardize the carefully constructed edifice of irrigation scheduling worked out over time. Allowing the land rich during droughts to claim all the water to which they have rights would reduce the efficiency of their water use at the expense of the land poor, who, because they have limited amounts of water to work with, are extremely careful managers.

Equity

Radical proponents of demand management advocate converting traditional rights to water to units capable of being leased, sold, rented, or otherwise transferred. Rarely discussed in their advocacy are the equity implications of these policies. In virtually all FMIS, water rights are attached to land and transfer informally on the transfer of land. Given the physical features of water, it is much easier to attach rights to land than to create shares of water. Although demand management advocates often cite the 700-year-old market in time-shares of water extant in Alicante in southern Spain (Gil Olcina 1994), this market is the exception to the rule. In practice, water rights are rarely alienated from landownership.

This is not to say that traditional farmers are unable to transfer water to adjust to variable supply and demand. In Mexico and in Chile, leases and sales of water among farmers for seasonal water use have existed for many years, even when such sales were neither encouraged nor legal (Easter and Hearne 1994; Brehm and Quíroz Castro 1995). What is notable in these transfers is their local control. Informal transfers of water occur within systems of local governance, low transactions costs, and high levels of compliance.

Outside of these local practices of water transfer, the implementation of transferable water rights raises questions concerning their effect on equity. One should be wary of large-scale centralized efforts to privatize water, given the history of resource privatization in Latin America. Historically, nineteenth-century reforms to privatize land laid the basis for the hacienda system and close to 200 years of class struggle and conflict. Although some campesino communities have managed to avoid falling within the orbit of haciendas, many retain inequities in water distribution stemming from the privatization of land. Certainly, there is no reason to believe demand management will redress existing inequities. Indeed, one can argue that it will enhance them.

Implementing demand management requires the standardization of measures of water volume, the recalibration of existing and new concessions, and the installation of physical devices to implement the new standards. Policymakers argue that standardizing measures will reduce transaction costs and increase the availability of water at low cost, much as the

European Union seeks a common currency to lower the costs of transacting across national boundaries with national currencies. Implementing demand management in FMIS may have the intended, or unintended, effect of more finely defining property rights. Economic historians have shown that the state can degrade growth by instituting property rights, bringing stagnation and economic collapse (North and Thomas 1973).

In the Colca valley and throughout highland Peru, communal control of water can have an important role in ameliorating inequities stemming from social and demographic differentiation. Inequitable water distribution often stems from land inequities since water rights are attached to land-ownership (Guillet and Mitchell 1994:2). Gross differences in social power can contribute to inequitable land distribution. Inequality in farm size can also surface from demographic differentiation. As households begin, grow, and mature over the course of their life cycles, changes in landholding reflect fluctuations in the demand for land associated with each stage (Chayanov 1966). A young household forms and expands, acquiring land to meet its growing needs. Later, as children mature and leave the household, pressures decline and landholdings may contract. The demographic cycle may thus contribute to inequality in farm size.

In the Colca valley village of Lari, for example, although indicators of differentiation exist, farmers perceive that "we are all equal." This perception accords well with observed behavior. As elsewhere in the valley, Lari displays the attributes of a classic minifundio pattern of smallholdings with some tendencies to inequality stemming from social and demographic differentiation (Guillet 1992:31–46; Instituto Nacional de Planificación 1983:14; Valderrama and Escalante Gutiérrez 1988:37–43). Communal water management principles are tilted to ensure that the land poor can derive a subsistence minimum. The irrigation of abandoned land is prohibited, and water distribution is limited during droughts. Priorities for water allocation reflect the importance of agriculture over pastoralism and domestic use, ensuring water for the irrigation of staple crops necessary for subsistence diets. Although large landholders are categorized as *mayoristas,* they do not constitute a clearly recognizable class.

These principles retard the accumulation of land, market entry, and the emergence of stratification. Of particular importance in this regard are limits on water imposed during droughts. Landowners who own large quantities of land in one irrigation cluster are severely affected by a limit on water imposed within the cluster. To circumvent limits, one could scatter holdings across irrigation sectors, and, in fact, diversification is a common form of risk reduction. By increasing the complexity of scheduling tasks, however, diversification brings other difficulties in its wake: the necessity of farmers to appear at numerous weekly meetings to claim water, to irrigate several quite distant fields, to coordinate delivery of water to fields on different days, to arrange for traction and transport animals, and so on. Even with hired labor it is difficult to coordinate all of the activities in space. Specialization in one crop intensifies the problem because it means that all tasks—irrigation, field preparation, seeding, weeding, and harvest—fall at the same time. The supply of labor, as well as draft and transport animals, is finite, and peak periods affect rich and poor alike.

Communal control of water in highland Peruvian communities does not necessarily ensure that water is distributed equitably. Water control is closely related to local stratification, and the politics of water distribution dominates many communities. Often, inequitable distribution is a result of hacienda or urban townspeople penetration. Formalized distribution systems during periods of peak demand, such as a rotation across fields, quells these tendencies.

But the incompatibilities of transferable and permanent rights to water with communal control over water would tilt the playing field toward large landholders who, relieved of constraints over their access to water, could accumulate even more power. One would be able to more freely accumulate land, enter markets, and coalesce with other large landholders at the expense of minifundistas. Converting rights to water attached to land and attenuated by communal controls to fully transferable and permanent rights would produce a windfall for large landholders. They would become instantly the holders of new marketable assets. If they possessed more land than they would be able to farm because of labor or capital constraints, they could sell off their water rights.

The Impact of Demand Management on Smallholder Agriculture

Assuming equity and efficiency issues can be resolved, demand management is at odds with the survival strategies of Latin American smallholders. Smallholder farming is highly efficient in its use of energy, produces more per unit area than large farms, and does so with less environmental degradation (Netting 1993). Where FMIS endure over time, part of their success has been the ability of farmers to control entrance into wider markets for land, labor, and foodstuffs. This has been achieved through passive defensive and/or active resistance (Scott 1990). Not surprisingly, smallholders today are resisting demand management actively and passively (Guillet 1997).

Communal controls over water are closely related to the mixed subsistence strategies and staple production necessary to reduce risk. Mixed subsistence strategies—in particular, mixed agropastoral subsistence essential to the rejuvenation of the lower Andean puna ecological zone through the recycling of organic matter—spread risk across two very different subsistence strategies. Within the agricultural zones, where peasant homesteads tend to be located, agriculture is combined with the keeping of small animal species, notably guinea pigs. Mixed staple production includes the well-known combination of potatoes and maize, as well as such lesser-known but equally important staples as *quinoa, tarwi,* and *cañihua.* A mixed set of staples allows nutritional and dietary levels to be maintained through the combination of traditional cultivars highly adapted to the vertical environment of the Andes. Besides diversification of staples across vertical space, one finds diversification in horizontal space: varieties of cultivars adapted to peculiar environmental conditions found in a particular ecological zone (Guillet 1981).

Irrigation by crop, for example, allows water application to be tailored to the moisture needs of a mix of subsistence staples. It can be adjusted to the pulsation of supply and demand for water during the irrigation season. At the beginning of the cycle, the ground is dry, and additional water is required to bring the moisture content of the soil up to levels necessary for seed germination. Villages and towns also periodically cease agricultural activity for festivities, thereby reducing demand temporarily.

Irrigation by crop does not preclude the capacity for change. New crops are allowed to enter the crop irrigation schedule but only under careful control. A good example is alfalfa, incorporated into the irrigation-by-crop sequence in Lari and elsewhere in the Colca valley. The incorporation of alfalfa into Lari's agriculture began on an experimental basis in the 1950s by land-rich farmers looking for a crop that could be grown with little labor. The introduction of alfalfa is a response to increased demand for meat by public works projects, mines, and coastal cities and the loss of communal land that provided natural grasses and crop stubble for forage. By the late 1970s, alfalfa cultivation had become firmly established in the economy of the village.

In the beginning, when the scale of alfalfa cultivation was small, alfalfa meadows were irrigated along with food crops. As the momentum picked up and the number of alfalfa fields increased, villagers began to demand a regular allocation of irrigation water. The response was to incorporate alfalfa into the irrigation-by-crop system by assigning it a place after early crops had been irrigated, prior to water distribution for the main crops.

This accommodation retained both the integrity of irrigation by crop and the centrality of maize in the crop and calendrical sequence. Adapting alfalfa to the existing calendar, rather than changing the calendar to meet the needs of alfalfa, was made easier by the fact that it can be seeded during the rainy season (January–March) and following the harvests (June–August) when there is no demand for water for irrigation. Eventually, alfalfa did come to be irrigated during the irrigation-by-crop sequence, competing with food crops, and the priority of agricultural over pastoral uses of water was accordingly modified. This shift reflected the value of alfalfa as an appropriate intensification of land and labor.

The introduction of alfalfa also produced shifts in the integration of agriculture and pastoralism, similar to those that are known to have occurred elsewhere. The system of communal grazing on the stubble of harvested fields was dismantled in a process of "enclosure" that is analogous to British common fields. Private control of fields is now fully entrenched in the economy. Yet there is no evidence of massive erosion and decline in soil fertility, key indicators of land degradation. Soil quality may, indeed, have been enhanced by the nitrogen-fixing qualities of alfalfa.

The introduction of alfalfa has not led to the widespread monocropping and land consolidation often associated with market forces, as ensued in the *campiña* of Arequipa with the expansion of the dairy industry (Love 1989). These tendencies were held in check in Lari for three reasons. First, for the majority of farmers, alfalfa has been a means for placing animal husbandry on a more secure basis, rather than for expanding it. Certainly, some farmers have responded to market incentives by cultivating alfalfa to fatten their own cattle or to rent out their fields to others. But although alfalfa cultivation per se is relatively risk free, the enterprise of cattle fattening runs the risks of animal disease and downturns in the demand for cattle. The majority of farmers avoid these risks by restricting alfalfa cultivation to land taken out of maize production and normally left fallow. The village remains heavily oriented toward subsistence, with households producing their own maize, broad beans, and barley for local consumption.

Second, distance from Arequipa keeps fresh milk from being produced in the Colca valley for delivery to the Leche Gloria plant in Arequipa. With the exception of limited cheese production, focused largely in Achoma and oriented to a local market, fresh milk production is quite low, seasonal, and almost entirely consumed in the home (Webber 1988).

Most importantly, although the shift to alfalfa has entailed major adjustments in water allocation and distribution, irrigation authorities have been very careful to safeguard the subsistence orientation of their agropastoral production. They are aware that a complete shift to alfalfa, as has occurred in the *campiña* of Arequipa, would reduce the ability of villagers to grow food for home consumption and force them to depend on other sources of income, of which there are very few in the region. Water is allocated to alfalfa during periods when demand for water for foodstuffs is low.

Farmers in Lari adopted alfalfa and made the transformations in their agropastoral system in an incremental way, monitoring the results as the process proceeded. Whereas communal control over communal grazing lands has weakened, reducing access to what were once extensive natural pastures, this has not been a critical issue, precisely because alfalfa offers, in both its fresh and dried forms, a much more secure and higher-quality source of forage. Thus, we find the emergence, anomalous by Andean standards, of private forms of tenure concomitant with increased and more secure access to productive resources.

Once again, one can see a collision between demand management and communal controls over water. In this case, it risks putting smallholder farmers on a technology treadmill. The technology treadmill is one of a set of processes of the industrialization of agriculture, including the adoption of more complex technology; the substitution of capital for labor; the tendency toward competition, specialization, and overproduction; and the increased interdependence between farm units and agribusiness (Barlett 1990). By breaking the control the community has over water management, the forces of competition and crop specialization would be unleashed to be followed by the others.

Many proponents of demand management welcome the replacement of smallholders by industrial farmers as a step toward the increase of agricultural production. This is a distorted view. Many anthropologists and development workers who have experience with smallholder agriculture are beginning to make their voice heard in policymaking circles. The UN *World Development Report* now acknowledges, for example, that small farms outproduce large farms. In Brazil, the productivity of a 10-hectare or smaller farm is U.S.$85.00 per hectare, while the productivity of a 500-hectare farm is $2.00 per hectare. In India, the productivity figure for a 5-hectare or smaller farm is 735 rupees per acre; for a 35-acre farm, 346 rupees per acre. In an industrial monoculture system, 300 units of input are used to produce 100 units of food, a productivity ratio of 0.33. In a polyculture system, five units of input are used to produce 300 units of food, a productivity ratio of 1.5. The polyculture system, called "low yielding" and incapable of meeting food needs, is five times more productive than the so-called high yielding monoculture. In a recent international conference on food production, in spite of all evidence pointing to the high diversity, productivity, and sustainability of small family farms, conference participants concluded that globalization is wiping out these efficient systems and replacing them with inefficient and unhealthy industrialized food systems that are under corporate control.[5]

Conclusion

The data presented here drawing out the implications of applying demand management to Andean highland irrigation systems suggests the prospects are much less sanguine than most observers predict. Applying Chilean models of transferable water rights to irrigation systems with communal water management, unmeasured water use, and on-demand access at low or no cost seems eminently logical. Yet it is a logic that runs counter to the smallholder production basic to many FMIS, in the Andes and elsewhere in Latin America. If the agenda of demand management is to produce an industrial, corporate, large-scale farmer, such s consequence would come at the expense of an efficient, productive, smallholder sector.

In its radical form of the privatization of water rights, demand management also pays short shrift to historical trends in the evolution of land, labor, and capital in Latin America. Rural communities still struggle with the effects of the neoliberal reforms of the early nineteenth century designed to free land from stagnant agrarian structures. The reforms resulted in the emergence of large-scale latifundias alongside overly small, minifundio farms, a displaced and impoverished rural labor force, and ensuing class tension and conflict. Organized resistance to these structural binds, once sporadic and easily repelled and increasingly organized and politically sophisticated, has, in this century, helped bring about societal revolution.

Alienating water rights from landownership and making them transferable and permanent would create serious potential problems leading to the emergence of a new class of "waterlords" out of land-rich farmers. Data from the Colca valley shows that smallholders have found ways to keep this potential in check by controlling access to water and attenuating the rights attached to land. In situations like these, if water rights attached to land were made transferable and alienable, the land rich would be rewarded disproportionately. In particular, communities would find it extremely difficult to ensure a subsistence minimum by prohibiting the irrigation of abandoned land and limiting the amount of water for irrigation during droughts.

Policy instruments may exist to retard the windfall that rich farmers would reap if water rights were made transferable. Tushaar Shah (1993), for example, has argued that a policy of flat tariffs can ameliorate tendencies toward the emergence of waterlords in groundwater markets. Although tariff policy may not necessarily work the same way in surface-water markets or in other societal contexts outside of India, where Shah's argument has been developed, creative thinking should be directed toward the requisite social and economic policies. Ironically, the Lari experience suggests that such policies already exist at the local level. If the will exists, they can be found and strengthened, and disseminated as policy measures, to accompany demand management.

In existing, long-standing FMIS, however, one should adopt, at the least, a healthy skepticism toward claims of efficiency made by advocates of demand management. FMIS have accumulated bodies of successful knowledge of effective water use in the household and communal management spheres. The Latin America experience suggests a "poor but efficient" irrigator thesis as a preferable starting point for conceptualizing and debating the issues involved in the demand management of FMIS.

Notes

1. Gorriz, Subramanian, and Simas 1995; Easter and Hearne 1994:16–22.
2. For a critique of fixed proportional flow dividers from a hydraulic engineering perspective, see Plusquellec, Burt, and Wolter 1994:93.
3. Conveyance is the movement of water from its sources (reservoirs, river diversions, wells, or pumping stations) through main and secondary canals to the tertiary offtake of a distribution system. Conveyance efficiency, Ec, is defined by the equation $Ec = Vd/Vs$, where Vs = volume diverted from sources plus inflows to the canal from other sources; and Vd = volume delivered to the distribution system.

Distribution is the movement of water from tertiary and distribution canals, channels, or pipes to individual field inlets. Distribution efficiency, Ed, is defined by the equation $Ed = Vf/Vd$, where Vf = volume furnished to the field. The combined efficiency of a conveyance and distribution system is described as "irrigation network efficiency," or En. It is defined as the water delivered to farm field inlets divided by the water diverted from the prime source: $En = Vf/Vs = Ec \times Ed$.

Field application is the movement of water from field inlets to crops. The field (or on-farm) efficiency, Ef, is defined by the equation $Ef = Vm/Vf$, where Vm = net volume needed to maintain the soil moisture, which is equal to the amount consumptively needed for evapotranspiration; that is, Vm = (crop water requirement) – (effective rainfall).

Another concept widely used in irrigation is overall or project efficiency, Eo. It is the ratio between the quantity of water consumptively used by crops and the total water diverted from the sources to a project area. It encompasses seepage and evaporation losses incurred in physically conveying water to crops, as well as losses due to deep percolation through the root zone to groundwater and field runoff: $Eo = Vm/Vs = Ef \times Ec \times Ed$ (Xie, Küffner, and Le Moigne 1993:5).

4. A *yuntada* is the land area that a team of oxen (*yunta*) is able to plow during one day.
5. Input and output data from UN sources are discussed in Shiva 1996:7; see Netting 1993 on general patterns of smallholder efficiency.

7

Ecotourism and Cultural Preservation in the Guyanese Rain Forest

Barbara J. Dilly

Ecotourism and the Meeting of the Global and the Local

The meeting of the global and local through trade, production, consumption, transportation, and communication are all evident in the expanding tropical rain forest ecotourism industry. Postindustrial developments in transportation and communication technology, economic affluence, and political stability at a global level expand the growth of social, cultural, and economic transactions between developed and developing countries through tourist activities (Boo 1990; Smith and Eadington 1992). The globalization of economic and social exchange in tourism is driven largely by the forces of Western capitalism in which a typically affluent and often "alienated" leisure class from developed countries becomes the consumers of exotic and pristine natural environments, "authentic" frontier experiences, and the traditional culture of local people in developing host countries.

Ecotourism is a particular type of tourism that reflects the globalization of environmental ideologies, and the policies and programs that encourage and support conservation of traditional cultures. Ecotourism is touted as an "authentic" cultural exchange between (often Western) tourists and local people in which environmental resources and traditional cultures are preserved at the same time economic development occurs. From this perspective, tourism is seen as an "industry that replaced manufacturing or extractive industries in industrial nations. . . . In developing countries, it replaces an agrarian economy" (Boo 1990:2). As a strategy of capitalist development, some developing countries, particularly those with large rain forest areas, are attempting to define policies that bypass

155

industrial development altogether and to replace extractive industries, like logging, with tourism (Smith and Eadington 1992:2).

This chapter addresses two perspectives that emerge from a global ecotourism axis. Rain forest ecotourism reflects and furthers a global concern for the health of the entire planet. At the same time, however, ecotourism intersects and corresponds with the frequently destructive penetration of Western capitalism into the most peripheral and pristine regions of the earth.

Despite the less dramatic environmental effects of ecotourism compared with those of such industries as logging and mining, critics have noted an exploitative side to ecotourism as well. Like other forms of tourism, ecotourism extends the consumer-based lifestyle of the "overdeveloped" nations to new locales and reproduces relationships of environmental and cultural domination in new ways. The promotion of ecotourism reinforces relationships of domination and subordination and, in fact, may be an outgrowth of such relationships. Through ecotourism, local cultures are frequently made dependent on outside cultures. Native people may lose their own initiative and self-reliance as they are "colonized" by outsiders or outside ideas (Nyoni 1987:53). Ecotourists, whether willingly or unwittingly, are agents of development who may strain local resources, distort local values, and create internal conflicts by furthering inequalities among locals.

Given the strong arguments made for and against ecotourism, analyses of the current tension among development ideologies, policies, and programs may prove to be as instructive as they have been destructive. It is axiomatic that the penetration of capitalism and Western culture into relatively natural environments and traditional cultures through ecotourism has had diverse effects and directions (Boo 1990). The theoretical and empirical analysis of ecotourism developments must recognize both positive and negative consequences to local economic, social, and cultural institutions (Cohen 1979; DeKadt 1979; McKean 1976).[1] A growing body of anthropological literature evaluates and examines theoretical and methodological approaches to the study of tourism and special cases such as ecotourism (Boo 1990; Cohen 1979; DeKadt 1979; Graburn 1995; Mac-Cannell 1992; McKean 1976; Nash 1995; Smith and Eadington 1992). Some tourism-generated activities change local cultures and environments, others act to sustain them. Concerns during the 1970s and 1980s that tourism effects were largely destructive of local environments and exploitative of local social and cultural structures were heightened as a result of evidence in the 1990s of the negative consequences of overdevelopment and the commodification of cultures as a result of shortsighted capitalist penetration into the periphery. In contradistinction, there is a growing awareness of specific global, national, and local tourism development policies that promote benefits for host peoples (Boo 1990; DeKadt 1979).

Recent research on ecotourism development in the Guyanese rain forest presents evidence that a growing awareness of the drawbacks of exploitative development is influencing tourism policies in Guyana. Examination of rain forest ecotourism in one of the farthest corners of the globe
raises the possibility that the hypothetical goal promoted by Valene Smith
and William Eadington (1992:3)—that both hosts and guests can enjoy
positive and worthwhile exchange—may be realized in practice. My initial
field observations show that ecotourism in the Guyanese rain forest may,
in fact, reduce the rate of negative culture change among interior
Amerindians, specifically social disintegration and decline in subsistence
food production that result from a variety of other global cultural forces
external to the host culture system. This study examines the social, political, and economic dynamics associated with ecotourism based on the experience of the Makushi people of Surama just outside the Guyanese international rain forest preserve Iwokrama (see Map 7.1). It explores the
practical implications of ecotourism as a means for sustaining traditional
cultures of the Makushi people and their neighbors and the natural environments upon which these people depend.

The Current Cultural Context

The examination of local decisionmaking and attitudes toward development of an ecotourism program by the Makushi people of Surama,
Guyana, illustrates how Makushi men and women choose among various
alternatives such as out-migration for wage labor, cooperation with the expansion of international nongovernmental organization agricultural development programs for developing countries, and ecotourism. Two existing
economic strategies that compete with, and may accompany, ecotourism
among the Makushi of the village of Surama within the cultural context
are examined here: (1) maintaining marginal traditional subsistence production of cassava and other foods, in addition to temporary and permanent out-migration of male labor to extractive industries such as logging
and mining, and (2) engaging in a surplus cassava production project, developed by an external international development program, aimed at generating income for women based on cassava as a cash crop to partially
compensate for the loss of male labor and/or to eventually retain male
wage labor in the village. The decisions made by local people are derived
from a core of ideas that is itself "cultural," having persisted, with some
modification as influenced by external realities, over the last 100 years.
    The Makushi are a Carib-language-speaking people of the north Rupu-
nuni District savannahs of interior Guyana and the frontier state of Roraima in Brazil.[2] Approximately 6,000 Makushi live in small villages near

Map 7.1   Communities in and around Iwokrama

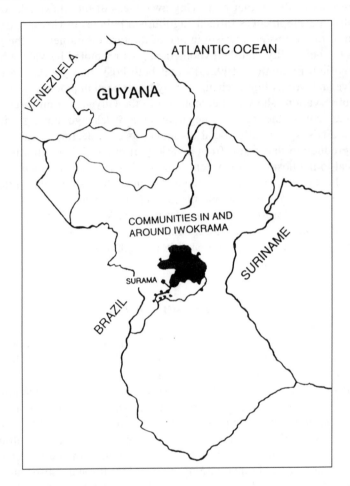

the foothills of the Pacaraima Mountains in the Guyanese interior. They are neighbors to an estimated 5,000 Arawakan-speaking Wapishana people in the south Rupununi savannahs in Guyana (Forte and Melville 1989:7). Most reside within 100 miles of the Brazilian border, which they regularly cross, legally and illegally, to work, to trade, and to visit with relatives. The population in any village at any given time is highly variable due to out-migration of adult labor to Brazil and the Guyanese coast. The periodic absence of children attending regional schools contributes to variability of the youth population in Makushi villages. Although their native languages are completely different and their natural environments are also variable, the Makushi and Wapishana peoples share common hunting and fishing areas and a similar way of life due to local subsistence agricultural production and trade. They also share acculturation processes due to historical domination and exploitation by English colonialists and Brazilian neighbors, although differences in these acculturation processes are also evident.

Historically, the Makushi are more influenced by the Anglican Church and the Wapishana by the Catholic Church; however, Evangelical churches are now winning converts in both villages (Forte and Melville 1989:7). According to ethnographic accounts (Forte and Melville 1989) and my observations in 1995 and 1996, the Wapishana people are more influenced by Brazilian culture than are the Makushi, due largely to their closer proximity to Brazil. The Makushi inhabit the savannah highlands and farm the rain forest foothills. Historically, the Wapishana typically engaged more in ranching than did the Makushi, due to their location in the lower savannahs and closer proximity to the Brazilian savannahs and a developing market (Forte and Melville 1989). Because they live adjacent to the Brazilian frontier state of Roraima, where Amerindian men are lured into mining and ranching by Brazilian companies, the Wapishana and Makushi people in the Rupununi District are not strangers to transnational economic structures of exploitation and development opportunities.[3]

In their traditional subsistence pursuits, the Makushi people were formerly much more mobile than they are today, ranging over a large area of Guyana and Brazil (Forte 1996). Residence shifted as cultivation of small family farms, hunting, and fishing locations rotated as the Makushi searched for better soils and more game. Fields were typically 2–6 miles from homesteads in higher elevations. Village sites were permanent or semipermanent social and religious centers (Forte 1996). Over the last 150 years, however, the Makushi became more sedentary, gradually shortening the distance to, and cycles of, their slash-and-burn plots in response to mission or government inducements to inhabit permanent settlements centered on church, school, and health care and sanitation facilities (Forte 1996). Because children's labor was an integral part of the subsistence agriculture, anthropologist Janette Forte argues that children's time at school was a factor that contributed greatly to decisions by men to engage in economic opportunities away from farming (Forte 1996:73).

Native culture change also occurred through the government policies that conscripted Guyanese Amerindian children to mission schools, greatly increasing cross-cultural contact among them and promoting intermarriage among the Makushi and the Wapishana peoples (Forte and Melville 1989). Diverse native-speaking Amerindians were required to communicate in English, which both broke down native cultures and promoted greater sharing of languages and cultural ideas among natives. Because of the attractiveness of Brazilian wage labor opportunities, modern Guyanese

Makushi speak Portuguese as well as their own language and some Wapishana. The Wapishana speak their language and English as well as Portuguese and some Makushi.

Following the acculturation demands of the English government and
church, which greatly affected the structure of social interaction, came the
reorganization of labor by capitalist development of extractive industries.
In the early 1900s, balata bleeding, a form of latex extraction similar to
rubber tapping, began the restructuring of Makushi and Wapishana labor
toward extractive industries. It also transformed the subsistence economy
through the payment and barter of exported goods such as flour, rice,
sugar, and matches for balata (Forte 1989:11). Peanut farming, which replaced balata bleeding in the 1960s, introduced cash income, which even
more greatly changed Makushi and Wapishana family farming and village
life (Forte 1989). Peanuts are planted on the same soil as the staple cassava after the first or second crop has been harvested, a production system
that provides for both cash crops and basic subsistence crops. However,
profitable peanut farming requires the labor of entire families, including
children, who often cultivate up to 10 acres of virgin forest at a time.
Peanuts are a fairly successful cash crop, but prices have not been high
enough in recent years to compete with logging and mining wages; hence,
out-migration of adult male labor.[4]

Cash payments from peanut farming introduced Makushi men to
Western technology and market goods. Income from peanuts provided
money to buy shotgun cartridges that men used to intensify their hunting
of deer, acouri, tapir, and labba, all of which ravage peanut plants. More
recently, mining and logging wage labor, in both Guyana and Brazil, offers
more cash incentives to men than does peanut farming. Hence, Makushi
men are increasingly drawn away from their families and communities into
individual employment in logging and mining to obtain shotguns and other
desirable goods.

Migratory wage labor, along with environmentally destructive extraction industries into the farthest reaches of the globe, brings social and economic distress to traditional subsistence pursuits, which most adversely affect the lives of women and children. The scene is illustrated again here.
Without male labor, which is essential to clear land for rotated plots, cash
crop and subsistence farming for the Makushi is not only less profitable, it
is less feasible for families. Hunting and fishing for dietary needs are also
limited by the absence of men. Increasingly, women and children are required to meet their protein needs in sedentary locations. Some women
have taken to raising chickens, but the decline in farming greatly affects
availability of agricultural staples in the region. A shortage of locally
grown food products has led to an increase in malnutrition. Native people
have little or no cash for food imports, which are scarce in the region.

Traditionally, the diversity of crops in Makushi agriculture provided for dietary needs. Two or three outlying farms per household in rotation produced several varieties of cassava in one field, as well as yams, sweet potatoes, corn, plantains, pineapples, papaws, peanuts, beans, maize, and peppers (Forte 1996). Traditionally, farms also produced tobacco, cotton, fish poison plants, and medicines (Forte 1996). Some cassava, plantains, mangoes, sugarcane, coconuts, peppers, corn, and seed plants are grown in nearby kitchen gardens if soil permits (Forte 1996). The diet is also supplemented with the eating of insects (Forte 1996:78). Not surprisingly, Forte reports that families that have retained traditional farming have more stable homes and more nutritious diets than those where male labor is absent.

The migration of Makushi male labor to Brazil, often for long periods of time, diminishes the social and economic viability of Amerindian communities. Many men never return, or return sporadically, often with serious alcohol dependencies that lead to domestic violence (Forte 1996). Male migration also presents a threat to Guyanese sovereignty, as it leaves communal hunting and farming territories unprotected from encroachment by Brazilian settlers, prospectors, and persons with criminal intent. Male absence leaves families vulnerable to starvation and violence, impoverishes communities of developmental potential, and threatens the traditional local ecology.[5]

The economic and social problems of the interior Amerindians are increasingly gaining national and international attention. Since Guyanese independence from Britain in 1966, Guyanese interior populations have been drawn more closely into the nexus of a developing Guyanese political economy. In 1989, local participation was encouraged through the development of an international rain forest reserve and research program in response to the globalization of concern regarding the destruction of the rain forest environment. The Iwokrama International Rain Forest Program operates out of a 900,000-square-mile rain forest preserve that is relatively isolated from the rest of Guyana (see Map 7.1). The desire to promote rain forest ecotourism was a major incentive for the establishment of the Iwokrama reserve. The intersection among international tourism, protection of the Iwokrama rain forest, and the local communities surrounding this preserve is a dramatic example of increasing globalization. The Iwokrama program is managed by the Guyana Natural Resources Agency in partnership with the Commonwealth Secretariat, the United Nations Development Programme, and the International Development Research Center of Canada. The reserve includes an international research camp that is an attraction for scientists in developed countries. But the reserve is also becoming the locus of various economic development projects as more people with diverse interests and agendas enter the area. The development of ecotourism is an outgrowth of the Guyanese government interests and indigenous concerns to maximize economic opportunities now emerging as a result of the Iwokrama site development.

Ecotourism Development in Interior Guyana

A model of global ecotourism that coordinates and sustains traditional Amerindian cultivation, hunting, and fishing with national and international rain forest protection strategies and the cultural rights of local people may be emerging in the Guyanese interior. Whereas its ultimate success is by no means certain, the current program incorporates the growing interests of international research scientists and other global visitors with national economic development agendas and the development needs of local people. An increase in visitors and a corresponding increased demand for food and lodging point to a need to recognize and plan for several possible effects of further globalization in the area. The Iwokrama research camp can accommodate the basic food needs of 20 guests per day through its local gardening, hunting, and fishing activities. Housing is limited, but additional cabins can easily be constructed. Rather than intensify food needs at the camp, however, the director of the Iwokrama program has demonstrated a willingness to coordinate accommodations for additional visitors in nearby villages, thereby serving as a basis for local ecotourism development in the area.

The Makushi of Surama are eager for such development opportunities. My students and I provided an opportunity for community awareness of longer-term benefits that the Iwokrama International Rain Forest Program might bring the Makushi of Surama. In response to my 1995 evaluation of the site, the small liberal arts church college I represented paid cash to the community council for two weeks of lodging for 30 persons in 1996. This money was used to develop a tourism infrastructure. A screened barracks for 8–12 persons with toilets and showers, similar to the facilities at the Iwokrama camp, awaited a 1998 student delegation. Plans for a kitchen and dining structure are under way.

Based on my field observations, however, it seems the development of an ecotourism niche in the rain forest frontier tourist market by the Makushi and their neighbors may be dependent upon whether they can guarantee a food supply for the guests, not facilities for cooking and dining. My 1996 group of 30 students transported their own food from Georgetown. We soon depleted our fresh fruits and vegetables. In response to my offer to purchase local supplies of such items, which I learned were primarily out of season in May, some locals made sacrifices from their own larders in return for cash. This was done in consultation with other community members. The price determined was the price normally established when selling food to fellow community members in need and below the market price to other outsiders. The locals wished to develop a positive relationship with our group, which paid the Makushi village council a generous accommodation rate per person for the use of the community center, fresh water, and the pit latrine. Additionally, Makushi individuals were paid for cooking, lecturing, and guiding nature tours at the same rate as the Iwokrama staff. These positions, which pay from U.S.$7.00 to $10.00 per day, are highly sought by locals.

The need to supply fruits and vegetables to meet the needs of visitors is a serious consideration in the development of an ecotourism program. Unless local surplus food production is guaranteed, an increasing number of visitors to the region may exacerbate present regional food shortages for locals as they sell their staples for cash. Opportunities for price gouging and competitive entrepreneurialism may discourage tourism, as well as threaten the local cooperative market exchange system.

Ideally, local production of food for guests should be based on the creation of sustainable agroecological models that ensure that local communities gain and secure favorable economic returns without environmental degradation. But these models will also have to realistically confront the fact that ecotourism and external sources of funding and support are linked to the vagaries of Western capitalism and touristic preferences. In such a structure of cultural and economic exchange, local native communities throughout the world have limited resources to adapt to, or limited power to resist, economic development projects introduced, implemented, or imposed by persons from the centers of power and influence in the world (Costa et al. 1995). However, a theory of ecotourism as an aspect of globalization would have us identify and examine the diverse effects and directions of external forces, recognizing that while some act to adversely change the culture, others act to sustain valued traits.

In my 1996 field study, I discussed with local Makushi women the availability of locally produced food for guests in the area and the best seasons for availability of local surplus. The women reported that they could not guarantee surplus unless they knew a year or six months in advance of the needs so that they could coordinate the labor necessary to make adjustments to their plantings. Even if large numbers of men would return to clear land and cultivate crops, the women acknowledged the plight of all farmers in warning that weather may not guarantee their crops. Fresh fruit and vegetable yields, of particular interest and demand by guests from developed countries, are the most difficult to predict. At this point, there are no detailed studies that examine the carrying capacity of the region to produce surplus fruits, vegetables, protein, and carbohydrate food sources for ecotourism guests given the current labor situation and hoe/machete technology.

Critics of ecotourism as an aspect of global development might argue that the nonlocal demand for food on the part of tourists interferes with local traditional food production strategies and results in further penetration of capitalism and Western cultures, heightening negative social effects. I argue, however, that preliminary evidence shows that ecotourism in the Guyanese rain forest can mediate the undesirable effects on local cultural systems already undergoing change as a result of global capitalist mining and logging industries. To better assess the effects of global ecotourism and other forms of global development on the region, rigorous longitudinal and latitudinal study of the 12 communities in and around Iwokrama should be conducted. My field studies indicate a commitment, so far, on the part of international guests and national hosts to carefully monitor all ecotourism developments.

A Development Alternative?
Intensified Cassava Production

The feasibility of revitalizing traditional cultivation practices to supply the food needs of local people and guests must provide competitive economic incentives for men to encourage them to remain in the community and to engage in farming rather than leave for mining or logging wage labor. In response to the lack of male laborers (itself a response to globalization), Makushi women around the village of Surama are currently engaged in a surplus cassava production project developed by the Guyanese government and the United Nations Children's Fund. Cassava is the staple crop for 500 million people worldwide, mostly women in underdeveloped nations, whose most important economic activity is engagement in small-scale farming on poor soils to produce subsistence food needs. In an attempt to intensify cassava production on lands near their homes and the Surama village center, 2.5 acres were cleared in 1996 using the traditional slash-and-burn methods.

Currently, community labor is coordinated one day a week at the cassava site to produce products to meet the carbohydrate need of local families composed of elderly widows and single mothers whose husbands have either abandoned them or are away for long periods of time. Intact households still farm and grow their own cassava, as well as participate in the development of the production center via community labor.[6] The proposed cassava production plan would rotate 20-acre fields in an area in close proximity to the permanent village center. Development of surplus cassava production draws Amerindian women into the capitalist economy of production for cash exchange rather than use. Surplus production of cassava is intended to meet local developmental needs to provide local peoples, particularly women, with cash for the purchase of food imports and other desired material goods. It is also expected to provide processed exports to expand Guyana's national economy.

The UN program developers argue that mechanized local processing of cassava products will yield farine and starch for local needs, will provide employment opportunities for men and women, and will produce cassareep, cassava bread, tapioca, and farine for commercial export. The program has trained local women in quality control, labeling, and processing techniques. A diesel engine used in the peeling and grating of the cassava and metal pails and drying pans were purchased from Brazil by the UN program. All are housed in a newly constructed traditional structure. Over a period of several months in late 1996, the cassava processing plant produced more than 3,000 pounds of farina, much of which was sold to other villages and miners in the region.[7] Local transportation of products is provided for free using the regional government office truck. The residents of Surama are encouraged by the results and have prepared more land in the area of the processing plant for excess planting.[8]

The recent cassava plant developments may encourage men to return to the village in hopes of gaining stable wage employment and regaining status. Should surplus production be sustained for any length of time, the local two-tier market structure will likely be transformed. The local subsistence economy is based on a series of "farmers markets," where locals sell a wide variety of crops to one another at prices currently agreed upon through the local political structure that protects locals from middlemen. There is another pricing structure for outsiders that is market driven, although current opportunities for participation are minimal. If a greater number of local people become dependent upon cash incomes earned through surplus production, the local noncompetitive market system will likely collapse. The guarantee of local food needs, equality in economic opportunities, and market stability will need to be addressed.

Development Prospects for the Region

Although access to, and incorporation into, a global market may be possible and desirable, the current surplus production project is also likely to lead to debt and dependency on imported goods, particularly food. A proposed road from Roraima in Brazil through the Rupununi region to Georgetown would provide Amerindians with access to markets. Although Georgetown residents and Amerindians welcome such a road in general, they recognize that the Brazilians potentially have the most to gain through access to a Caribbean port. Guyanese government policies toward Amerindians are more favorable than Brazil's policies toward its native population (Davis 1976). Brazil's economy is also much more developed than that of Guyana. As Brazilians gain more influence in the area, it is feared that more Amerindian men would be lured into Brazilian economic development schemes of various sorts and become dependent on Brazilian consumer goods, drawing them more into the political economy of Brazil than Guyana. The road from Brazil to Georgetown would further exacerbate threats to Guyanese sovereignty, threaten rain forest protection, and destabilize Amerindian communities. The road would also accelerate the linkage of local Amerindian communities to national and international markets and politics with unpredictable effects for local people. Therefore, it is unclear whether international and national programs to promote environmentally and socially sound ecotourism can resist or reverse some of the negative trends in the globalization of traditional egalitarian economies.

Questions also remain regarding development programs that promote a gender-based division of labor in traditionally egalitarian societies. Extended male absence from family and community for wage labor in extractive industries leaves women to sustain the agricultural sector and creates a variety of social and economic problems. It is reasonable to assume that the program designed to employ women to produce surplus cassava for export, if successful without male labor returning to the village, may still serve to further impoverish women whose husbands are absent. It is uncertain whether men would return and try to take over or transform the cash crop cassava production and processing if it were economically successful. If men do not return and intensified cassava production is successful over a long period, women will gain greater control of resource allocation, business decisions, and distribution of economic rewards. Without male contributions to their economic livelihoods, women will also gain more independence and economic security, but they may not be able to stabilize their families and preserve their culture.

Rather than stabilizing a local and regional network of interdependence and making women more economically self-sufficient, attention to cash crop processing by women is likely to reduce their ability to produce a variety of basic foods for household needs, as well as create dependence on unstable markets and unreliable transportation to them. Reliance on processing of cash crops by female-headed households is also likely to induce further nucleation of more permanent households. This will reduce the possibility that kitchen gardens can contribute significantly to local nutritional needs, despite an attempt on the part of the cassava processing project to develop more kitchen garden production.

The effects of intensifying agricultural practices that provide cash crop income for women and/or develop local surplus for incoming ecotourists need to be more closely examined at all levels of local, national, and international interaction. Such feasibility studies need to be comparative over the 12 nearby communities all seeking to benefit from development of an ecotourism industry in the area. These comparative social impact studies of the effects of various international and national economic development programs are likely to demonstrate that social organization and the local ecology are less likely to change with ecotourism than with intensified cassava production or any other experiment that emphasizes women's labor and accepts the absence of men as a long-term reality. It is not clear what numerical gender balance is necessary for traditional forms of gender equality to be sustained in the area. It is already apparent, from my observations, that for those few men who remain in the community, strategies to revitalize Makushi culture through development of women's social and economic roles are often at the cost of male decisionmaking and leadership roles. Tensions exist between male and female leaders primarily over influence of the direction of outside development assistance, particularly the externally directed but locally staffed ethnobotany project that promises to be the location for the first Internet system in the village.

Based on my field observations, there are already indications that, as the women gain more power over funding for surplus food production and cultural preservation programs, as well as ethnobotany and ecotourism development programs, many of the men who remain experience potentially diminished roles. Conflicts between men and women at the level of community leadership are evident and may jeopardize ecotourism developments. These conflicts can be reduced with ecotourism activities that develop and coordinate cooperative roles in social and economic development based on traditional forms of gender equality. Such ecotourism programs employ men as hunting and fishing guides and lecturers for photography and nature tours. Women play traditional roles in lodging, cooking, and demonstration of food production. Both women and men can play key leadership roles as lecturers in native ecology and customs, as well as logistics coordinators. This study strongly suggests that the success of ecotourism developments in traditional societies depends on coordination and development of the talents of both men and women in the community.

With careful coordination and consideration of local cultural values, the development of ecotourism based on local decisionmaking and local market control may yet prove to be the most viable strategy for Amerindians in the Guyanese interior to sustain their local ecologies and cultures within the context of transnational economic development agendas. There are many variables, however, that are beyond the control of local decisionmakers. Ecotourism may prove highly seasonal, providing only periodic income from visitors. Rain forest tourism may also become highly competitive, with peoples in developing nations throughout the world competing with one another in a global market coordinated and dominated by international tourism agents. Or the current interest in rain forest tourism could diminish altogether as affluent and alienated consumers search for the next fashionable destination and experience.

Although the women and some men of the village demonstrated to me and my 30 students over two weeks in May 1996 that they are highly qualified and motivated to deliver a cultural ecology program for undergraduate education, at this point, the infrastructure is not ready for market-driven tourism. And whether ecotourism offers equal development potential among the 12 villages as a growing number of tourists seek diverse experiences also remains to be seen. Presently, the development of ecotourism and surplus production opportunities is uneven, a fact that has not gone unnoticed by the general director of the Iwokrama International Centre for Rain Forest Conservation and Development. At the instigation of the Iwokrama staff, a Regional Development Council was created, made up of representatives and stakeholders of each of the communities surrounding Iwokrama for the purpose of evaluating consultants' reports and for regular interaction. The Iwokrama staff recognizes that better decisions can be made as natives learn to evaluate alternatives that have rapidly become available.

Fortunately, the national political structure of Guyana, of which the Iwokrama reserve is a part, accommodates local and regional native political structures and seeks to broaden opportunities for village development through ties to the Iwokrama programs. It is recognized that without careful regional management, competition among villages for specialized production to enhance cash flow and ecoadventure niches is likely to be divisive. Without social impact studies that carefully monitor its social, cultural, and economic consequences, ecotourism development could be as suspect as cash cropping in promoting negative changes in social behavior.

It is important to recognize that the greater the contact with local hosts, the greater the changes in local behavior as a result of tourism. After each contact, the nature of local culture changes, either becoming more artificial or more like that of their visitors (Butler 1990). Seasonal tourism confined to small areas can minimize local culture change, whereas seeking to avoid seasonal peaking by dispersing tourists over space and time can have more profound and permanent changes (Butler 1990:49-66). In addition to the effect on local culture, participants and directors of ecotourism programs need to also carefully assess the broader consequences of attempts by villagers at economic development through market tourism. Market tourism for village people can cause them to be periodically unemployed (particularly during the rainy season) and to purchase too many supplies on credit to accommodate boom-and-bust tourism cycles.

Ideally, Guyana's links to global ecology movements should continue to be carefully coordinated and evaluated through a central government office that incorporates the input of anthropologists. Ecotourism is a high priority of national economic development programs with policies designed to encourage local participation. Although many opportunities for cultural preservation can be obtained from ecotourism, there are dangers to the rain forest ecosystem if the local interior economy becomes too growth oriented. Successful interior developments may place further demands on interior resources to fund national government strategies for the development of ecotourism and other programs on the coast. Each new national and global demand requires careful analysis of opportunities and threats posed in each village ecology.

Conclusion

Market tourism poses a threat to the particular and authentic identities of local villages, because, as Marie-Francoise Lanfant and Nelson Graburn (1992) argue, it is the market that decides what will be the image and local identity of hosts. Touristic products are created to attract potential clients and to match local identity aspects with customer desires (Lanfant and Graburn 1992:99). Anthropologists can help by evaluating ecotourism programs, identifying market-driven ecotourism agendas, and contributing to the design of environmental education programs led by tour directors or college faculty who are motivated toward "colonizing" niches for adventure on the global scene. Unreliable programs led by tour leaders or researchers who shift agendas or communicate one thing to natives and quite another to their nonnative neighbors or the Iwokrama management can strain community social systems and exacerbate vicious competition between natives and nonnatives, as well as promulgate facile understanding and shallow cultural exchange.

Applied anthropologists can identify global and local structures of exploitation and unequal opportunities. Local, but nonnative, tourism enterprises generally have greater access to development funds and communication with outside systems, and they are usually in a better position to exploit market opportunities, as well as their native neighbors, in the development of ecotourism, making some rich at the expense of others.[9] And because any resources directed toward native self-determination that demonstrate economic success can also draw in exploitative global networks of tourism, national and local decisionmakers must constantly assess the structures of interaction among local, national, and global actors. This analysis, then, takes the "knowledge-based platform" of tourism scholarship, which argues that tourism must be studied not just in its forms and consequences, but in its holistic connection to other global and social phenomena (Smith and Eadington 1992:11).

In the final analysis, the success of an ongoing ecotourism project appears to be dependent upon the local leadership of key individuals who can identify national and international opportunities and structures of support and who can demonstrate great creativity and skill in coordinating cultural ecology educational programs for outside guests without commodifying local culture. This is no small task, yet the leaders of Surama demonstrate such global awareness and local authority. The motivations, attitudes, and behavior or ethos of tourists greatly affect the goals of mutual understanding and equality among tourists and hosts, but ultimately, the perspective of the host inhabitants will define the just forms of exchange (Nyoni 1987:51).

In a 1997 conversation with the director of the International Iwokrama Program, I learned that the Makushi are confident that the International Research Program can attract tourists and visitors to the Guyanese interior who will benefit their community and the surrounding communities. In addition to a screened barracks with flush toilets and showers, the Makushi have built boats and a bird watching tower in preparation for a growing ecotourism market. A tribal spokesman assured me that the visit by my group did not generate or foment any new conflicts among the village residents, but neither did it serve to resolve any of the old conflicts between leadership factions, issues that will demand attention in the future. It is encouraging to note that my observations were appreciated and recorded by the Iwokrama program director and his staff.

Applied anthropologists can and should play a major role in defining appropriate policies that respond to the globalization of ecotourism by training local peoples to gather systematic data for social impact surveys. This will aid in local evaluation of the intersection of outside agents that aid and inform as well as complicate local economic decisionmaking. Anthropologists can quickly identify not only the locus of native knowledge but the inequalities in power in the negotiation of short-term and long-term institutional relationships among community stakeholders in an increasingly more complex nexus of native economic decisionmaking in which many outside individuals and organizations compete for influence. Recognizing that the effects of tourism are more determined than determining (Nash 1995:189), anthropologists can also help articulate cross-cultural relationships in ecotourism in which native peoples themselves have voice and power. This preliminary analysis shows that the Makushi and their neighbors have several options for development, and they will no doubt seek to maximize all of them as individuals negotiate their own best economic strategies as well as contribute to the needs of families, communities, and the region.

The globalization of ecotourism shows that even within the most peripheral regions of the globe, agents of global capitalism compete for the central role in economic development. It may be, however, that, unlike other forms of tourism developed over the last century, ecotourism is less likely to supplant traditional subsistence patterns with an exploitative service sector that redefines social and cultural institutions. In the globalization of capitalism, typically one form of economic development has given way to another form as modes of subsistence production were replaced or transformed by capitalist production in developing regions. Multiple modes now coexist and may continue in somewhat complementary roles in the future.

Ecotourism development, like all development, is clearly a double-edged sword. The potential rewards for host communities are great, but the potential for cultural disruption is equally strong. Ecotourism, with its potential to extend economic development into the most peripheral regions while sustaining local cultures and environments, poses new challenges to institutions providing international assistance to these regions.[10] The evaluation of such global phenomena as ecotourism will require a more sophisticated transcultural conceptualization of globalization processes that incorporates intersections of cultural contact at many levels. Applied anthropologists, working with local people, clearly have a role in formulating these conceptualizations and guiding this type of development. The extent to which ecotourism can provide economic opportunities and also sustain or supplement valued elements of traditional lifestyles is dependent upon many global processes, mostly external, but not wholly hostile, to host societies. Local people must learn themselves how to assess the effects of global processes and to evaluate their effects to maximize options. Whether culture becomes merely a commodity, a conduit, or a contestant in the globalization of ecology through ecotourism will be revealed through theoretical refinement of transcultural processes, methodological sophistication of cultural change analysis, and the human agency of individual stakeholders.

Notes

1. The World Tourism Organization concluded that diverse models of "alternative forms of tourism" must be analyzed in terms of their consequences to sustainability (Nash 1995:183). G. Dann, D. Nash, and P. Pearce (1988:4–5) argue that scientific analysis of tourism forms must include theoretical awareness and methodological sophistication in which all aspects of cultural contact and change are considered.

2. There are six Carib-speaking peoples living in Guyana in separate geographical areas interspersed among linguistically distinctive Arawakan- and Warau-speaking peoples (Forte 1996:105).

3. Many Makushi people also reside in Brazil, sharing a culture and a language across two national cultures. The Guyanese Makushi speak their native language and, out of necessity, English and Portuguese. They frequently cross over the border without legal documentation to visit their relatives or to work and to shop for scarce goods in Brazil.

4. Low peanut prices do not entice Amerindian males who reside farther into the mountains and who often sell their farm produce surplus directly to nearby miners. For those Amerindians in the savannahs, peanuts are bought by the

Regional Development Council and flown to Georgetown, but transportation to Annai's savannah airstrip is often slow and irregular (Forte 1996).

5. Currently, the community structure is able to respond to the negative effects of the absence of individual males who seek economic opportunities in Brazil. Community members endeavor to protect and aid single-parent households that experience hardship as a result of male absence. The problem has grown so severe, however, that leaders recently imposed sanctions against those who do not tell other community members where they are going and when they expect to return. This is to reduce tensions that result when their wives give them up for dead and take up with other men, only to have the husband return and demand his conjugal rights.

6. According to J. Krippendorf (1982), the healthiest development strategies retain and strengthen farm economies.

7. This data comes from a report from the director of the Iwokrama International Rain Forest Program based on information received from Makushi village leaders.

8. A serious consideration to the success of the program is the recognition that interior rain forest soils are highly acidic. Through the process of slash-and-burn clearing and rotation, nutrients that raise the soil pH for root crops are released from the ash of burned trees. Small, isolated clearings are not a threat to the rain forest ecology, particularly when rotated fallow periods are long. However, intensified cultivation in a relatively small area must recognize the nutritional deficiencies of the soil, as well as the loss of rain forest biodiversity. Intensified domestic monocrops also grow increasingly more vulnerable to pests and diseases. The surplus production experiment relies on continuous production on soils surrounding the processing plant. Rain forest soils quickly lose fertility. The program developers argue that pen animal manure and cassava skins can be applied directly to the new plantings to sustain soil fertility. But these materials do not appear to be in adequate supply in the area surrounding Surama. There are no penned animals, for example, only a few privately owned animals that graze a larger fenced area.

9. A nearby ecotourism resort owned and managed by an Englishman can take advantage of an increased number of tourists to the area because of several reasons: (1) he is funded by outsiders; (2) he offers several levels of accommodations, including tile baths and a swimming pool; and (3) he is located near an airstrip on the savannahs.

10. Currently, international church groups and other global nongovernmental organizations provide infrastructural support toward educational and health care developments, such as schools and wells for permanent site water supplies.

8

Global Space and Local Response: The Uses of *Convite* in the Dominican Deep South

Manuel Vargas

This chapter will focus on the experience with agricultural development in Blue Mountain and Green Savannah, two adjacent peasant villages located in a flat, dry coastal area of the Dominican Republic known as the "Deep South" (see Map 8.1). Two main phenomena will be discussed. The first is how the cultivation of hybrid sorghum has impacted the lives of Montañeros (the dwellers of Blue Mountain) and Sabaneros (those of Green Savannah). The second is the way in which those peasants have used *convite,* a traditional form of labor pooling, as an ideological weapon for long-term survival in the new social space created by the arrival of sorghum cultivation. My use of a reflexive style is due to the fact that I was directly involved as an agronomist in the early stages of that modernization project, hence the need to reflect on how my deeds impacted the lives of those dwellers.[1]

My interpretation of these issues is in accord with Mark Hobart's (1993) argument that the plasticity of local knowledge or tradition can enhance the effectiveness of human agency when dealing with the hegemonic claims inherent to modernization. Like Paul Richards (1993), I find it fruitful to look at farming as a performative act linked to social projects.

I agree with Michael Foucault's assertion that people (peasants included) attempt to overcome alienation using the technologies of production, of sign systems, of power, and of self (1988:18). But unlike him, I argue that ideology is crucial for the care of self in contested social spaces like the ones marked by the increasing globalization and modernization of peasant communities. Furthermore, so my argument goes, care of the self is achieved through the use of symbolically mediated actions of resistance in daily life.

A context is necessary for our story.

Map 8.1   The Deep South in its larger context

The Social Context of Sorghum Cultivation

As with most development initiatives in the Republic, state-sponsored agricultural modernization has reached the farms of most Montañeros and Sabaneros several years after it was well under way in other geographic areas.

Sorghum cultivation was not an exception to this pattern of neglect. Indeed, although the promotion of the drought-resistant cereal as a panacea for rural poverty began in the Republic's northern and western regions as early as 1966, it did not start in the Deep South until 1978.[2] Rather than accidental, this time difference is embedded in the unique relationship the southern region has had with the larger society since 1844, when the nation became independent from Haiti. We need not tell such a complex story here. Suffice it to say that, despite the Deep South's significant contribution to the national economy, most of its residents have hitherto enjoyed very little of the fruits of national progress. Paradoxically, poverty is pervasive in a frontier zone the rich natural resources (e.g., bauxite, salt, precious woods) and cheap labor of which have made possible the accumulation of wealth for national and foreign capitalists alike. This asymmetric situation was originally caused by a host of phenomena, such as the extractive nature of most industries operating in the area, the weak linkage between regional leaders and the national centers of power, and the outside perception of the Deep South as a backward territory the residents of which do not conform to the sanctioned national ideals of "civilization" (e.g., skin color, religion, agricultural practices, architecture). A relatively small electorate has been a key component in the perpetuation of the region's low status vis-à-vis other geographic areas. As locals often say, "Our votes do not reach the presidential palace." The dwellers' present sense of remoteness from Santo Domingo, the nation's capital, mirrors their lived experience in a region euphemistically called the "poorest" in the Republic.

The arrival of sorghum in Blue Mountain and Green Savannah in the fall of 1979 was mediated by the interplay of two related phenomena, namely, economic and political priorities at the national level and new local expectations. Indeed, at the time, the cereal was desperately needed to support the growing poultry industry based in Santo Domingo. Corn, the grain hitherto utilized for the privately owned poultry industry, was not profitable enough for Dominican peasants to grow on their small farms. By the same token, imports made through U.S. Public Law 480 did not satisfy the increasing demand for corn. Hence, the promotion of sorghum cultivation became a priority for the individuals whose capital was invested in the prosperous meat industry. In that context, public investment in the promotion of sorghum cultivation was explicitly aimed at protecting the interests of powerful entrepreneurs.

As shown in Table 8.1, whereas the importation of corn increased at an annual rate of nearly 20 percent during the 1973–1983 period, the national production of corn remained stagnant during the same period. By contrast, the national production of sorghum increased so significantly that by the year 1982, it had become nearly equal to the production of corn.

Such a rapid increase in production was directly caused by the services and facilities provided by the government to sorghum growers, including

Table 8.1   Sorghum and Corn Production and Importation of Corn, 1973–1983 (in metric tons)

Year	Sorghum Production	Corn Production	Corn Imports
1973	9,205	51,864	53,318
1974	15,273	59,045	66,638
1975	16,364	43,682	32,364
1976	15,591	82,045	57,318
1977	17,729	61,590	100,954
1978	18,409	49,455	105,045
1979	23,059	38,318	110,363
1980	25,136	45,500	185,545
1981	34,214	39,000	165,682
1982	34,580	37,182	192,000
1983	40,477	53,627	226,474

Source: The Dominican Republic's Ministry of Agriculture archives.

land preparation at low prices, free technical assistance, low-interest credit, and a secure market. Likewise, extraordinary measures were also taken to secure both a good harvest and the transfer of the precious grain to the capital for processing. For instance, in 1979, unexpected heavy rains came in Blue Mountain when an impressive combine was packing the brownish sorghum grains into plastic sacks. The fermentation of the cereal was certain, unless something special was done expeditiously. I still remember seeing a huge grain drier arriving in the village to save the raw material. The machine, owned by the government, was so tall that it was necessary to utilize all kinds of tricks to pass it across some of the steel bridges. That display of state interest in the crops grown by peasants was alien to the Deep South. Clearly, there was an economic motivation behind those unprecedented official actions. The events unequivocally revealed the interplay between economics and politics in the project under consideration.

But this characterization of the political economy of sorghum cultivation, its accuracy notwithstanding, does not tell the whole story. To avoid reductionism, we need to pay close attention to the role played by local expectations, social projects, and personal commitments in the arrival of sorghum in Blue Mountain and Green Savannah. Of course, these are complex phenomena the full discussion of which is beyond the scope of this narrative. For the task at hand, what calls for our attention is that the aforementioned official assistance to peasant agriculture signified more than a structural act motivated by economic rationality alone. Rationality aside, agricultural modernization reached in many ways the affective dimension of reality in the two villages.[3] The following synopsis should illustrate this point.

Simply put, prior to the arrival of sorghum, most locals had received minimal government aid.[4] The only meaningful exception to this pattern took place in 1966, when Blue Mountain and Green Savannah were totally obliterated by a terrible hurricane. Following the natural disaster, the government built new houses and gave them away to Montañeros and Sabaneros. Although the relocation of Blue Mountain to a safer location in 1967 was a government intervention, almost nothing was done to develop the Deep South thereafter. This was especially true of agriculture. For instance, whereas the extension service began operating in other regions in the mid-1960s, the first extension agent arrived in Green Savannah in 1977. It is fair to say that expectations of direct government support to peasant agriculture is a recent phenomenon in the Deep South. Small wonder that one often hears local dwellers saying loudly that they live "in a dark hole" and sorely calling "strangers" those from other regions.

Such a strong sense of exclusion from mainstream society suffered a major transformation in 1978, when the Dominican Revolutionary Party and its newly elected president—Antonio Guzmán Fernández—utilized the slogan *El Cambio* (The Change) to symbolize social justice. The new state policies aimed at redistributing wealth through both the creation of public jobs and the increase of investment in agriculture, health, and education created a short-lived national consensus. The implementation of modernizing agricultural projects in regions like the Deep South was a key component of those policies. It was in the context of such an enthusiastic populist mobilization that Montañeros and Sabaneros perceived the new cash crop as more than a new source of profit; they also saw it as a symbol of recognition by the national government, the powerful Other. This is to say that reason and feelings were closely interwoven in the arrival of sorghum.

That sorghum cultivation was locally seen as a favor from the government is illustrated by the way in which Vicente, a Montañero, recalled in 1990 his original perception of the official project. "We never thought that the government was really willing to help us this way," Vicente told me when we discussed the local response to the new cash crop. "I never thought that those important people from up there cared about poor people like us."

Although sorghum cultivation brought new elements of bureaucratic control into Blue Mountain and Green Savannah (e.g., paperwork for loans and standardized procedures for land preparation, harvest, and payment), it never was a totally faceless process. In part because of the excellent rapport the agronomist working directly in the villages had with the local peasant leaders, in part because of the utopian overtone of this specific state intervention in the Deep South, reciprocity and recognition overshadowed struggle in the first two years of sorghum cultivation. Granted, the extraction of surplus value from peasants was taking place. But it does not follow that development had a hideous face. At least not at first.

When I was appointed as the regional director of the Ministry of Agriculture (henceforth SEA) in August 1978, I became a broker between the entrepreneurs operating at the national level and the local actors (i.e., peasants, agronomists, staff). But my involvement in the promotion of sorghum cultivation was more than a professional undertaking dictated by impersonal structures. Indeed, both my personal commitments and professional interests played a key role in the formulation, implementation, and evaluation of the project. In the first place, I shared the utopian goal of social justice claimed by the new president. Furthermore, I was genuinely convinced that agricultural modernization was beneficial for Montañeros and Sabaneros. It was because of such beliefs that I accepted enthusiastically the job offered to me by the minister of agriculture, a good friend of mine. When he told me, "I want you to go to the Deep South and make a revolution," I gained a sense of mission. To say the least, I felt recognized as a man of noble ideals and professional competence. Many members of my generation felt and acted in similar ways.

However, because my main goals were to increase sorghum production (hence supporting national progress) and help peasants make a monetary profit as large as possible (hence increasing their nominal and real income), I overlooked most of the social ramifications of agricultural modernization in Green Savannah and Blue Mountain. Although certainly mediated by a genuine belief in social justice, mine was primarily a short-sighted, naive, technocratic interest. I saw Montañeros and Sabaneros mainly as agricultural producers in need of technical and financial assistance to make a profit. In other words, my validation criteria and social myopia at the time prevented me from seeing that farming in the two villages was not just an economic activity, but an integral part of a complex social fabric that began to disintegrate along with the prosperity brought about by sorghum. Of course, peasants did not passively watch the collapse of their communities. Instead, they resisted alienation in myriad ways, including the imaginative use of tradition.

The Creation of a New Social Space

Sorghum made a good start in the Deep South. Indeed, a combination of favorable weather, effective technical and financial assistance, good prices, pure luck, and the like, made possible two excellent consecutive harvests of the grain.[5] The new crop provided Montañeros and Sabaneros with the opportunity to earn an unprecedented amount of money in a rather short period of time. As shown in Table 8.2, from being an unknown crop in 1978, the cereal in the year 1987 was responsible for the circulation of

Table 8.2   Sorghum Production and Circulation of Money, Blue Mountain, 1979–1987

Year	Production (quintales)	Price (Dominican Republic pesos)	Total Money Circulation (Dominican Republic pesos)
1979	19,007	5.50	104,539
1980	15,300	5.85	89,505
1981	52,720	5.85	308,412
1982	93,784	7.00	656,466
1983	72,000	7.45	536,400
1984	105,000	14.00	1,470,000
1985	160,000	17.00	2,720,000
1986	136,000	19.80	2,692,800
1987	105,345	82.33	8,673,054

Source: SEA, Blue Mountain.

nearly nine million Dominican pesos in the zone. Using an average exchange rate of six Dominican pesos to one U.S. dollar, that sum at the time represented close to $1.5 million. Altogether, during the 1979–1987 period, the circulation of money generated by sorghum was $2.5 million per year. That means that, on the average, each of the 360 sorghum growers handled nearly $7,000 anually. Prior to sorghum cultivation, only a few wealthy ranchers had access to that large a sum of money.

Needless to say, such a large amount of money circulating in any peasant village had major social and cultural consequences. To mention but a few, at least 30 Montañeros bought houses in Santo Domingo, others sent their children to college, and nearly all purchased new home appliances and furniture. It is fair to infer that the local profit was far more modest than the one made by the owners of the poultry industry.

The early economic success of sorghum cultivation brought dwellers closer to a world formerly out of reach. It was a world of new consumer goods, better education, more money, rapid secularization of power, new symbols of progress, and new social relations. A happy mood was shared by those who opted for modernization and won the bet, however skeptically. I felt genuinely part of the local sense of accomplishment epitomized by the bright colors chosen by sorghum growers to paint their dwellings after the first two harvests. After all, those were some of the intended consequences of the state intervention in the area.

But along with the happy world unveiled by modernization in Blue Mountain and Green Savannah, a less triumphant reality was concealed. It was the unpleasant world of inequality and alienation created by the unintended consequences of development. In order to comprehend and contest this rather hidden reality, Montañeros and Sabaneros had to suspend their belief in the utopian claims made by the state. To take care of themselves in such a dangerous situation, they also had to use their relative power. It is such a gesture of contestation that I call "ideology." Within this theoretical framework, ideologies and utopias go hand in hand. They both use, in imaginative ways, the taken-for-granted cultural practices of daily life as a raw material to redefine social projects (Berger 1995:35; Ricoeur 1991).

Elsewhere, I have discussed both the idiosyncratic way in which Montañeros and Sabaneros engaged sorghum cultivation and the larger meaning of their differential response to the new cash crop.[6] I have suggested that we play close attention to the changing nature of such experiences in order to comprehend the interplay between structure and agency in the Deep South. For present purposes, I will examine just four dimensions of the new social space in the two villages—namely, the lack of food security, the dependence on cash for production and consumption, the increasing control by public and private agencies, and the erosion of women's role in farming.

First of all, the diversity of the long-lived system of production eroded concurrently with the increase of modernization. To be sure, the shrinking of diversity cannot be attributed exclusively to sorghum cultivation. Indeed, other erosive factors include the massive deforestation and heavy use of chemicals (especially pesticides) accompanying the adjacent cotton plantation since 1957, the hurricane of 1966, the large-scale felling of trees for commercial charcoal making, the establishment of a sisal plantation, and the local effect of environmental changes taking place elsewhere in the country and in the Caribbean region. Yet the evidence clearly shows that the sharpest deterioration of the traditional system of production took place soon after sorghum arrived.

Putting those differences aside for heuristic purposes, let us take a look at the system of production in the area prior to modernization. During the period 1966–1970 (see Figure 8.1), at least 17 different crops were grown in the two villages. Some of them (e.g., peanuts, squash, rice) were used for self-consumption and for trade. Likewise, wild and tame animals were used by Montañeros and Sabaneros as sources of food, transportation, and power (e.g., horses were utilized for plowing). Off-farm work (mainly at the cotton plantation and in the harvest of peanuts) helped dwellers earn the cash needed to purchase goods and services. Both females and males, children and adults, participated in those activities according to the division of labor existing at the village and household levels. Needless to say, a sophisticated knowledge of the natural world, coupled with the performance of elaborate rituals—witchcraft included—was also utilized to protect crops and animals against the evil eye, spells, pests, and so forth. In both villages, *convite* provided a large portion of the labor necessary for special tasks (e.g., felling trees to make a new farm, mending fences, harvesting).

Such an impressive diversity in production and consumption had mostly faded away by 1990 (see Figure 8.2). To begin with, a significant decline in the number of crops and animals took place. As of 1990, several crops had totally disappeared from the local landscape (e.g., peanuts, rice, yams). Others were planted by just a few peasants (i.e., bananas, eggplant, plantain). Second, there was a drastic fall in hunting and gathering activities. Third, the volume of animal products entering the market decreased significantly. Fourth, there has been a major reduction in the number of children per household. Finally, the presence of the government and private companies increased, especially connected with the numerous activities associated with market transactions taking place between the villages and the larger society.

The decline in diversity significantly reduced the amount of food available locally. In fact, in both formal and informal interviews with me, several women from Blue Mountain indicated that members of their households in 1990 were eating twice a day instead of three times a day (or more), as they used to do before 1979. Further, when I asked them to

Figure 8.1 A Comprehensive System of Production, Blue Mountain and Green Savannah, 1966

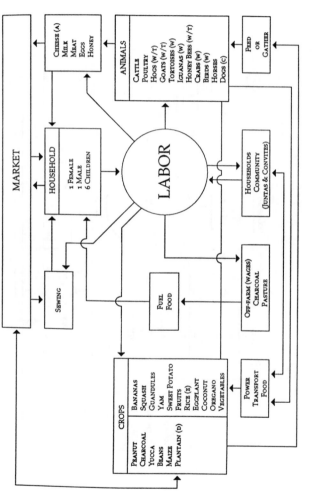

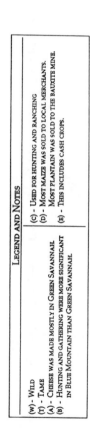

LEGEND AND NOTES

(w) - WILD
(t) - TAME
(A) - CHEESE WAS MADE MOSTLY IN GREEN SAVANNAH.
(B) - HUNTING AND GATHERING WERE MORE SIGNIFICANT
      IN BLUE MOUNTAIN THAN GREEN SAVANNAH.

(c) - USED FOR HUNTING AND RANCHING
(d) - MOST MAIZE WAS SOLD TO LOCAL MERCHANTS.
      MOST PLANTAIN WAS SOLD TO THE BAUXITE MINE.
(E) - THIS INCLUDES CASH CROPS.

Figure 8.2 A Comprehensive System of Production, Blue Mountain and Green Savannah, 1990

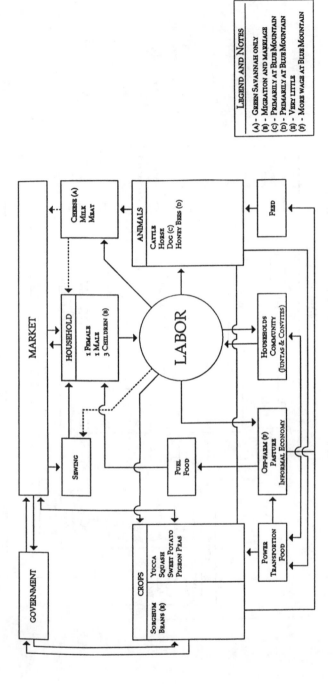

LEGEND AND NOTES

(A) - GREEN SAVANNAH ONLY
(B) - MIGRATION AND MARRIAGE
(C) - PRIMARILY AT BLUE MOUNTAIN
(D) - PRIMARILY AT BLUE MOUNTAIN
(E) - VERY LITTLE
(F) - MORE WAGE AT BLUE MOUNTAIN

MARKET

GOVERNMENT

HOUSEHOLD
1 FEMALE
1 MALE
3 CHILDREN (B)

CHEESE (A)
MILK
MEAT

ANIMALS
CATTLE
HORSE
DOG (C)
HONEY BEES (B)

FEED

LABOR

SEWING

CROPS
SORGHUM
BEANS (E)
YUCCA
SQUASH
SWEET POTATO
PIGEON PEAS

FUEL
FOOD

HOUSEHOLDS
COMMUNITY
(JUNTAS & CONVITES)

OFF-FARM (F)
PASTURE
INFORMAL ECONOMY

POWER
TRANSPORTATION
FOOD

list the types and amount of food they used to eat prior to and after modernization, I discovered the occurrence of two important phenomena: first, the intake of carbohydrates had increased significantly; second, the intake of vegetables, eggs, and meat had declined abruptly. For instance, one Montañera told me that a typical breakfast before modernization consisted of yucca, sweet potato, squash, eggs, and milk; nowadays, however, she and her three children usually eat a piece of bread, some milk, and occasionally a soup that she purchases at the food store, provided cash is available. Another woman said that her kids "have lost the custom to have breakfast." During my fieldwork, I saw several children who went to school on an empty stomach, expecting to receive before noon some boiled wheat or lentils donated by international agencies. Let me illustrate with the following example how this drastic fall in the local production of food is a source of existential vulnerability for locals.

In March 1988, during my preliminary fieldwork in Blue Mountain, there was a moment at which water scarcity reached dramatic levels. In addition to the severe drought, the only well in town was broken. That was the first time in my life I saw people unable to eat because of the lack of water needed to cook their food. The combination of crop failure and dryness made life particularly difficult for those who could not afford to purchase water from the only private supplier. Then, all of a sudden, an official truck arrived in town and began distributing free food to nearly everyone who could prove that they were poor enough. Ironically, the donated packages contained foodstuffs that used to be cultivated or gathered before modernization, namely, rice, beans, corn flour, and sardines. It did not take long for Montañeros to realize that the government was using the free food as a deterrent for political unrest. Even though they took the food, I witnessed many Montañeros—women and men alike—reflecting upon the meaning of that unusual "gift" from the government. One person said to others: "Who would have thought that we will be receiving from Santo Domingo the food that we used to grow ourselves?" The local sense of honor was at stake. I witnessed the same phenomenon during my visit to the area in August 1997.

The second major ramification of such drastic changes is that those Montañeros and Sabaneros who neglected their traditional plots must now purchase agricultural products (staple food) from merchants. Likewise, in order to grow sorghum, they need to purchase hybrid seeds,[7] fertilizers, pesticides, and other inputs that are produced by private companies— multinational corporations included. This creates considerable need for cash. It is in that context that the meaning of a total failure of sorghum cultivation becomes apparent. Since all peasant agriculture in the area is rain-fed, the threat of crop failure is almost constant. When this happens, debt is certain. It goes without saying that the burden created by the lack of cash increases when the family has one or more of its members studying in the capital city.

Such a constant demand for money in daily life has increased the power of local moneylenders. Furthermore, because no private institution thus far finances peasant farming, most farm credit is provided by BAGRICOLA, the state bank. As shown in Table 8.3, the number of local borrowers from the bank more than tripled from 1980 to 1988. It is worth noticing that that number decreased significantly in 1989. Further, the area planted with sorghum ceased to continually rise in 1984, fluctuating thereafter. The reason for this is twofold: some peasants from both villages made the decision not to continue sorghum cultivation, and BAGRICOLA made tougher its conditions to lend money.

Chiefly because of lack of irrigation, the possibility of going into debt with BAGRICOLA is very high. Evidence of this is the fact that, by 1990, nearly all sorghum growers from both villages had lost at least one harvest of the grain because of drought, heavy rain, pests, lack of equipment, and the like. Prior to sorghum cultivation, the only crop that made such a situation possible was peanuts. A major difference between these crops, however, is that whereas hybrid sorghum demands a capital-intensive technological package, it is possible to grow peanuts with very little cash, provided one has the seeds and animal traction.

Table 8.3   Sorghum Production Financed by the Agricultural Bank, Blue Mountain and Green Savannah, 1980–1989

Year	No. of Cultivators	Area (in tareas)[a]	Total Amount (pesos)	% of Payback
1980	106	6,258	401,700	40
1981	141	9,032	560,100	45
1982	191	14,844	852,500	55
1983	316	59,680	1,404,200	60
1984	332	37,246	1,742,700	60
1985	311	52,185	1,697,000	35
1986	354	38,635	1,851,400	75
1987	360	41,144	1,869,200	85
1988	347	31,726	2,883,900	85
1989	276	24,846	3,243,900	95

Source: Agricultural Bank, personal communication.
a. One tarea equals 628 square meters.

With sorghum, it is nearly impossible to have a crop failure without increasing your debt to BAGRICOLA. For instance, nearly 85 percent of Montañero sorghum growers owed money to the bank in 1990. Getting off of the credit treadmill and out of debt is a difficult task that very few peasants in the Deep South can achieve. This is what Montañeros and Sabaneros metaphorically call *"quedar enganchado con el banco"* (literally, to end up hooked with the bank). The image of "being hooked" expresses the vulnerability and anxiety felt by peasants once they internalize the ramifications of a permanent economic debt. Small wonder that peasants usually point at their genitals to show metaphorically the part of their personal and social body where they are "hooked."

The situation has worsened in recent years. Indeed, when I visited the Deep South in August 1997, I was not surprised to learn that the official bank was lending money to less than 30 percent of the sorghum growers. The local perception, in my view accurate, is that now that the government can grow sorghum on its own plantation using the recently built irrigation canal (see p. 193), it is too risky to lend money to peasants who depend so much on the unstable rainfall. It is worth noticing that the government is now promoting sorghum cultivation in areas with irrigation. As I was told by locals, "Now the sorghum from the Deep South is not as important."

The ultimate meaning of the new articulation is that peasants are dependent on a thick structural web to cultivate a grain that, at first, they perceived as just "a favor from the government." Obviously, the peasant system of production has become inextricably linked to agencies representing not only the economic interests of a social class, but those of multinational corporations as well.

A crucial dimension of governmental influence in the local system of production refers to a process I term "begging for seeds." What this means is that, since modernization, there has been a growing number of peasants (more Montañeros than Sabaneros) that depend on SEA to obtain some of the seeds they need to plant crops other than sorghum. Prior to the abandonment of their traditional farms, peasants relied on one another to obtain most of the seeds they planted. For instance, a peasant that saved some of the red beans from the previous harvest shared part of the stash with others who had some maize seeds. When the rainy season was about to start, peasants engaged in a generalized process of reciprocity. Even though there are some peasants from Blue Mountain who still save seeds for the next planting season, most of them have to wait for the government in order to obtain the seeds they need. One rather moving scene I saw more than once was peasants asking the local agronomist to bring from Santo Domingo the seeds of some crops they used to grow in the same parcels where they now grow sorghum.

And last is the crucial issue of women's and children's direct participation in farming activities. As discussed above, the labor provided by
women and children was vital for the preservation of the traditional system
of production. By contrast, the high level of mechanization inherent in
sorghum cultivation displaces them from most of the activities taking
place in the modernized fields. To use Marxian terminology, the high organic composition of capital present in the cultivation of the new cereal
has reduced the need for "living" labor. For women, this is a major loss of
power within the household. It is not surprising, then, that most women
(67.6 percent) surveyed in 1989 said that their lives *as women* have worsened since sorghum cultivation. Significantly, most of them said that during the same period of time, life *in the villages* has improved.

Concomitant with the objective dimension of the aforementioned unintended consequences of modernization, there is an emotional sphere that
cannot fully be discussed here. Suffice it to say that when the public agencies take sorghum from the Deep South to the cities, that operation con-
notes more than a simple distribution of a raw material. The meaning of
this becomes apparent if one realizes that most Montañeros and Sabaneros,
many of whom are illiterate, used to trade with merchants who paid them
cash. With sorghum, peasants retain only a form that indicates their enti-
tlement to the commodity taken away. The anxiety created by such a rather
nebulous situation reaches dramatic terms when, as it often happens,
BAGRICOLA takes four months or longer to make effective the payment
to sorghum growers. I witnessed peasants who had to go as many as five
times to the nearest city before receiving the final payment. It is not uncommon to see Montañeros and Sabaneros returning from the city with a
deep feeling of frustration, if not total rage, after being told that the profit
they made is far lower than they expected. The bitter expression "This is
the last time I grow sorghum" usually follows such humiliating experiences with the bureaucratic world.

It took most Montañeros and Sabaneros several years to realize that
modernization had consequences they had not fully anticipated. However,
they did not reach such a conclusion through rational analysis alone; their
feelings were also vital in the process of discovering their new reality. Indeed, their eye-opening experiences included the vulnerability felt before
the power structure in general, their discovery of uneven terms of exchange between local and national institutions in particular, and their concerns about social fragmentation and loss of tradition (e.g., the increase in
crime, alcohol consumption, inequality, and, from the elders' perspective,
the laziness of the younger generation). When the dwellers realized that
their whole lives were at risk, they intentionally began using both their traditional practices and their new knowledge to take care of themselves.

The Uses of *Convite:*
Looking to Tradition to Cope with Progress

Resistance to the unintended consequences of sorghum cultivation has taken myriad forms in both villages, ranging from resilient ambiguity to simulation to stubborn actions. An indication of the latter is the case of Eduardo, a pioneer sorghum grower who, in 1982, hijacked the state-owned combine in response to the fact that his sorghum was not harvested at the right time. But the majority of peasants have chosen to cope with their situation by using two strategies that circumvent direct confrontation. The first, which I term "looking to tradition to cope with progress," is the decision to use *convite* to remain dwellers of a contested social space. The second, which I call "talking to the government," consists of manipulating the connections peasants have with the same structures and individuals they see as having too much control over their lives. For lack of space, I will discuss the ideological use of *convite* only.

In its traditional form, *convite* is as old as the Dominican peasantry. *Convite* is a multivocal discourse; it encompasses both economic rationality and ethical norms aimed at constructing a sense of ontological security. Likewise, *convite* functions as a vehicle for the symbolic construction of what Anthony Cohen (1994:93) calls "an identity of aspiration."

For the sake of clarity, let's put *convite* in the actual context of social relations in Blue Mountain and Green Savannah. After doing so, I will interpret two salient ideological uses of *convite* in the social projects of Montañeros and Sabaneros.

In 1983, a group of about 25 Montañeros who defined themselves as "poor peasants" formed an association they first called "The Hope." Its nickname was "The Little One." That was the second peasant association in town; the first, organized in 1970, was named "The Experience" as a way of making explicit that its members had learned how to defend themselves. The reference to knowledge in that act of naming is relevant. Significantly, in 1987, members of The Little One decided to change its name to "New Progress." When I asked the local leaders why they chose those two names, they told me that whereas the former was intended to signify that there was some hope that life will improve, the latter indicated that there was a need to choose a path of progress different from the one symbolized by sorghum cultivation.

Although in 1990 (when I concluded my second field study in the area) The Experience was formally associated with the well-to-do sorghum growers (the rich) and New Progress with those who claimed to be growing food or planting pasture (the poor), an extraordinary collaboration existed between the two associations. For instance, nearly a quarter of the peasants belonged to both groups. More important, for several years, both associations had the same man as their president. Class conflict notwithstanding, solidarity and manipulation of social capital were taken seriously in the village.

Manipulation of labor through *convite* is the key instrument of resistance to obliteration used by members of New Progress who represent themselves as poor. It is this institution that illustrates in the clearest way the interrelation of tradition, solidarity, and power at the local level.

The first ideological aim of *convite* is to lower expenses and increase efficiency by having several people working at once on lengthy and difficult tasks. It is not uncommon for a *convite* to last for 10 or more hours of intense work. Under normal circumstances, the "owner" of a *convite* must provide food, water, and coffee to all people involved. Equal work intensity is expected of everyone participating in the activity. Participants in a traditional *convite* do not earn wages. Reciprocity and a sense of honor form the backbone of this long-lived institution.

Second, *convite* provides peasants with a social space in which to exchange information, develop community-forming ties, revitalize traditional values, express themselves, and reinforce male bonds. While working together, peasants talk (and gossip) about politics, sex, cockfighting, the "rich people," family members, and the like. Generally speaking, the spirit of peasants during a *convite* is high and even cheerful. They sing traditional songs, sometimes accompanied by a drum. Only exceptionally one sees rum being served by the host during the noon break.

A word of caution is needed here to avoid essentialism. Its lasting characteristics notwithstanding, *convite* is not a fixed, systematic, or ahistorical practice. Rather, as an ideological praxis based on local knowledge, *convite* is manipulated and altered by peasants in order to face concrete challenges in changing, fluid social spaces in creative ways. Let me explain what I mean by this.

In Blue Mountain and Green Savannah, labor pooling is nowadays utilized primarily to plant the same crops peasants used to grow before modernization. In fact, during the 14 months of my fieldwork (1989–1990), only two *convites* were explicitly devoted to activities dealing with sorghum cultivation. Furthermore, for the most part, the cultivation of traditional crops is carried out in new farms created through the use of slash-and-burn techniques. Those new farms are located deep in the dry forest. They are mostly utilized for the creation of use value. In reality, they represent "insurance" for tough times.

As mentioned above, wages are not paid in the traditional *convite,* but that is no longer always the case in Blue Mountain. Indeed, since at least 1988, some participants in the activity are paid either by the host or by those campesinos who are unable to reciprocate the help they received to

work in their farms. But rather than being local dwellers, those wage earn-
ers are farm workers who migrated to the Deep South to work on activities
related to sorghum cultivation or on the adjacent sisal and cotton plantations mentioned earlier. Prior to that date, it was unthinkable for local
dwellers to hire labor. In fact, until recently, the local ethos prescribed that
a man of honor was not supposed to use paid labor to cultivate his farm.

The situation just characterized is significant for at least two reasons.
First, rather than seeing an evolutionary, progressive trajectory of modernization, one is witnessing Montañeros and Sabaneros actually "acting out
ambiguity," so to speak. In other words, instead of rejecting modernization
altogether, they accepted it at first and neglected temporarily the traditional system of production described above. Second, without abandoning
sorghum cultivation, they have returned to their traditional practices "to
cope with progress."

The result of all of this is a hybrid system of production. In theory,
whereas sorghum cultivation is carried out using capital-intensive technology and commercial credit, the traditional plots are cultivated using labor-
intensive technology. In practice, however, inputs and outputs circulate
freely between the two phases of the system.

It is fair to say that because of its revitalization of "living labor," *convite* is still the blood of the whole system. An indication of this revitalization signified by *convite* is that each time I participated in the activity, I
heard expressions such as "I love our association," "Only lazy people are
against our group," "We are a family," and so forth.

Of course, one ramification of all of the above is the change of power
relations within the villages in general and in *convite* in particular. What I
mean by this is that those with more money can potentially buy labor and
control the *convite,* hence eroding its ethos of solidarity and reciprocity.
For instance, in 1990, I witnessed one of the peasants with double membership in the two local associations attempting to purchase several
convites in order to fell the trees from the secondary vegetation and plant
sorghum immediately on his farm. But when Montañeros realized what he
was doing, they simply confronted him and forced him to stop. In doing
so, they prevented, perhaps only for a short time, patron-client relationships within their association.

But how effective is this hybrid system for long-term survival? What
ideological role does *convite* play in this new social space? I do not have
the answer to these questions. Whether *convite* is going to be ideologically
effective in the long run is impossible for me to predict. But I propose to
explore that probability by looking at a process taking place in the Deep
South, namely, the impact of national and international migration on the
social fabric of Blue Mountain and Green Savannah. Due to space constraints, my discussion of this will be highly schematic.

During my visit to Blue Mountain and Green Savannah in August 1997, it was obvious that many changes had taken place in the two villages since I concluded my fieldwork in 1990. New bars and stores have been opened. New houses have been built. Several farmers have bought tractors. At least one combine is locally owned. Modernization is visible there. But the change that impacted me the most was the new telecommunications center in Blue Mountain, with its brand-new fax machine and six telephones. The center is busy all the time. As a local friend of mine told me, "Now we are part of the world!"

At first, I thought that my friend was talking about the new center of communications only. But soon I learned that migration from the Deep South did not stop in San Domingo. Instead, a significant number of women from Green Savannah have made the long journey to Europe (mainly Italy); young men and women from both villages have migrated to Central and South America (e.g., Panama, Venezuela), the Caribbean (e.g., Puerto Rico, Haiti, St. Vincent), and, of course, the United States. The result is a new era in the globalization of the local social spaces. To use Michael Kearney's terminology (1996:118), a "hyperspace" is being constructed in the Deep South.

I do not mean to suggest that international migration from the two villages was caused by the arrival of sorghum only. Yet I cannot overlook the displacement of women and children from farming that took place when agricultural modernization began in 1979.

Is this new phase of globalization detrimental to the campesinos of Blue Mountain and Green Savannah? Is migration from the area a loss or a gain for Montañeros and Sabaneros as people? What can be done to prevent disintegration of the hybrid system of production resulting from the interplay of tradition and modernization in the region? And how can the ethnographic information presented here be used to support the long-term survival practices of those dwellers?

Perhaps the best place to look for answers to the above questions is in the real-life world of the transnational community emerging in the Deep South. In other words, I suggest looking at what Sabaneros and Montañeros themselves are already doing to survive in their new reality to determine the effects of recent developments. Let me illustrate this with three examples.

First, as of this writing, the "modified" *convite* is still utilized to keep the hybrid system of production operating in the Deep South (mostly in Blue Mountain). Indeed, during my recent visit, I witnessed dozens of my Montañero friends who are members of New Progress enthusiastically walking toward their farms at dawn amid a severe drought that had killed hundreds of cows and left the open fields covered by only the reddish dust so typical of the area. I saw them waiting for the rain to come and pondering the wisdom of planting sorghum at the expense of growing food. Although several of them told me that they quit growing sorghum for good, most intended to plant the cereal as soon as it rained, provided technical and financial assistance was available. Meanwhile, I was told, *convite* is vital for survival. In other words, the hybrid system of production is still operating in the area.

When I inquired about the financial support they have to cultivate their farms, I was not surprised to learn that a portion of the remittances sent from abroad was being invested in farming and ranching. Significantly, part of that money is used to support *convite*. Furthermore, those remittances provide the funds that the official bank is now unwilling to provide. To be sure, this is not a new phenomenon in the Dominican Republic. On the contrary, research (Georges 1990; Portes and Guarnizo 1990) shows that Dominicans abroad are actually supporting many small business enterprises back home. It is worth noting that the cash needed for international migration from the Deep South came in part from the large amount of money circulating in the area because of sorghum cultivation.

The second example is very telling. A year ago, I received a fax message from Blue Mountain. The sender, a prominent Montañero peasant leader, wrote to let me know that two young men from the village received scholarships to study in California. Curiously, each of them is studying agroforestry. I was surprised to hear that because I knew that one of them wanted to study computer science. When I asked the young man why he decided to study agroforestry instead, his answer was unambiguous: "This way I can help my community to protect the land." Of significance is the fact that his scholarship is in part sponsored by the Dominican Ministry of Agriculture, the same agency that brought sorghum into the Deep South in 1979. This example is a clear indication of what Anthony Giddens (1984) refers to as the "enabling and constraining dimensions of structuration." Indeed, the state apparatus is simultaneously facilitating the extraction of surplus value from the Deep South and opening new opportunities—however limited—to some local dwellers.

Finally, *convite* is being used as an ideological weapon to defend the land in the Deep South. This new development is as complex as the unexpected ramifications of sorghum cultivation. To make a long story short, in 1996, representatives of a powerful family with a long tradition of animosity toward peasants arrived in Blue Mountain claiming legal ownership of most of the land in the village, including the area where the government built new homes after the 1966 hurricane. Ironically, that family is pressing peasants to return the land on which they grow sorghum.

Local response to this unanticipated challenge has been both strong and imaginative. For instance, graffiti with radical slogans and symbols of resistance have been painted at strategic locations so that outsiders passing through the area can see them. By the same token, local leaders have used their political connections "to talk to the government" in the nation's capital. Some young students have even set fire to tires to show their determination to resist. But what called my attention most was the fact that prominent local leaders have suggested planting some of the traditional crops they cultivated before sorghum arrived in the area as a way to show that they are peasants willing to die for their land. *Convite* has become a key emblem of this ideology. However, the ultimate goal of this "return to tradition" is not to restart the system of production transformed by the arrival of sorghum. Instead, the aim is to use those crops and labor pooling to symbolically represent the decision to stay as dwellers of a new, contested social space where the global and the local interface.

It is in this fluid, complex global space that the ideological uses of *convite* must be understood. Like Arturo Escobar (1995:222), I believe that it is by looking "for alternative practices in the resistance grassroots groups" that anthropology can make a contribution to the survival of campesinos like Montañeros and Sabaneros.

To conclude, I want to stress that, as of today, Montañeros and Sabaneros have been able to put to work both their social imagination and their tradition to face with authenticity a complex, dangerous situation involving powerful structures and human beings. Rather than being provided with a "true consciousness" by outsiders, we see these campesinos using their traditional and newly acquired knowledge to take care of themselves.

Notes

1. The fieldwork (1988–1990) was funded by the Wenner-Gren Foundation for Anthropological Research.

2. The cultivation of hybrid sorghum for commercial purposes was first suggested by a team of international consultants in the aftermath of the 1965 civil war that led to the second U.S. military intervention to the Dominican Republic. The new cash crop was then seen as a partial solution to the pervasive poverty in the nation's countryside.

3. The affective dimension of reality in Blue Mountain and Green Savannah when sorghum arrived was signified by three related phenomena: (1) the shared sense of vulnerability since the total obliteration of both villages by a hurricane in 1966 (including the death of nearly 60 people); (2) the circumstance that Montañeros' agricultural practices at the time were perceived as backward and their farms as worthless because of lack of irrigation and rather poor soils (hence the dwellers' sense of exclusion); and (3) the fact that whereas most Montañeros in 1979 were locals, nearly 90 percent of Sabaneros were brought by the government as colonists from the country's northern region as part of a racially based state-sponsored campaign the aim of which was to "Dominicanize" the Deep South, which then, as now, was seen by many as a Haitian-like region. One practical implication of this is that sorghum cultivation provided Montañeros with both recognition from the larger

society and the opportunity to demonstrate their worth as peasants and citizens alike. Hitherto, most Montañeros took pride in their cattle rather than in their crops. By contrast, most Sabaneros constructed their sense of self through the protection of their long-lived farms where "food" was cultivated. See note 6 below.

4. It is worth mentioning that a cotton plantation was established in the area in 1957. Owned by an influential capitalist from Central America, the plantation utilized a highly sophisticated technological package (e.g., chemical fertilizers, pesticides, tractors, airplanes), which was in sharp contrast with the labor-intensive technology used by peasants at the time. Most Montañeros worked for wages on the plantation. Likewise, peanut cultivation was introduced in the area by a private company in the late 1950s. Although both enterprises had a major impact on the lives of Montañeros and Sabaneros, they did not transform significantly the traditional local system of production. For instance, Montañeros started using tractors and pesticides on their farms only after they became sorghum growers.

5. As of this writing, all peasant agriculture in the arid Deep South is rain-fed. Although the government built a small-scale irrigation canal in 1994, only the nearby state-owned plantation can utilize it. For instance, when I visited the area in August 1997, I witnessed Montañeros and Sabaneros desperately coping with the devastating effects of a seven-month drought. Next to their deserted farms, by contrast, was the healthy sorghum planted on the official plantation. The average annual precipitation in the area is 700 millimeters. Most rainfall occurs between August and October, when sorghum is planted. It is worth mentioning that most dwellers don't have legal titles for the land they cultivate.

6. Briefly, during the period 1979–1982, nearly 80 percent of Montañeros abandoned their long-lived system of production and became sorghum growers. Many of them even sold their livestock to grow the cereal. In contrast, nearly 78 percent of Sabaneros rejected sorghum cultivation for at least three years and, significantly, did everything possible to preserve their traditional production patterns after many of them adopted the new cash crop. In 1982, three years after the launch of modernization, the majority of Sabanero peasants made the decision to plant sorghum. My argument is that the differential response was conditioned by the idiosyncratic ethnically linked ideologies in the villages. Indeed, whereas most Montañeros are locals, the majority of Sabaneros migrated to the Deep South in the mid-1950s as part of a racially based state program of colonization of the frontier region using peasants from the Republic's northern region. On this, see Vargas 1996.

7. As of this writing, a significant proportion of the hybrid seeds was cultivated in the northern region, primarily by a national firm that had an agreement with the American firm that produces the seed brand Pioneer. There were other national companies that imported hybrid sorghums as well. Montañeros and Sabaneros utilized at least three different brands of sorghum seeds.

9

Working in the Field: Perspectives on Globalization in Latin America

Benjamin Orlove

The chapters in this volume offer two general sorts of insights on globalization and the rural poor in Latin America. They clarify the current situation and trajectory of important sectors of Latin American society, especially the rural poor. They also serve as the basis for more general reflections on the anthropological contributions to the study of globalization. These two sorts of insights complement each other, since the specific details that these chapters provide about specific groups point toward the broader potential for the insights that anthropology can offer about this topic.

Anthropological Contributions to the Study of Globalization

The authors in this volume have closely overlapping definitions of "globalization," that odd term that consists of a brief root noun, "globe," followed by suffixes that transform it three times. In the first shift, the root becomes an adjective, "global," or "globelike" in scale; in the second, a verb, "globalize," to become global; in the last, a noun once again, "globalization," the process of globalizing. These multiple suffixes point to the difference between globalization and "world systems," the previous planetary-scale term that held great importance in anthropology. As the grammatical structure suggests, globalization is a process. In contrast, world systems, with the associated terms of "core" and "periphery," is a noun, one that implies the existence of structures. There were certainly processes associated with this structure—appropriation, exploitation, domination, resistance, revolution, and the like—but the basic framework was one of structures rather than processes.

This contrast raises a difficulty for anthropologists. In a large-scale structural framework like world-systems theory, the standard anthropological tools of ethnographic fieldwork can be of great use. They can provide descriptions of particular portions of these large structures and thus contribute to an understanding of the nature and dynamic of these structures. However, it is less clear what anthropology might contribute to a process-centered perspective, particularly one such as globalization that emphasizes growing interconnectedness and homogeneity. World-systems theory, with its emphasis on structural relations, supported accounts of how human groups were organized differently in different places. Globalization might be taken to suggest that such differences are irrelevant and likely to disappear. The research techniques of anthropology provide detailed descriptions of local, social, and cultural arrangements—topics that might be presumed to be of some interest to world-systems theories that seek to account for differentiation, but topics of little interest to globalization theorists. In this regard, the question of representativeness offers a particularly telling challenge to anthropology: how can a study of a small number of individuals reformulate the conceptualization of the entire planet, with its billions of human inhabitants?

However, the chapters in this book demonstrate at least three kinds of uses of anthropology in the study of globalization, even granted the problem of representativeness. First, anthropological accounts can provide a fuller, richer view of the processes of globalization. They can put a human face, or many human faces, on what otherwise would be anonymous, impersonal statistics. In this way, they offer a more powerful account of these processes. With respect to poverty, anthropologists might indicate the human experience behind the loss of income or security. David Guillet's account of small-scale farmers in southern Peru, for example, shows that new forms of regulation of irrigation water, designed to increase efficiency and remove obstacles to market-based development, make established communities vulnerable to the loss of the basis of their livelihood. Manuel Vargas documents the challenges faced by peasant farmers in the Dominican Republic who can neither maintain their long-established agricultural economy nor find viable alternatives in cash crop production or migration. Similarly, Liliana Goldin shows how structural adjustment policies in Guatemala have encouraged production arrangements (putting-out systems, offshore assembly plants) that place increasing demands on unpaid household labor, with great strain for household relations.

Second, the anthropological accounts can challenge some of the claims of integration and homogenization. By linking individuals, groups, and economies more closely, globalization does not necessarily lead to social fragmentation, especially the disruption of local institutions and communities. In other words, anthropologists can show that the planetwide process of globalization does not necessarily produce uniform results. These findings draw on both anthropological research techniques and anthropological analysis of the linkages between local organization and wider economic and political contexts. To take a concrete instance, anthropologists show that impoverishment proceeds in different ways in different places, rather than simply always accompanying globalization. Ronald Waterbury discusses a group of small farmers in southern Mexico whose incomes have risen through the production of fresh vegetables for urban and tourist markets. Barbara Dilly documents some economic expansion in another impoverished area, the interior of Guyana, through the development of ecotourism programs. In a similar vein, Goldin documents that some Maya communities in Guatemala have taken advantage of niches in export markets through the production of craft items or the cultivation of fresh fruits and vegetables. The authors all concur that these pockets of relative prosperity are fragile; demand is less stable in the new global order, and productive resources may become scarce.

The third kind of use of anthropology in the study of globalization is, I believe, the most important. It follows closely on the second point above. Some claims about globalization have linked the economic processes of globalization with changes in political organization and in ideology. In this view, globalization influences not only trends in the distribution and access to capital and other productive resources, not only trends in income levels and distribution, but also changes in the bases of valuation. Phrased in other terms, globalization transforms economic goals as well as economic resources, and it therefore transforms political organization and ideology.

Anthropologists are uniquely qualified to examine these political and ideological shifts, many of which occur at the local level and would be missed by specialists in other disciplines. As the chapters in this volume show, anthropologists can describe and analyze certain key facets of globalization: local institutional responses to global economic forces; the formation of new political spaces in a globalized world; and emergent forms of ideology, especially heightened patterns of generational consciousness and local appropriations of new images of globalization as modernity. In other words, as the chapters in this volume indicate, the poor come to understand their condition in different contexts and in different ways; their actions are similarly variable and context dependent.

Local Institutional Responses

New forms of economic production emerge in the context of globalization. The contributions to this volume point to the adaptability of local institutions to target new or changing markets; this adaptability has economic and ideological components. A mix of economic and ideological dimensions emerges in local institutional responses in Mexico. As James McDonald points out, some small-scale dairy farmers in central Mexico have obtained new forms of technology and reworked state-linked *ejido* institutions to move successfully into the supply of milk for yogurt production, in part through a mobilization based on the ideology of social justice and communitarianism of the center-left Party of the Democratic Revolution. The ideology of modernization seems an important element here as well. In this case, the reinforcement of community ties rests in part on strictly spatial considerations, where the bulkiness and perishability of fresh milk encourages concentration of dairying.

Guillet and Waterbury show other cases of local institutional responses in which local communities organize themselves to obtain or manage key productive resources. Guillet shows the importance of local associations of users of irrigation water in a semiarid region of highland Peru. Though based on traditional institutions, these associations negotiate with the state and seek accommodation within changes in resource law that favor large-scale private water uses; they balance the use of water to produce new cash crops, as well as traditional subsistence food items. Waterbury discusses a peasant village in southern Mexico that has developed a local cooperative in order to obtain the electricity to pump water and irrigate vegetable plots that supply new urban and tourist markets. This cooperative has been more forceful than other local organizations in bargaining with state agencies and obtaining credit. In these two cases, the reinforcement of community institutions comes from organizational considerations; the spatial considerations (delivery of irrigation water and electricity) are not absent, but they are not as primary as in the two previous cases.

Nonetheless, these four instances all indicate the reinforcement, rather than the weakening, of local institutions in the face of globalization. Some communities are certainly undermined by globalization, as Vargas documents with particular force; nonetheless, it is important to recognize that this erosion of community is not universal.

New Political Arenas

It has been predicted that globalization will lead to an erosion of politics in an era when markets and firms are stronger than the state, when media saturation limits awareness of local political issues, and when migration creates crosscutting ties that erode citizenship. These chapters contradict this claim and point to two new political arenas. The first consists of the nongovernmental organizations (NGOs), groups that operate in the public arena in relation to such political issues as social mobilization, resource allocation, and policy formulation, but that are independent of political parties and state agencies. In their study of indigenous mobilization in Panama, Philip Young and John Bort show the importance of such NGOs as the Centro de Estudios y Acción Social-Panamá in opposing the expansion of mining activity on traditional lands. Similarly, Dilly documents the efforts of international environmental NGOs to promote the establishment of protected areas and ecotourism programs in Guyana.

Closely linked to these NGOs are what have been termed "new social movements," the newness of which lies in their distance from earlier class-based forms of mobilization and state- and party-linked forms of activism. These movements have an affinity to NGOs that can promote them and channel their efforts. Some of these new social movements are linked to ethnic mobilization. Vargas shows a new self-consciousness of local customary practices in the southern portion of the Dominican Republic. Local people in this region now conceptualize their use of *convite* forms of exchange labor as a sign of their distinctiveness within the national society and as a basis for their mobilization for redistribution of state resources. Young and Bort show the emergence of a more politically engaged leadership among the Ngóbe indigenous people of Panama. This leadership draws on global movements of indigenous peoples to strengthen their claims for greater autonomy in the management of their territory. This linkage to global movements is not restricted to ethnic movements. Dilly's discussion of environmentalism in Guyana shows the ability of local communities to draw on global environmental ideologies to reshape land use claims and to plan new economic activities. In sum, globalization does not lead automatically to a postpolitical world in which markets dominate, but rather it can lead to new political forms such as NGOs and new social movements.

New Ideologies

The third and final contribution of these chapters to the study of globalization can be seen in the discussion of new ideologies. Though some might claim that globalization would lead to the erosion of all ideological commitments in an era of market-oriented consumerism, these chapters show that global media and NGOs can permit the spread of ideologies that local people adapt and rework. It is striking that two chapters discuss the emergence of local ideologies that critique global consumerism. Young and Bort show that many Ngóbe link the reemergence of their distinctive ethnic identity with a rejection of some international commodities and fashions. In particular, the Mama Chi religious movement raised questions about patterns of alcohol consumption. Goldin shows similar debates

among Protestants in Maya communities in Guatemala, who also reject alcohol and actively debate consumption in such questions as dress, housing,
and leisure activities.

Other chapters show the ideological dimensions of new forms of
market-based economic evaluation. In other words, globalization does not
simply impose new economic arrangements; instead, local people debate
the value of these arrangements. McDonald's discussion of dairy farmers
in central Mexico shows that many of them place a positive valuation on
the acquisition of an entrepreneurial orientation and a capitalist rationality.
In contrast, Waterbury's study of southern Mexico shows local opposition
to these economic ideologies, while Guillet's discussion of Peruvian farmers indicates fearfulness about the encroachment of these frameworks. Put
another way, globalization does not simply impose a single economic ideology; rather, local people examine the market-oriented capitalist ideology
and develop a variety of responses to it.

In sum, these studies by anthropologists in Latin America and the
Caribbean show the complexity of local responses to globalization. They
provide a richer, more nuanced account of globalization. They demonstrate
that local communities can be reinforced, as well as undercut, by the economic linkages associated with globalization. Most important, they show
that the political and ideological responses to globalization, often operating at the local level, are more diverse than has often been assumed. Without anthropological studies such as the ones in this volume, much less
would be known about local institutional responses to new forms of access
to resources and markets. Similarly, there would be weaker understandings
of the emergence of arenas, such as NGOs and new social movements, that
offer alternatives to national governments and political parties as forms of
political expression. The varied and often critical local response to man-
agerial and capitalist ideologies would also be little known.

The distinctly anthropological contribution of these chapters is more
apparent when contrasted with the work of other social scientists. Lester
Thurow's *The Future of Capitalism: How Today's Economic Forces Shape
Tomorrow's World* (1995), for instance, reflects his background as an economist. He states explicitly that there are five major forces in the contemporary world. Two of these are economic forces (the shift from resource-
based to information- and image-based industries and the growth of
international finance and trade), two are political (the end of communism
and the shift to a multipolar world), and the fifth is the emergence of a
new demographic pattern (with three subforces here: population growth,
international migration, and increasing life expectancy). These forces all
point to the global movements of objects, capital, ideas, and people, and
they all weaken the power of the nation-state. Thurow notes the increasing
gap in income and wealth between the small sectors that benefit greatly

from the new global order and the larger groups that are displaced by this order, and he fears that this gap will create political discontent and economic stagnation; he hopes that massive investment in education and infrastructure will allow the opportunities of the new global order to bring sustainable benefits to a wide social spectrum. The chapters in this volume point to another source of such widening of benefits: the organizational efforts of local people, often in association with NGOs and new social movements. This source lies outside the state sector that Thurow emphasizes.

In his 1995 *Jihad vs. McWorld: How Globalism and Tribalism are Reshaping the World,* Benjamin Barber, a sociologist, traces a number of forces in the contemporary world. As his title suggests, he is particularly concerned with the relationship between the growing uniformity of consumption patterns (and the spread of corporate power) and the resurgence of local identities (and the spread of fundamentalisms). He sees the two processes—homogenization and differentiation—as linked responses to a number of forces in the contemporary world. These forces include economic changes associated with economic growth and new technologies (particularly the development of worldwide markets for natural resources), the shift from industrial to service economies, and the growth of electronic media. These economic changes, in turn, weaken the nation-state, thus creating the paradox of the simultaneous rise of global and local identities. Barber fears that these identities might lead to warfare and political chaos, though he also hopes that the weakened nation-state will somehow permit the emergence of a new kind of public sphere and new forms of citizenship that rest on networks of smaller communities. By contrast, the chapters in this volume offer a more complex view of these local identities. Indigenous activists, whether in Panama, Guatemala, or Guyana, do not reject national identities, as Barber suggests, but seek a renegotiation of relations between indigenous peoples and the nation-state. The identities that challenge consumerism, as in Guatemala, or that question capitalist and entrepreneurial rationality, as in Mexico, are similarly not the extreme rejection of and withdrawal from modernity that Barber implies, but rather active efforts to construct new frameworks that reposition local people in the global order.

These chapters generally support the overview of globalization provided by an anthropologist. Arjun Appadurai's *Modernity at Large: Cultural Dimensions of Globalization* (1997) also notes a number of forces at work in the contemporary world. The anthropologist Appadurai emphasizes the growth of international mass migration and electronic mass media in the shift to the present cultural moment, one in which national identities, ideologies, and institutions are weakened. In his analysis of this moment, he lists five "scapes." The first three are economic and social: the ethnoscapes of translocated persons (tourists, immigrants, refugees, exiles, guests workers, etc.) (Appadurai 1997:33); the financescapes of rapid international capital and currency markets; and the technoscapes of mobile machines and techniques. The last two, closely linked to each other, lie more in the realm of the social: the mediascapes of circulating information and images, and the ideoscapes that frame these in terms of ideologies and movements. Appadurai fears the growing "incivility and violence" (Appadurai 1997:23), though he hopes that the possibilities of cultural freedom and expression can lead to an awareness of new forms of justice in postnational public spheres. It is precisely these public spheres that the anthropologists in this volume have described: the spheres of economic debate within communities, the spheres of ideological contestation, the spheres of NGOs and new social movements.

The three above-cited works examine economic processes of production, distribution, and exchange. To oversimplify them slightly for the sake of argument, one could say that Thurow, the economist, emphasizes the trends in objective economic indicators (e.g., gross national product, investment, productivity, distribution of wealth), while Barber, the sociologist, discusses major reactions to the neoliberalism that accompanies globalization. For Barber, these reactions form two opposed trends: consumerism and capitalist rationality, on the one hand, nativist reaction and withdrawal, on the other. For Appadurai, the questions of value come forward more strongly. Unlike Thurow, he does not limit himself to market valuations and the concomitant tendency to treat all objects as commodities. Unlike Barber, he sees that there are more alternatives to the local views toward globalization than an acceptance or a rejection of this form of market valuation. Appadurai shows that local peoples have complex perceptions of globalization, that they are engaged in complex forms of commentary on and critique of globalization, and that they often seek to expand public debate about globalization.

The authors in this volume share with Appadurai the interest in local forms of cultural and ideological engagement with globalization. However, they are distinctive in that they have tended to study the people who remain in place, rather than the people who migrate or who are displaced. The authors in this volume, moreover, find the commentary on globalization not only in symbolic representations and performative activities in spheres of expressive culture; they look to economic production and political mobilization. The authors who discuss culturally elaborate responses to globalization, such as Goldin in her examination of Protestantism in Guatemala or Young and Bort in their treatment of Ngóbe indigenous activism, link their accounts to economic processes of resource control and employment opportunities. In a similar fashion, there are accounts of local cultural debates over the economic justice of the world market even in the chapters that seem most directly tied to conventional economic anthropological studies of production and work, such as Waterbury's account of fruit and vegetable production and McDonald's study of dairying. In these cases, collective social action emerges as a response to economic change linked to globalization. In some of these cases, the authors note in this collective action a form of local commentary on the failure of market and state mechanisms to meet local needs; this commentary, in turn, draws on global and local ideologies. These local comments on and critiques of globalization, linked not only to cultural discourse but also to economic and political practice, may be one of the most important processes associated with globalization, and one that anthropologists are well positioned to document and to analyze.

References

Aberle, D. F. 1966. *The Peyote Religion Among the Navaho.* Chicago: Aldine Publishing Co.

Aguilar, Silvio. 1995. "Continúan en la Extrema Pobreza 408 Municipios." *Noticias,* January 18.

Ahmed, Akbar S., and Chris N. Shore, eds. 1995. *The Future of Anthropology: Its Relevance to the Contemporary World.* London: Athlone Press.

Anonymous. 1993. "Continua la injusticia." *Drü* 6(35–36):19.

Aparicio, J. R. 1995. "Notindio." *Drü* 8(45):16.

Appadurai, Arjun. 1997. *Modernity at Large: Cultural Dimensions of Globalization.* Minneapolis: University of Minnesota Press.

Appendini, Kirsten. 1992. *De la Milpa a los Tortibonos: La Restructuración de la Política Alimentaria en México.* Mexico: El Colegio de México.

Aramburú, Carlos. 1984. "Expansion of the Agrarian and Demographic Frontiers in the Peruvian Amazon." In *Frontier Expansion in Amazonia,* ed. M. Schminck and C. Wood, pp. 153–179. Gainesville: University of Florida Press.

Arsen, David D. 1996. "The NAFTA Debate in Retrospect: U.S. Perspectives." In *Policy Choices: Free Trade Among NAFTA Nations,* ed. Karen Roberts and Mark I. Wilson, pp. 37–58. East Lansing: Michigan State University Press.

Asturias de Barrios, Linda, coords. 1996. *Producción agrícola en Santa María Cauqué.* Guatemala: Asociación de Investigación y Estudios Sociales (hereafter ASIES).

Asturias de Barrios, Linda, Brenda Tevalán, and Sergio Romero. 1996. "Socioeconomic Impacts on Non-Traditional Export Crops in Guatemala: A Literature Review." Draft paper for the Integrated Pest Management Collaborative Research Support Program, Guatemala, July.

Avance Económico (Peru). 1996. "Perspectiva macroeconómico." Accessible at http://ekeko.rcp.net.pe/AVANCE/revista.htm.

AVANCSO (Asociación para el Avance de las Ciencias Sociales en Guatemala). 1994. *El Significado de la Maquila en Guatemala.* Cuadernos de Investigación No. 10. Guatemala: AVANCSO.

AVANCSO/PACCA. 1992. "Growing Dilemmas: Guatemala, the Environment, and the Global Economy." Guatemala: AVANCSO.

Baer, Werner, and William Maloney. 1997. "Neoliberalism and Income Distribution in Latin America." *World Development* 25(3):311–327.

Barber, Benjamin. 1995. *Jihad vs. McWorld: How Globalism and Tribalism Are Reshaping the World.* New York: Ballantine.

Barham, Bradford, Mary Clark, Elizabeth Katz, and Rachel Schurman. 1992. "Nontraditional Exports in Latin America." *Latin American Research Review* 27(2):43–82.

Barkin, David. 1987. "The End of Food Self-Sufficiency in Mexico." *Latin American Perspectives* 14(3):271–298.

Barlett, Peggy F. 1990. "Industrial Agriculture." In *Economic Anthropology,* ed. Stuart Plattner, pp. 253–291. Stanford, CA: Stanford University Press.

Beals, Ralph L. 1975. *The Peasant Marketing System of Oaxaca, Mexico.* Berkeley: University of California Press.

Bennett, John W. 1988. "Anthropology and Development: The Ambiguous Engagement." *Development* 4 (1988):6–16.

Berger, Bennett M. 1995. *An Essay on Culture: Symbolic and Social Structure.* Berkeley: University of California Press.

Binger, Brian, and Elizabeth Hoffman. 1989. "Institutional Persistence and Change: The Question of Efficiency." *Journal of Institutional and Theoretical Economics* 145:67–84.

Bodley, John H. 1990. *Victims of Progress.* 3rd ed. Mountain View, CA: Mayfield.

Bohren, Lenora, and Pam Puntenny. 1996. "Targeting Anthropology in the Marketplace." *Society for Applied Anthropology Newsletter* 6:3.

Bonfil Batalla, Guillermo. 1990. "Aculturación e Indigenismo: La Respuesta India." In *Indianismo e Indigenismo en América,* ed. José Alcina French, pp. 189–209. Madrid: Alianza Editorial.

Boo, Elizabeth. 1990. *Ecotourism: The Potentials and Pitfalls.* Country Case Studies, vol. 2. Washington, DC: World Wildlife Fund.

Bort, John R. 1976. "Guaymí Innovators: A Case Study of Entrepreneurs in a Small Scale Society." Unpublished Ph.D. diss., Department of Anthropology, University of Oregon, Eugene.

Bort, John R., and Philip D. Young. 1985. "Economic and Political Adaptations to National Development Among the Guaymí." *Anthropological Quarterly* 58(1): 1–12.

———. 1982. "New Roles for Males in Guaymí Society." In *Sex Roles and Social Change in Native Lower Central American Societies,* ed. C. and F. Loveland. Urbana: University of Illinois Press.

Bourgois, Philippe. 1989. *Ethnicity at Work: Divided Labor on a Central American Banana Plantation.* Baltimore: Johns Hopkins University Press.

———. 1985. *Ethnic Diversity on a Corporate Plantation: Guaymí Labor on a United Brands Subsidiary in Bocas del Toro, Panama, and Talamanca, Costa Rica.* Cultural Survival Occasional Paper No. 19. Cambridge, MA: Cultural Survival.

Bousquet, Earl. 1996. "Stories by Earl Bousquet." *Guyana News,* March 6, 1996.

Brecher, Jeremy, and Tim Costello. 1994. *Global Village or Global Pillage: Economic Reconstruction from the Bottom Up.* Boston: South End Press.

Brehm, Monica Rios, and Jorge Quíroz Castro. 1995. "The Market for Water Rights in Chile: Major Issues." World Bank Technical Paper No. 285. Washington, DC: World Bank.

Britnell, George E. [1951] 1958. "Problemas del Cambio Económico y Social en Guatemala." In *Economía de Guatemala,* Seminario de Integración Social Guatemalteca, pp. 47–77. Guatemala: Editorial del Ministerio de Educación Pública.

Brown, Michael. 1996. "On Resisting Resistance." *American Anthropologist* 98(4): 729–735.

Butler, Richard. 1990. "Tourism, Heritage, and Sustainable Development." In *Heritage Conservation and Sustainable Development,* ed. J. G. Nelson and S. Woodley, pp. 49–66. Waterloo: University of Waterloo, Heritage Resources Center.

Butterworth, Douglass. 1977. "Selectivity of Outmigration from a Mixteca Community. *Urban Anthropology* 6(2):129–139.

———. 1975. "Rural-Urban Migration and Microdemography: A Case Study from Mexico." *Urban Anthropology* 4(3):265–283.

Calí, Francisco. 1992. "Interview with Francisco Calí: 'We Must Join Hands . . .'" *Report on Guatemala* 13(3):2–4.

Calva, Jose Luis. 1993. *La Disputa por la Tierra: La Reforma del Articulo 27 y La Nueva Ley Agraria.* Mexico: Editorial Fontarama.

Carlos, Manuel L. 1981. "State Policies, State Penetration, and Ecology: A Comparative Analysis of Uneven Development and Underdevelopment in Mexico's Micro Agrarian Regions." Mexican Studies No. 19. La Jolla: U.S.-Mexico Studies Center, University of California, San Diego.

Carter, Michael, and Bradford Barham. 1997. "Level Playing Fields and *Laissez Faire:* Postliberal Development Strategy in Inegalitarian Agrarian Economies." *World Development* 24(7):1133–1149.

CEPAL (Comisión Económico para América Latina). 1994. "Social Panorama of Latin America." *CEPAL News* 14(7):1–3.

CEPAL/INEGI (Instituto Nacional de Estadística, Geografía, e Informática). 1993. *Magnitud y evolución de la pobreza en México, 1984–1992.* Mexico City: UN-CEPAL and INEGI.

Cernea, Michael. 1996. *Social Organization and Development Anthropology.* Environmentally Sustainable Development Studies and Monograph Series No. 6. Washington, DC: World Bank.

———. 1991. "Knowledge from Social Sciences for Development Policies and Projects." In *Putting People First: Sociological Variables in Rural Development,* 2nd ed., ed. Michael Cernea, pp. 1–41. Oxford: Oxford University Press.

Chayanov, A. V. 1966. *Theory of Peasant Economy.* Homewood, IL: Richard Irwin.

COESPO (Consejo Estatal de Población de Oaxaca). 1993. *Oaxaca: Población y Futuro,* No 13. Oaxaca: Consejo Estatal de Población de Oaxaca.

Cohen, Anthony. 1994. *Self-Consciousness: An Alternative Anthropology to Consciousness.* New York: Routledge.

Cohen, E. 1979. "The Impact of Tourism on the Hill-Tribes of Northern Thailand." *Internationales Asienforum* 10(5):5–38.

Collins, Jane L. 1993. "Gender, Contracts, and Wage Work: Agricultural Restructuring in Brazil's Sao Francisco Valley." *Development and Change* 21(1):53–82.

———. 1988. *Unseasonal Migrations: The Effects of Rural Labor Scarcity in Peru.* Princeton, NJ: Princeton University Press.

Conroy, Michael, Douglas Murray, and Peter Rosset. 1996. *A Cautionary Tale: Failed U.S. Development Policy in Central America.* Boulder, CO: Lynne Rienner Publishers.

Cook, Scott, and Leigh Binford. 1990. *Obliging Need: Rural Petty Industry in Mexican Capitalism.* Austin: University of Texas Press.

Cook, Scott, and Martin Diskin, eds. 1975. *Markets in Oaxaca.* Austin: University of Texas Press.

Cordera, Rolando, and Carlos Tello. 1984. *La Desigualdad en Mexico.* Mexico: Siglo XXI.

Cornelius, Wayne A., and David Myhre, eds. 1998. *The Transformation of Rural Mexico: Reforming the Ejido Sector.* La Jolla: U.S.-Mexico Studies Center, University of California, San Diego.

Cornelius, Wayne A., Ann L. Craig, and Jonathan Fox, eds. 1994. *Transforming State-Society Relations in Mexico: The National Solidarity Strategy.* La Jolla: U.S.-Mexico Studies Center, University of California, San Diego.

Coronel Ortiz, Dolores. 1997. "Redes de Comercialización e Intercambio de las Hortalizas en la Central de Abastos de la Ciudad de Oaxaca." Master's thesis, Ciencias en Desarrollo Rural Regional, Universidad Autónoma Chapingo.

Costa, Alberto C. G., Conrad Kottak, Rosane M. Prado, and John Stiles. 1995. "Ecological Awareness and Risk Perception in Brazil." In *Global Ecosystems: Creating Options Through Anthropological Perspectives,* ed. Pamela J. Puntenney, pp. 71–87. National Association for the Practice of Anthropology (NAPA) Bulletin No. 15. Washington, DC: American Anthropological Association.

Dann, G., D. Nash, and P. Pearce. 1988. "Methodology in Tourism Research." *Annals of Tourism Research* 15:1–28.

Davis, Sheldon H. 1976. *Victims of the Miracle: Development Against the Indians of Brazil.* Cambridge: Cambridge University Press.

de Janvry, Alain, Elisabeth Sadoulet, and Linda Wilcox Young. 1989. "Land and Labour in Latin American Agriculture from the 1950s to the 1980s." *Journal of Peasant Studies* 16(3):396–424.

DeKadt, E., ed. 1979. *Tourism: Passport to Development?* Oxford: Oxford University Press.

DeWalt, Billie, and Martha Rees. 1994. *The End of Agrarian Reform in Mexico: Past Lessons, Future Prospects.* La Jolla: U.S.-Mexico Studies Center, University of California, San Diego.

Dornbusch, Roger. 1988. "Peru on the Brink." *Challenge* (November–December 1988):31–37.

Drü 1997. "Ley 10 del 7 de marzo de 1997, por la cual se crea la Comarca Ngóbe-Buglé y se toman otras medidas." 10(54):4–18.

Durand, Jorge, and Douglas Massey. 1992. "Mexican Migration to the United States: A Critical Review." *Latin American Research Review* 27(2):3–42.

Durham, William. 1995. "Political Ecology and Environmental Destruction in Latin America." In *The Social Causes of Environmental Destruction in Latin America,* ed. M. Painter and W. Durham, pp. 249–264. Ann Arbor: University of Michigan Press.

Durrenberger, E. Paul. 1980. "Chayanov's Economic Analysis in Anthropology." *Journal of Anthropological Research* 36(2):133–148.

Easter, William, and Robert Hearne. 1994. "Water Markets and Decentralized Water Resources Management." Department of Agricultural and Applied Economics, College of Agriculture, University of Minnesota.

ECLAC (Economic Commission for Latin America and the Caribbean). 1997. *Progress in the Privatization of Water-Related Public Services: A Country-by-Country Review for South America.* Santiago: ECLAC.

Edwards, Sebastian, and Simon Teitel. 1986. "Growth, Reform, and Adjustment: Latin America's Trade and Macroeconomic Policies in the 1970's and 1980's." *Economic Development and Cultural Change* 34(3):423–431.

Embriz, Arnulfo, et al. 1993. *Indicadores Socioeconómicos de los Pueblos Indígenas de Mexico.* Mexico: Instituto Nacional Indigenista.

Escobar, Arturo. 1995. *Encountering Development: The Making and Unmaking of the Third World.* Princeton, NJ: Princeton University Press.

Escobar, Arturo, and S. Alvarez. 1992. *The Making of Social Movements in Latin America*. Boulder, CO: Westview Press.

Esteva, Gustavo. 1980. *La Batalla en el Mexico Rural*. Mexico: Siglo XXI.

FAO (Food and Agricultural Organization). 1988. *Potentials for Agricultural and Rural Development in Latin America and the Caribbean*. Rome: FAO.

Fernandez-Kelly, María Patricia. 1983. "Mexican Border Industrialization, Female Labor Force Participation, and Migration." In *Women, Men, and the International Division of Labor*, ed. June Nash and María Patricia Fernandez-Kelly. Albany: State University of New York Press.

Fonseca Martel, Cesar. 1983. "El control comunal del agua en la cuenca del rio Cañete." *Allpanchis* 22:61–73.

Forte, Jannette. 1996. *About Guyanese Amerindians*. Georgetown, Guyana: Janettte Forte.

Forte, Jannette, and Ian Melville. 1989. *Amerindian Testimonies*. Georgetown, Guyana: Janette Forte.

Foucault, Michel. 1988. *Technologies of the Self: A Seminar with Michel Foucault,* ed. Luther H. Martin, Huck Gutman, and Patrick H. Hutton. Amherst: University of Massachusetts Press.

Fox, Jonathan. 1994. "Targeting the Poorest: The Role of the National Indigenous Institute in Mexico's Solidarity Program." In Cornelius, Craig, and Fox 1994 (op. cit.), pp. 179–216

———. 1993. *The Politics of Food in Mexico: State Power and Social Mobilization*. Ithaca, NY: Cornell University Press.

Fox, Jonathan, and Josefina Aranda. 1996. *Decentralization and Rural Development in Mexico: Community Participation in Oaxaca's Municipal Funds Program*. La Jolla: U.S.-Mexico Studies Center, University of California, San Diego.

Fox, Jonathan, and Julio Moguel. 1995. "Pluralism and Anti-Poverty Policy: Mexico's National Solidarity Program and Left Opposition Municipal Governments." In *Opposition Government in Mexico: Past Experience and Future Opportunities,* ed. Peter Ward and Victoria Rodriguez, pp. 180–203. Albuquerque: University of New Mexico Press.

Friedrich, Paul. 1977. *Agrarian Revolt in a Mexican Village*. Chicago: University of Chicago Press.

Garcilaso de la Vega. [1609] 1966. *Royal Commentaries of the Incas and General History of Peru*. 2 vols. Austin: University of Texas Press.

Garrard Burnett, V. 1990. "Positivismo, Liberalismo e Impulso Misionero: Misiones Protestantes en Guatemala, 1880–1920." *Mesoamerica* 11:13–31.

Gates, Marilyn. 1993. *In Default: Peasants, the Debt Crisis, and the Agricultural Challenge in Mexico*. Boulder, CO: Westview Press.

Gelles, Paul. 1994. "Channels of Power, Fields of Contention: The Politics of Irrigation and Land Recovery in an Andean Peasant Community." In *Irrigation at High Altitudes: The Social Organization of Water Control Systems in the Andes,* ed. W. Mitchell and D. W. Guillet, pp. 233–274. Arlington: American Anthropological Association.

———. 1988. "Los hijos de Hualca Hualca: Historia de Cabanaconde." Serie Aportes No. 1. Arequipa: Centro de Apoyo y Promocíon al Desarrollo Agrario.

Georges, Eugenia. 1990. *The Making of a Transnational Community: Migration, Development, and Cultural Change in the Dominican Republic*. New York: Columbia University Press.

GEXPRONT/AGEXPRONT (Asociación Gremial de Exportadores de No Tradicionales de Guatemala). 1998. "Exportaciones de Productos No Tradicionales

Según Ingreso de Divisas, 1990–1997." Internet address, Fuente BANGUAT: www.quezalnet.com/gexpront/ingreso dd.htm.

———. 1997. "Origin of the Capital." Guatemala: Quota Office, July.

Giddens, Anthony. 1984. *The Constitution of Society: Outline of the Theory of Structuration.* Berkeley: University of California Press.

Gil Olcina, Antonio. 1994. *La propiedad de aguas perennes en el sureste ibérico.* Alicante: Universidad de Alicante.

Gjording, Chris N. 1991. *Conditions Not of Their Choosing: The Guaymí Indians and Mining Multinationals in Panama.* Washington, DC: Smithsonian Institution Press.

Gledhill, John. 1991. *Casi Nada: A Study of Agrarian Reform in the Homeland of Cardenismo.* Austin: University of Texas Press.

Glewwe, Paul, and Dennis de Tray. 1989. *The Poor in Latin America During Adjustment: A Case Study of Peru.* Living Standards Measurement Study Working Paper No. 56. Washington, DC: World Bank.

Goldin, Liliana. 1997a. "Economic Restructuring and New Forms of Market Participation in Rural Latin America." In *The Politics of Social Change and Economic Restructuring in Latin America,* ed. R. P. Korzeniewics and W. Smith. Boulder, CO: North South Center and Lynne Rienner Publishers.

———. 1997b. "Fabricando Identidades: Mayas y Ladinos en la Producción Industrial." Paper presented at the Second Congress of Maya Studies, Guatemala, August.

———. 1996. "Economic Mobility Strategies Among Guatemalan Peasants: Prospects and Limits of Nontraditional Vegetable Cash Crops." *Human Organization* 55(1):99–107.

———. 1992. "Work and Ideology in the Maya Highlands of Guatemala: Economic Beliefs in the Context of Occupational Change." *Economic Development and Cultural Change* 41(1):103–124.

———. n.d. "Maquila Age Maya: The Changing Nature of 'Community' in the Central Highlands of Guatemala." Unpublished manuscript, State University of New York at Albany.

Goldin, Liliana, and Brent Metz. 1991. "An Expression of Cultural Change: Invisible Converts to Protestantism Among Highland Guatemala Mayas." *Ethnology* 30(4):325–338.

Goldin, Liliana, and María Eugenia Saenz de Tejada. 1993. "Uneven Development in Western Guatemala." *Ethnology* 32(3):237–252.

González, Luis. 1972. *Pueblo en Vilo: Microhistoria de San José de Gracia.* Mexico: El Colegio de México.

Goodland, Robert, H. Daly, and S. el Serafy. 1992. *Population, Technology, and Lifestyle: The Transition to Sustainability.* Washington, DC: Island Press.

Gorriz, Cecilia, Ashok Subramanian, and José Simas. 1995. "Irrigation Management Transfer in Mexico: Process and Progress." World Bank Technical Paper No. 292. Washington, DC: World Bank.

Graburn, Nelson H. H. 1995. "Tourism, Modernity, and Nostalgia." In *The Future of Anthropology: Its Relevance to the Contemporary World,* ed. Akbar S. Ahmed and Cris N. Shore, pp. 158–178. London: Athlone Press.

Grammont, Hubert C. de, coord. 1995. *Globalización, Deterioro Ambiental, y Reorganización Social en el Campo.* Mexico: Juan Pablo Editor.

Grammont, Hubert C. de, and Hector Tejera Gaona, coords. 1996. *La Sociedad Rural Mexicana Frente al Nuevo Milenio.* 4 vols. Mexico: Plaza y Valdes Editores.

Greenberg, James. 1997. "A Political Ecology of Structural-Adjustment Policies: The Case of the Dominican Republic." *Culture and Agriculture* 19(3):85–93.

Guillet, David. 1998. "Rethinking Legal Pluralism: Local Law and State Law in the Evolution of Water Property Rights in Northwestern Spain." *Comparative Studies in Society and History* 40(1):42–70.

———. 1997. "The Politics of Sustainable Agriculture in Europe: Water Demand Management in Spain." *South European Society and Politics* 2(1):97–117.

———. 1994. "Canal Irrigation and the State: The 1969 Water Law and Irrigation Systems of the Colca Valley of Southwestern Peru." In *Irrigation at High Altitudes: The Social Organization of Water Control Systems in the Andes,* ed. W. Mitchell and David W. Guillet, pp. 167–187. Arlington: American Anthropological Association.

———. 1992. *Covering Ground: Communal Water Management and the State in the Peruvian Highlands.* Ann Arbor: University of Michigan Press

———. 1981. "Surplus Extraction, Risk Management, and Economic Change Among Peruvian Peasants." *Journal of Development Studies* 18:3–24.

Guillet, David W., and W. Mitchell. 1994. "Introduction: High Altitude Irrigation." In *Irrigation at High Altitudes: The Social Organization of Water Control Systems in the Andes,* ed. W. Mitchell and David W. Guillet, pp. 1–20. Arlington, VA: American Anthropological Association.

Hardoy, Jorge E., Diana Mitlin, and David Satterwaite. 1992. *Environmental Problems in Third World Cities.* London: Earthscan Publications.

Harrell, Marielouise, Cutberto Parillon, and Ralph Franklin. 1989. "Nutritional Classification Study of Peru: Who and Where Are the Poor?" *Food Policy* (November 1989):313–329.

Hernández, Edin. 1997. "Artesanías en busca del mercado perdido." *Crónica,* May 16.

Hewitt de Alcántara, Cynthia. 1976. *Modernizing Mexican Agriculture: Socioeconomic Implications of Technological Change, 1940–1970.* Geneva: United Nations Research Institute for Social Development, Report No. 765.

Hobart, Mark. 1993. "Introduction: The Growth of Ignorance." In *An Anthropological Critique of Development: The Growth of Ignorance,* ed. Mark Hobart, pp. 1–30. New York: Routledge.

Holmstrom, Mark. 1984. *Industry and Inequality. The Social Anthropology of Indian Labour.* Cambridge: Cambridge University Press.

Hopenhayn, Martin. 1993. "Postmodernism and Neoliberalism in Latin America." *Boundary 2* 20(3):93–109.

Howe, Jim. 1986. *The Kuna Gathering: Contemporary Village Politics in Panama.* Austin: University of Texas Press.

Hughes, L. H. 1950. "The Mexican Cultural Mission Program." UN Educational, Scientific, and Cultural Organization Monographs on Fundamental Education No. 3. Paris: United Nations.

IDB (Inter-American Development Bank). 1996. "Peru: General Social and Economic Data." (Internet address, IDB home page: http://iadb6000.iadb.org/~http/pics/logomed.gif.

IFPRI (International Food Policy Research Institute). 1995. "A 2020 Vision for Food, Agriculture, and the Environment in Latin America," ed. James L. Garrett. Food, Agriculture, and the Environment Discussion Paper No. 6. Washington, DC: IFPRI.

Instituto Nacional de Planificación. 1983. *Diagnóstico microregional de las provincias altas de Arequipa-Cailloma.* Arequipa: Instituto Nacional de Planificación.

Jaén C. B. 1994. "Salvar la tierra Ngóbe." *Drü* 7(42):14.

———. 1991. "Los proyectos estatales y el pueblo Ngóbe." *Drü* 4(22):13.

Janick, J., R. W. Schery, F. W. Woods, and V. W. Ruttan. 1974. *Plant Science: An Introduction to World Crops.* 2nd ed. San Francisco: W. H. Freeman.

Johnston, Barbara. 1997. *Life and Death Matters: Human Rights and the Environment at the End of the Millennium.* Walnut Creek, CA: Altamira Press.

———. 1994. *Who Pays the Price: The Sociocultural Context of Environmental Crisis.* Washington, DC: Island Press.

Johnston, Bruce, and John Mellor. 1961. "The Role of Agriculture in Economic Development." *American Economic Review* 51(4):566–593.

Jones, Jeffery R. 1990. *Colonization and the Environment: Land Settlement Projects in Central America.* Tokyo: United Nations University Press.

Kearney, Michael. 1996. *Reconceptualizing the Peasantry: Anthropology in Global Perspective.* Boulder, CO: Westview Press.

Kirkby, Anne V. T. 1973. *The Use of Land and Water Resources in the Past and Present Valley of Oaxaca, Mexico.* Memoirs of the Museum of Anthropology No. 5. Ann Arbor: University of Michigan.

Korten, David. 1995. *When Corporations Rule the World.* London: Kumarian Press.

Krippendorf, J. 1982. "Towards New Tourism Policies." *Tourism Management* 3:135–148.

Lanfant, Marie-Francoise, and Nelson H. H. Graburn. 1992. "International Tourism Reconsidered: The Principle of the Alternative." In *Tourism Alternatives: Potentials and Problems in the Development of Tourism,* ed. Valene L. Smith and William R. Eadington, pp. 89–112. Philadelphia: University of Pennsylvania Press.

Lees, Susan. 1975. "Oaxaca's Spiraling Race for Water." *Natural History* 84(4).

Lewis, Arthur. 1954. "Economic Development with Unlimited Supplies of Labor." *Manchester School* 22 (May):139–192.

Lipton, Michael. 1977. *Why Poor People Stay Poor: Urban Bias in Rural Development.* Cambridge, MA: Harvard University Press.

Loker, William. 1996. "Campesinos and the Crisis of Modernization in Latin America." *Journal of Political Ecology* 3:69–88.

Love, Thomas F. 1989. "Limits to the Articulation of Modes of Production Approach: The Southwestern Peru Region" In *State, Capital, and Rural Society: Anthropological Perspectives on Political Economy in Mexico and the Andes,* ed. Benjamin S. Orlove, M. W. Foley, and Thomas F. Love, pp. 147–179. Boulder, CO: Westview Press.

MacCannell, Dean. 1992. *Empty Meeting Grounds.* New York: Routledge.

Mander, Jerry. 1996. "The Dark Side of Globalization: What the Media Are Missing." *The Nation,* July 15–22, pp. 9–13.

McDonald, James H. 1997. "Privatizing the Private Family Farmer: NAFTA and the Transformation of the Mexican Dairy Sector." *Human Organization* 56(3): 321–332.

———. 1996. "The Milk War: The Effects of NAFTA on Dairy Farmers in the United States and Mexico." In *Policy Choices: Free Trade Among NAFTA Nations,* ed. Karen Roberts and Mark I. Wilson, pp. 75–105. East Lansing: Michigan State University Press.

McKean, P. 1976. "Tourism, Culture Change, and Culture Conversion." In *Ethnic Identity in Modern Southeast Asia,* ed. D. Banks. The Hague: Mouton.

McKinley, Terry, and D. Alarcón. 1995. "The Prevalence of Rural Poverty in Mexico." *World Development* 23(9):1575–1585.

McMichael, Philip. 1996. *Development and Social Change: A Global Perspective.* Thousand Oaks, CA: Pine Forge Press.

Mendizábal, Ana Beatriz, and Jürgen Weller, coords. 1992. *Exportaciones Agrícolas No Tradicionales del Istmo Centroamericano: ¿Promesa o Espejismo?* Panama: CADESCA.

Michie, Barry H. 1994. "Reevaluating Economic Rationality: Individuals, Information, and Institutions." In *Anthropology and Institutional Economics,* ed. J. M. Acheson. Lanham, MD: University Press of America.

Moguel, Julio. 1994. "Salinas' Failed War on Poverty." *NACLA Report on the Americas* 28(1):38–41.

Moreno García, Heriberto. 1981. *Cotija.* Mexico: Monografía Municipal del Estado de Michoacán.

Morley, Samuel. 1992. "Structural Adjustment and the Determinants of Poverty in Latin America." Occasional Paper. Washington, DC: Vanderbilt University and the Inter-American Development Bank, July.

Murray, Douglas. 1994. *Cultivating Crisis: The Human Costs of Pesticide Use in Latin America.* Austin: University of Texas Press.

Nash, Dennison. 1995. "Prospects for Tourism Study in Anthropology." In *The Future of Anthropology: Its Relevance to the Contemporary World,* ed. Akbar S. Ahmed and Cris N. Shore, pp. 179–202. London: Athlone Press.

Nash, June. 1983. "The Impact of the Changing International Division of Labor on Different Sectors of the Labor Force." In *Women, Men, and the International Division of Labor,* ed. June Nash and María Patricia Fernandez-Kelly. Albany: State University of New York Press.

Netting, Robert McC. 1993. *Smallholders, Householders: Farm Families and the Ecology of Intensive, Sustainable Agriculture.* Palo Alto, CA: Stanford University Press.

North, Douglass C. 1990. *Institutions, Institutional Change, and Economic Performance.* Cambridge: Cambridge University Press.

North, Douglass C., and Robert P. Thomas. 1973. *The Rise of the Western World: A New Economic History.* Cambridge: Cambridge University Press.

Nyoni, S. 1987. "Indigenous NGOs: Liberation, Self-Reliance, and Development." In *Development Alternatives,* ed. Anne Gordon Drabek, pp. 51–66. Oxford: Pergamon Press.

Ong, Aihwa. 1987. *Spirits of Resistance and Capitalist Discipline: Factory Women in Malaysia.* Albany: State University of New York Press.

Ostrom, Elinor. 1990. *Governing the Commons: The Evolution of Institutions for Collective Action.* Cambridge: Cambridge University Press.

Otero, Gerardo, ed. 1996. *Neoliberalism Revisited: Economic Restructuring and Mexico's Political Future.* Boulder, CO: Westview Press.

Ottey, B. 1977. "Los Maestros Voluntarios Guaymíes." Nota de Trabajo No. 1. Unpublished document for the Interamerican Development Institute Plan Guaymí.

Paerregaard, Karsten. 1994. "Why Fight over Water? Power, Conflict, and Irrigation in an Andean Village." In *Irrigation at High Altitudes: The Social Organization of Water Control Systems in the Andes,* ed. W. Mitchell and David W. Guillet, pp. 189–202. Arlington, VA: American Anthropological Association.

———. 1989. "Exchanging with Nature: T'inka in an Andean Village." *Folk* 31:53–75.

Pasaran Jarquín, Carlos. 1998. "Sequía en el Granero." *Noticias,* January 22.

Pastor, Manuel, and Carol Wise. 1992. "Peruvian Economic Policy in the 1980s: From Orthodoxy to Heterodoxy and Back." *Latin American Research Review* 27(2):83–118.

Paus, Eva, ed. 1988. *Struggle Against Dependence: Nontraditional Export Growth in Central America and the Caribbean.* Boulder, CO: Westview Press.

Peck, Jamie, and A. Tickell. 1994. "Jungle Law Breaks Out: Neoliberalism and Global-Local Disorder." *Area* 26(4):317–326.

Petersen, Kurt. 1992. *The Maquiladora Revolution in Guatemala.* Occasional Paper Series No. 2. New Haven, CT: Orville H. Schell Jr. Center for International Human Rights at Yale Law School.

Petras, James, and S. Vieux. 1992a. "Myths and Realities: Latin America's Free Markets." *Monthly Review* 44(1):9–20.

———. 1992b. "Twentieth Century Neoliberals: Inheritors of the Exploits of Columbus." *Latin American Perspectives* 19(3):25–46.

Plusquellec, Herve, Charles Burt, and Hans W. Wolter. 1994. "Modern Water Control in Irrigation: Concepts, Issues and Applications." World Bank Technical Paper No. 246. Washington, DC: World Bank.

Polanyi, Karl. 1944. *The Great Transformation.* Boston: Beacon Press.

Porter, Gina, and Kevin Phillips-Howard. 1997. "Comparing Contracts: An Evaluation of Contract Farming Schemes in Africa." *World Development* 25(2):227–238.

Portes, Alejandro, and Luis E. Guarnizo. 1990. *U.S. Bond Immigration and Small Enterprise Development in the Dominican Republic.* Occasion\al Paper No. 5. Baltimore: Johns Hopkins University, Department of Sociology.

Power, Grant. 1997. "Globalization and Its Discontents." *Development* 40(2):75–80.

Prud'homme, Jean-François, coord. 1995. *El impacto social de las políticas de ajuste en el campo mexicano.* Mexico: Plaza y Valdés.

Przeworski, Adam. 1992. "The Neoliberal Fallacy." *Journal of Democracy* 3(3): 45–59.

Ramales, Rosy. 1996. "Pobreza y Marginación, Coincidencias entre los Estados con Guerrilla." *Noticias,* July 1.

Randall, Laura, ed. 1996. *Reforming Mexico's Agrarian Reform.* Armonk, NY: M. E. Sharpe.

Reichert, Joshua S. 1981. "The Migrant Syndrome: Seasonal United States Wage Labor and Rural Development in Central Mexico." *Human Organization* 40(1):56–66.

República de Panamá, Dirección de Estadística y Censo. 1993. *Panamá en Cifras: Años 1987–1991.* Panama: Contraloría General de la República.

———. 1975. *Censos Nacionales de 1970.* Volumen III. Panama: Contraloría General de la República.

Reyes Osorio, Sergio, et al. 1974. *Estructura Agraria y Desarrollo Agrícola en Mexico.* Mexico: Fondo de Cultura Económica.

Richards, Paul. 1993. "Cultivation: Knowledge or Performance?" In *An Anthropological Critique of Development: The Growth of Ignorance,* ed. Mark Hobart, pp. 61–78. New York: Routledge.

Ricoeur, Paul. 1991. "Imagination in Discourse and Action." In Paul Ricoeur, *From Text to Action: Essays in Hermeneutics, Volume 2,* trans. Kathleen Blamey and John B. Thompson, pp. 168–187. Evanston, IL: Northwestern University Press.

Rios Vásquez, Othón. 1993. "Estudio de la Migración de Trabajadores Oaxaqueños a los Estados Unidos de America." In *Migración y Etnicidad en Oaxaca,* ed. Jack Corbett et al., pp. 25–34. Publications in Anthropology No. 43. Nashville, TN: Vanderbilt University.

Rodríguez Gómez, M. Guadalupe. 1995. "Las reformas al Articulo 27 y los tanques rancheros: Nuevos espacios de confrontación en Los Altos de Jalisco." Paper presented at the International Congress of the Latin American Studies Association, Washington, DC.

Rodríguez Hernández, Oscar. 1994. "Industrializan el Agua Destinada a la Agricultura." *El Sur,* December 4.

Rohter, L. 1996. "Known for Social Programs, Costa Rica Turns to Austerity." *New York Times* News Service, September 30. Internet address, LatinoLink: http://www.latinolink.com/biz/0930bcos.htm.

Rosenbaum, Brenda, and Liliana Goldin. 1997. "New Exchange Processes in the International Market: The Re-Making of Maya Artisan Production in Guatemala." *Museum Anthropology* 21(2):72–82.

Sachs, Wolfgang. 1992. *The Development Dictionary: A Guide to Knowledge as Power.* London: Zed Books.

Safa, Helen. 1983. "Women, Production, and Reproduction in Industrial Capitalism: A Comparison of Brazilian and U.S. Factory Workers." In *Women, Men, and the International Division of Labor,* ed. June Nash and María Patricia Fernandez-Kelly. Albany: State University of New York Press.

Sagasti, Francisco. 1995. "Knowledge and Development in a Fractured Global Order." *Futures* 27(6):571–610.

Sánchez Gómez, Martha Judith. 1995. "Actividades Económicas y Estrategias de Reproducción entre Comunidades Hablantes de Zapoteco en los Valles de Oaxaca." In Grammont 1995 (op. cit.), pp. 161–194.

Sanderson, Steven E. 1986. *The Transformation of Mexican Agriculture: International Structure and the Politics of Rural Change.* Princeton, NJ: Princeton University Press.

———. 1981. *Agrarian Populism and the Mexican State: The Struggle for Land in Sonora.* Berkeley: University of California Press.

Sandor, Jon. 1989. "Investigation of Agricultural Soils at Lari, Colca Valley, Peru." In *Cognitive and Behavioral Studies of Soil Management in the Colca Valley, Peru,* ed. David W. Guillet. Technical Report to the National Science Foundation Anthropology Program. Washington, DC: Catholic University of America, Department of Anthropology.

———. 1987. "Report on Soils in Agricultural Terraces in the Colca Valley, Peru." In *Prehistoric Agricultural Fields in the Central Andes,* pp. 163–192. Oxford: British Archaeological Reports, International Series.

Sandor, Jon A., and Louanna Furbee. 1996. "Indigenous Knowledge and Classification of Soils in the Andes of Southern Peru." *Soil Science Society of America Journal* 60:1502–1512.

Santos Martínez, Adalberto. 1992. "El Problema del Agua." *Cambio* 84 and 85.

Sarsanedas, J. 1995. "Basta ya." *Drü* 8(44):2.

Schiller, Nina Glick, Linda Basch, and Cristina Blanc-Szanton. 1992. *Towards a Transnational Perspective on Migration: Race, Class, Ethnicity, and Nationalism Reconsidered.* New York: New York Academy of Sciences.

Schultz, Theodore. 1964. *Transforming Traditional Agriculture.* New Haven, CT: Yale University Press.

Scott, James. 1990. *Domination and the Arts of Resistance.* New Haven, CT: Yale University Press.

———. 1985. *Weapons of the Weak: Everyday Forms of Peasant Resistance.* New Haven, CT: Yale University Press.

Shah, Tushaar. 1993. *Groundwater Markets and Irrigation Development.* Oxford: Oxford University Press.

Shiva, Vandana. 1996. "New Delhi Conference on Global Food Security." *IFGNEWS* (International Forum on Globalization) 1:6–7.

Siglo 21. 1996. "La mitad de los mexicanos no dispone de las calorías indispensables al día." July 16, p. 17.

Sklair, Leslie. 1989. *Assembling for Development. The Maquila Industry in Mexico and the United States.* Boston: Unwin Hyman.

Smith, Carol. 1990. *Guatemalan Indians and the State, 1540 to 1988.* Austin: University of Texas Press.

————. 1977. "How Marketing Systems Affect Economic Opportunity in Agrarian Societies." In *Peasant Livelihood,* ed. R. Halperin and J. Dow. New York: St. Martin's Press.

Smith, Valene L., and William R. Eadington, eds. 1992. *Tourism Alternatives: Potentials and Problems in the Development of Tourism.* Philadelphia: University of Pennsylvania Press.

Solomons, Noel, and R. Gross. 1987. "Urban Nutrition in the Tropics: A Call for Increased Attention to Metropolitan Population in the Developing World." *Food and Nutrition Bulletin* 9(March–June):43–44.

Sorroza, Carlos. 1990. "Cambios Agropecuarios y Crisis Alimentaria en Oaxaca (1949–1985)." *Estudios Sociológicos* 9(22).

Spalding, Rose. 1984. *The Mexican Food Crisis: An Analysis of the SAM.* La Jolla, CA: U.S.-Mexico Studies Center, University of California, San Diego.

Stavenhagen, Rodolfo, et al. 1968. *Neolatifundismo y Explotación: De Emiliano Zapata a Anderson Clayton & Co.* Mexico: Editorial Nuestro Tiempo.

Stephen, Lynn. 1991. *Zapotec Women.* Austin: University of Texas Press.

Stoll, David. 1990. *Is Latin America Turning Protestant? The Politics of Evangelical Growth.* Berkeley: University of California Press.

Stonich, Susan. 1993. *I Am Destroying the Land! The Political Ecology of Poverty and Environmental Destruction in Honduras.* Boulder, CO: Westview Press.

Tanski, Janet M. 1994. "The Impact of Crisis, Stabilization, and Structural Adjustment on Women in Lima, Peru." *World Development* 22(11):1627–1642.

Tardanico, Richard. 1993. "Dimensions of Structural Adjustment: Gender and Age in the Costa Rican Labour Market." *Development and Change* 24(3):511–540.

Taylor, William B. 1972. *Landlord and Peasant in Colonial Oaxaca.* Stanford, CA: Stanford University Press.

Tellez, Luis, coord. 1993. *Nueva Legislación de Tierras, Bosques y Aguas.* Mexico: Fondo de Cultura Económica.

Thompson, John B. 1990. *Ideology and Modern Culture.* Stanford, CA: Stanford University Press.

Thrupp, Lori Ann, Gilles Bergeron, and William F. Waters. 1995. *Bittersweet Harvest for Global Supermarkets: Challenges in Latin America's Agricultural Export Boom.* Washington, DC: World Resources Institute.

Thurow, Lester C. 1996. *The Future of Capitalism: How Today's Economic Forces Shape Tomorrow's World.* New York: William Morrow.

Treacy, John. 1992. "Teaching Water: Hydraulic Management and Terracing in Coporque, the Colca Valley, Peru." In *Irrigation at High Altitudes: The Social Organization of Water Control Systems in the Andes,* ed. W. Mitchell and David W. Guillet, pp. 99–114. Arlington, VA: American Anthropological Association.

————. 1989. "The Fields of Coporaque: Agricultural Terracing and Water Management in the Colca Valley, Arequipa, Peru." Ph.D. diss. Department of Geography, University of Wisconsin.

Trenbath, B. R., G. R. Conway, and I. A. Craig. 1990. "Threats to Sustainability in Intensified Agricultural Systems: Analysis and Implications for Management." In *Agroecology: Researching the Ecological Basis for Sustainable Agriculture,* ed. Stephen Gliessman, pp. 337–365. New York: Springer-Verlag.

Turkenik, Carole. 1975. "Agricultural Production Strategies in a Mexican Peasant Community." Unpublished Ph.D. diss., University of California, Los Angeles.

Ulin, Robert C. 1988. "Cooperation or Co-optation: A Southwest French Wine Co-operative." *Dialectical Anthropology* 13:253–267.

Valderrama, Ricardo F., and Carmen Escalante Gutiérrez. 1988. *Del tata mallku a la mama pacha: Riego, sociedad, y ritos en los Andes peruanos.* Lima: Centro de Estudios y Promoción del Desarrollo.

Valdés, Alberto, and Tom Wiens. 1996. "Rural Poverty in Latin America and the Caribbean." Paper presented at the World Bank Annual Conference on Development in Latin America and the Caribbean, Washington, DC, May 30.

Vandermeer, John, and Ivette Perfecto. 1995. *Breakfast of Biodiversity: The Truth About Rainforest Destruction.* Oakland, CA: Food First Books.

Vargas, Manuel. 1996. "Culture, Ideology, and Dwelling in Two Dominican Villages." *New West Indian Guide* 70(1–2):5–38.

Vasques, M. 1995. Personal communication with John Bort.

Voget, F. W. 1956. "The American Indian in Transition, Reformation, and Accommodation." *American Anthropologist* 58:249–263.

Von Braun, Maarten, D. Hotchkiss, and D. D. Immink. 1989. *Nontraditional Export Crops in Guatemala: Effects on Production, Income, and Nutrition.* Washington, DC: IFPRI.

Wallace, A. F. C. 1956. "Revitalization Movements." *American Anthropologist* 58:264–281.

Warren, Kay. 1992. "Transforming Memories and Histories: The Meaning of Ethnic Resurgence for Mayan Indians." In *Americas: New Interpretive Essays*, ed. Alfred Stepan, pp. 189–219. New York: Oxford University Press.

Waterbury, Ronald. 1996. "El Desestablecimiento De La Religión Comunitaria En Una Comunidad Oaxaqueña." Paper presented at the Second Biennial Conference of the Welte Institute for Oaxacan Studies, Oaxaca, Mexico, August 2.

———. 1989. "Embroidery for Tourists: A Contemporary Putting-Out System in Oaxaca, Mexico." In *Cloth and Human Experience*, ed. Jane Schneider and Annette Weiner, pp. 241–271. Washington, DC: Smithsonian Institution Press.

———. 1975. "Non-Revolutionary Peasants: Oaxaca Compared to Morelos in the Mexican Revolution." *Comparative Studies in Society and History* 17(4): 410–442.

———. 1970. "Urbanization and a Traditional Market System." In *Social Anthropology of Latin America*, ed. Walter Goldschmidt and Harry Hoijer, pp. 126–153. Los Angeles: Latin American Center, University of California, Los Angeles.

Waterbury, Ronald, and Carole Turkenik. 1976. "The Marketplace Traders of San Antonino: A Quantitative Analysis." In Cook and Diskin 1975 (op. cit.), pp. 209–229.

Webber, Ellen Robinson. 1988. "Alfalfa and Cattle in Achoma: A Study of Stability and Change." In *The Cultural Ecology, Archaeology, and History of Terracing and Terrace Abandonment in the Colca Valley of Southern Peru*, vol. 2, ed. William Denevan, pp. 91–111. Technical Report to the National Science Foundation (Anthropology Program). Madison: Department of Geography, University of Wisconsin.

White, T. Anderson, and C. Ford Runge. 1995. "The Emergence and Evolution of Collective Action: Lessons from Watershed Management in Haiti." *World Development* 23(10):1683–1698.

———. 1993. "Common Property and Collective Action: Lessons from Cooperative Watershed Management in Haiti." *Economic Development and Cultural Change* 43:1.

Whiteford, Scott, and Francisco A. Bernal. 1996. "Campesinos, Water, and the State: Different Views of La Transferencia." In Randall 1996 (op. cit.), pp. 223–234.

Wilkie, James W. 1993. *Statistical Abstract of Latin America,* vol. 30, part 1. Los Angeles: UCLA Latin American Center Publications.

Wilson, B. R. 1973. *Magic and the Millennium.* New York: Harper & Row.

Winterhalder, Bruce. 1994. "The Ecological Basis of Water Management in the Central Andes: Rainfall and Temperature in Southern Peru." *Irrigation at High Altitudes: The Social Organization of Water Control Systems in the Andes,* ed. W. Mitchell and David W. Guillet, pp. 21–68. Arlington, VA: American Anthropological Association.

Wolf, Eric R. 1969. *Peasant Wars of the Twentieth Century.* New York: Harper & Row.

Womack, John. 1969. *Zapata and the Mexican Revolution.* New York: Alfred A. Knopf.

World Bank. 1992. *World Development Report, 1992: Development and the Environment.* New York: Oxford University Press.

Xie, Mei, Ulrich Küffner, and Guy Le Moigne. 1993. "Using Water Efficiently: Technological Options." World Bank Technical Paper No. 205. Washington, DC: World Bank.

Young, Frank W., Donald K. Freebairn, and Reuben Snipper. 1979. "The Structural Context of Rural Poverty in Mexico: A Cross-State Comparison." *Economic Development and Cultural Change* 27(4):669–686.

Young, Philip D. 1985. "Guaymí Socionatural Adaptations." In *The Botany and Natural History of Panama,* ed. W. G. D'Arcy and M. D. Correa A., pp. 357–365. St. Louis: Missouri Botanical Garden.

———. 1978a. "Los Rituales Guaymíes: Perspectivas Simbólicas y Culturales." *Revista Patrimonio Histórico* 2(1):7–38.

———. 1978b. "La trayectoria de una religión: El movimiento de Mama Chi entre los Guaymíes y sus consecuencias sociales." *La Antigua* 11:45–75.

———. 1976. "The Expression of Harmony and Discord in a Guaymí Ritual: The Symbolic Meaning of Some Aspects of the Balsería." In *Frontier Adaptations in Lower Central America,* ed. M. Helms and F. Loveland, pp. 37–53. Philadelphia: Institute for the Study of Human Issues.

———. 1975. "Guaymí Nativism: Its Rise and Demise." *Proceedings of the XLI International Congress of Americanists, Volume 3,* pp. 93–101. Mexico, D.F.

———. 1971. *Ngawbe: Tradition and Change Among the Western Guaymí of Panama.* Illinois Studies in Anthropology No. 7. Urbana: University of Illinois Press.

———. 1970. "Notes on the Ethnohistorical Evidence for Structural Continuity in Guaymí Society." *Ethnohistory* 17(1–2):11–29.

Young, Philip D., and John R. Bort. 1979. "The Politicization of the Guaymí." *Journal of the Steward Anthropological Society* 11(1):73–110.

———. 1976. "Edabali: The Ritual Sibling Relationship Among the Western Guaymí." In *Ritual and Symbol in Native Central America,* ed. Philip D. Young and J. Howe, pp. 77–90. University of Oregon Anthropological Papers No. 9. Eugene: University of Oregon Press.

Zamora, Guillermo. 1997. *Caso CONASUPO: La leche radiactiva.* Mexico: Editorial Planeta.

Zuvekas, Clarence. 1997. "Latin America's Struggle for Equitable Economic Adjustment." *Latin American Research Review* 32(2):152–169.

About the Contributors

Peggy F. Barlett is professor of anthropology at Emory University in Atlanta. Author of *American Dreams, Rural Realities: Family Farms in Crisis* and *Agricultural Choice and Change: Decision Making in a Costa Rican Village* and editor of *Agricultural Decision Making: Anthropological Contributions to Economic Development,* she has studied agricultural development and economic decisionmaking from the perspective of family farmers in the United States and Latin America. Her current interests include sustainable development, globalization, institutional change, and the intersection of adult development and masculine and feminine definitions of personal success.

John R. Bort teaches in the Department of Anthropology at East Carolina University. He has worked with the Ngóbe peoples of Panama since 1972. His major resesarch interests are artisanal fisheries, aquaculture, and culture change among traditional and indigenous populations in Central America.

Barbara J. Dilly is visiting assistant professor of anthropology at the University of Northern Iowa. Her research interests include ethnology of rural minorities, comparative agricultural community studies, and ecotourism.

Liliana R. Goldin is associate professor of anthropology and Latin American and Caribbean studies at the University at Albany, SUNY. She has published widely on issues of economic restructuring in rural Latin America, economic strategies of Mayas and non-Mayas in Guatemala, and the processes of economic and cultural change. She is currently working on a monograph titled *Ideology in Production: Making Perspectives in Rural Guatemala.*

David Guillet is professor of anthropology at Catholic University in Washington, D.C. He is the author of *Covering Ground: Communal Water Management* and *The State in the Peruvian Highlands* (1992).

James H. McDonald is assistant professor of anthropology at the University of Texas at San Antonio. His research examines different dimensions of sociocultural change in the Mexican political economy. His work appears in journals including *Human Organization, Critique of Anthropology, American Anthropologist,* and *Culture and Agriculture.*

Benjamin Orlove is an anthropologist in the Department of Environmental Science and Policy at the University of California at Davis. His most recent books are *The Allure of the Foreign: Imported Goods in Post-Colonial Latin America* (1997), an edited volume on the economic and cultural roots of the boom in imports in Latin America after independence, and *In My Father's Study* (1995), a family memoir. He is currently at work on *Lines in the Water: An Ecological History of the Lake Titicaca Fishermen.*

Manuel Vargas, a native of the Dominican Republic, is associate professor and coordinator of the African and African-American Studies Program at Rollins College in Winter Park, Florida. During the period 1970–1984 he worked as an agronomist.

Ronald Waterbury is professor of anthropology at Queens College of the City University of New York. He first began fieldwork in San Antonino in 1965 while he was a graduate student serving as field director of the UCLA Oaxaca Markets Project. He has been following developments in the community ever since, focusing on changing household economic strategies, how these changes interrelate with the external political economy, and how they ramify through the internal sociocultural system.

Philip D. Young teaches in the Department of Anthropology at the University of Oregon in Eugene. He has worked with the Ngóbe peoples of Panama since 1964. Among his major research interests are political ecology, social movements, and culture change among the indigenous peoples of Central America.

Index

About the Book

With global sociopolitical and economic change contributing to an accelerating crisis in Latin America's rural communities, rural residents are responding creatively with a range of survival strategies: new forms of collective action, involvement in social movements, the development of resource management programs, and participation in broader markets. The analyses and case studies in this book illustrate these strategies in the context of declining wages, rapid population growth, and reduced access to land and resources.

The authors also examine the implications and ideological justification of current development approaches. A concluding chapter explores the connections between globalization and the underlying forces of urbanization, liberalization, and democratization.

William M. Loker is associate professor of anthropology at California State University, Chico.